Skrifter utgivna vid Juridiska Fakulteten i Lund
Nr 175
Acta Societatis Juridicae Lundensis

How to Teach European Comparative Legal History

Workshop at the Faculty of Law Lund University 19–20 August 2009

Editors

Kjell Å. Modéer and Per Nilsén

Juristförlaget i Lund
Distribution: eddy.se AB

Address for orders: eddy.se AB
Bookorder
Box 1310
S-621 24 Visby
+46 (0)498 253900 (tel)
+46 (0)498 249789 (fax)
order@bokorder.se

Publisher's address: Juristförlaget i Lund
Box 207
221 00 Lund
+46 (0)46 222 10 16 (tel)
Vilhelm.Persson@jur.lu.se
www.juristforlaget.se

ISBN 978-9154405527
9 789154 405527

Grafisk form: *Alf Dahlberg*/Pan Eidos
Layout: Hans-Heinrich Vogel
Tryck: Wallin &Dalholm Boktryckeri AB
Lund 2011
ISBN 978–91–544–0552–7

Content

Introduction

The initiative to arrange this workshop was taken at the Annual meeting of the *American Association of Legal History* at Ottawa in November 2009. The sessions at these American meetings are increasingly intertwined with European legal history. An increasing part of the speakers comes from Europe, and several of the American speakers are elaborating on themes from European legal history. One of the sessions in Ottawa was on *Codification and Nationalism in Europe*. The panelists were Remco van Rhee, Maastricht, Ancieto Masferrer, Valencia, and Dirk Heirbaut from Ghent – all of them were co-organizers of this workshop – and the commentator was James Q. Whitman from Yale Law School, one of the most experienced comparative legal historians in the USA.

At one of the traditional substantial receptions during this meeting the European participants concluded that there was a need for an internal discourse on Comparative Legal History in Europe. Many universities today include classes in European Legal History to their curriculum, and at the same time many teachers in legal history are increasingly confused both due to lack of good class material and to their problems to articulate attractive perspectives on legal history on the European level. A lot of work on educational material in this field is made or on its way or planned for a near future. So it's important for all of us to learn from our experiences and be inspired by our visions. That was the aim of the workshop to which some 20 European legal historians were invited. The acceptance of the invitation to this workshop demonstrated the need for legal historians to discuss how to handle the concepts of time and space in relation to law in our time when legal education and its curriculum are discussed and changed – more frequent than ever.

The aim behind this initiative was of course also to construct a network between legal historians on the European level. Up to now legal historians have networked on the national or on a regional level. The British legal historians meet biannually with participants mostly from all the common law countries, not so many from the European continent. The German speaking legal historians also meet biannually at the German *Rechtshistorikertag*, with many German-speaking colleagues from Europe – and Japan! Also the legal historians in the Low Countries meet regularly – but in their mother's tongue. And the legal historians around the Baltic Sea meet regularly since some 10 years ago. At those meetings the conference languages are English or German.

In Ottawa the need to create a parallel to the *American Association of Legal History* also was discussed. We were happy to welcome the president of the American Association, Professor Maeva Marcus, from the George Washington University at Washington D.C. to this workshop. Her outsider's perspectives on European legal history were of great value for the discussions in the workshop. We are happy to welcome the inauguration of the European Society of Comparative Legal History at Valencia University in July this year.

After the workshop one of the participants, PD Dr. Miloš Vec at the Max Planck of European Legal History, published an article on the workshop in *Rechtsgeschichte. Zeitschrift des Max-Planck-Instituts für Europäische Rechtsgeschichte*. The article is republished in this volume.

The workshop was arranged within the Pufendorf Seminar in Legal History at Lund.

Lund in June, 2010.

Kjell Å. Modéer *Per Nilsén*

Theoretical and Methodological Aspects

Kjell Å. Modéer

Is European Comparative Legal History Running Wild? From Function and Texts to Perspectives and Contexts

1.

This workshop on comparative legal history within legal education has a context. It all started some 15–20 years ago. International law increasingly invaded Western legal jurisdictions. The end of the cold war and the break down of the Soviet Union resulted in mobility and transparency between national territories. Also postcolonial situations became relevant within the law. Lots of refugees and immigrants came from Asia, Latin America and Africa to West European countries where they in *diasporas* developed religious and legal cultures in conflict with those in the traditional nation states, with their well developed homogeneous national identities and more or less complete welfare states models. Their position as minorities was also protected by international human rights conventions and obligations. It also resulted in a new attitude to the third world and its legal systems. A new legal colonialism started out from the Western paradigm. In Europe it expanded the human rights concept into a global strategy. Another important part of the context was the Maastricht Treaty 1992 and the creation of the European Union January 1, 1995. Acceptance of cultural diversities resulted in legal discourses on heterogeneity and differences.

In the Scandinavian countries the Danish legal scientists Henrik Zahle and Hanne Petersen pioneered with the concept polycentricity, which especially looked into the effects of the multicultural situation related to the legal sources. It resulted in a different and more complex approach within legal education, where the traditional monolithic legal systems were challenged not only within the nation states but also in relation to the supranational EU law. Already in the late 1980's initiatives were taken within the legal education related to a common European curriculum. The Bologna treaty regarding exchange of law students was signed in 1988, before the break down of the Berlin Wall, and before master-classes in European Law (including competition law), Human Rights Law and European Legal History started to pop up as mushrooms at the European Law Schools. In that respect legal theory and legal history pioneered. Today this European strategy is commonplace.[1] From a legal science perspective it developed an increasing schizophrenia between the national homogeneous monolithic legal system and its identity within the legal community on one hand and the claims from the *diasporas* on the other. In that respect we all are aware of the current conflicts between secular and religious legal systems within family law. How to handle multiculturalism is an essential part of the discussions for this workshop.

2.

I would like to start out from Anthony T. Kronman's latest book, published in 2007, *Education's End,* which very critically demonstrates the problems of the legal education in the modern professional American law school, where law as a human discipline has been abolished – due to rationality and functionality. Secular humanism, political correctness and the dominance of science have resulted in an academic environment lacking humanism.[2] Comparative law, however, is bringing humanity into the law. It gives the lawyers perspectives within a mother-system related to their own professional cognitive structure. Kronman is referring to metaphysical perspectives of the law; it brings you up to the meta-perspectives of the legal constructs. In retrospect Pierre Legrand pioneered with his epistemological analysis of the common law and civil law systems. The negative reaction his postmodern perspectives had to traditionally orientated legal scientists, in fact validates the dominating position of the paradigm of the nation state and its mother-system.

Comparative European Legal history challenges the legal concepts of the modernity, where the cognitive systems were dominated by the nation state and the valid law. Within that concept comparative law as well as legal history had an underdog position. In the current late modernity, however, comparative law and legal history has got a quite new and positive position within legal science. The purpose of this workshop is to try to investigate the consequences of this development within legal education.

---

1 http://www.europaeische-juristenausbildung.de.

2 Anthony T. Kronman, Education's End: Why Our Colleges and Universities Have Given Up on the Meaning of Life. Yale University Press, New Haven/London 2007.

3.

When Konrad Zweigert and Hein Kötz in the early 1970's published their well-known *Introduction to Comparative Law* they elaborated on an evolutionary perspective on comparative law. Western legal systems were constructed into legal families. The Nordic legal systems were as we all know looked upon as one of these mainly Western legal families with their own style. Similarities and harmonization characterized the Western legal families. Their concept of *style* was a heritage from Max Weber. They defined this concept in five points. The first characteristic was "the historical background and development of the legal system (the reception of Roman Law as opposed to customary law)". In an article in the early 1990's Hein Kötz also emphasized the relation between comparative law and legal history.[3] It started a new discourse related to the aims on the European level within private law to find the historical basis to construct a European civil code. The Ole Lando Commission on European Contract Law, Christian von Bar's Study Group on a European Civil Code as well as the Ugo Mattei and Mauro Bussani's Common Core of European Private Law at Trento University, all are efforts to construct such a code and may be taken as examples in that direction.

At the German Legal Historians' biannual meeting, *Deutscher Rechtshistorikertag*, in Regensburg some ten years ago a half-day session with several contributions was devoted to Legal History and Comparative Law.[4] We were many in the auditorium who optimistically had expected to be witness to a new marriage between the two disciplines. The problem was that the representatives of the two disciplines came with too much of scientific cargo of its own. Comparative law asked for support from legal history, and *vice versa*. Today, ten years later, we find another situation, with much more of interaction between the disciplines within the law curriculum. The problem may also have been that comparative law looked upon legal history as a competing discipline among the *Grundlagenfächer*. Legal history as well as Comparative law fought to find

[3] Hein Kötz, „Was erwartet die Rechtvergleichung von der Rechtsgeschichte". *Juristen-Zeitung* 1992, 20 ff.

[4] Mattias Reimann, „Rechtsvergleichung und Rechtsgeschichte im Dialog", 7 *Zeitschrift für Europäisches Privatrecht* (1999); 496 ff.; Klaus Luig, „Was kann die Rechtsgeschichte der Rechtsvergleichung bieten?", 7 *Zeitschrift für Europäisches Privatrecht* 1999, 521 ff.; Michele Graziadei, „Comparative Law, Legal History, and the Holistic Approach to Legal Cultures", 7 *Zeitschrift für Europäisches Privatrecht* (1999), 531 ff.; Albrecht Cordes, „Was erwartet die (mittelalterliche) Rechtsgeschichte von der Rechtsvergleichung und anderen vergleichend arbeitenden Disziplinen?", 7 *Zeitschrift für Europäisches Privatrecht* (1999), 545 ff.; William Ewald, „Legal History and Comparative Law", 7 *Zeitschrift für Europäisches Privatrecht* (1999), 553 ff.; David Johnston, „Roman Law, Comparative Law and Legal History, 7 *Zeitschrift für Europäisches Privatrecht* (1999), 513 ff.

its space within the law curriculum. Zweigert and Kötz in their *Introduction to Comparative Law* used the same argument legal history used to do.

In my opinion legal history and comparative law today are involved in a merging process. The ongoing Europeanization and globalization of the law have resulted in a new legal meta-sphere, a supranational and transnational dimension of the law, which gives you quite new perspectives of the law. They are perspectives where time and space are interacting.

4.

Comparative law, however, didn't find its way into the current law curriculum thanks to the European Union. It has a longer story of its own. This story is well documented in Mathias Reimann's and Reinhard Zimmermann's impressive *Oxford Handbook of Comparative Law* – a very rich volume which demonstrates the multiplicity and variety in the perspectives of comparative law.[5]

It was Vivian Grosswald Curran at University of Michigan, who made me aware of the modern development of comparative law related to the cognitive structures of the German law émigrés brought to the UK and the USA in the 1930's and 40's.[6] Max Rheinstein, Stefan Riesenfelt, Albert Ehrenzweig, Rudolf Schlesinger, Hessel E. Yntema, among others – all of them brought international law and comparative law into the parochial American legal culture. Curran has recently in a review article to Zimmermann's *Uprooted Jurists* emphasized their importance for the development of international law and comparative law in the post-war United States.[7] The concept of comparative law they demonstrated was very much related to the black letter law. The functional way of doing comparative law was not only very fact orientated. It also fitted well into the paradigm of the legal realism. They urged to find similarities between legal systems, as e.g. demonstrated by Max Rheinstein in his huge comparative studies within family law.[8]

---

[5] Mathias Reimann & Reinhard Zimmermann (ed.), *The Oxford Handbook of Comparative Law*. Oxford University Press: Oxford 2006.

[6] Vivian Grosswald Curran, "Cultural Immersion: Difference and Cathegories in U.S. Comparative Law", *American Journal of Comparative Law* 1998.

[7] Vivian Grosswald Curran, "Voices Saved from Vanishing", *University of Pittsburgh Law Review*, vol. 70 (2009), 435 ff.

[8] Max Rheinstein, *Marriage Stability, Divorce, and the Law*, The University of Chicago Press: Chicago 1972; Kjell Å Modéer, "Secularization, Liberalization and Modernization: Family Law in Scandinavian Welfare-States in the 1960s–1970s", in Harry N. Scheiber & Laurent Mayali (eds.), *Japanese Family Law in Comparative Perspective*, [Studies in Comparative Law] Robbins Collection (UCal/Berkeley) 2009, 205 ff.

The new comparative paradigm developed throughout the last 20 years, however, is keener to emphasize the study of differences. The differences between the traditional nation states legal systems and the Other's are visible in a quite new manner in the heterogeneous and multicultural late modern societies. So also the contexts have changed dramatically.

5.

The new comparative as well as historical perspectives make it necessary to use the disciplines comparative law and legal history in a new way. We are all aware of the new position of comparative law within the late modern paradigm of legal science. But how can – or shall – we handle it within the legal education?

If we look into the normal composition of the students in a Comparative European Legal History class at a Swedish faculty of law we find a very mixed breed. Some students come from Western Europe of course, but also increasingly a crop of overseas students (from e.g. Australia, Canada and the USA) and some from what we may call "the new Europe" (the former satellite states to the Soviet Union). Interestingly enough, very, very few students from the law program at the faculty of law are taking this class. It demonstrates what has been called the "hidden epistemic" of the law curriculum. As long as the students learn that the law curriculum is monolithically orientated to the valid law of the mother-system, as long they also are interpreting the context as nation-orientated.

And the teachers, in this case they are all from Lund and are by the students regarded as a part of the mother-system. So the foreign students actually meet the same situation as the German law émigré students did when they arrived in the common law countries in the 1930's. We may have learnt from this example that the real experience is that open-minded teachers actually can learn as much as the students in such a class. In the current discourse related to comparative legal education this student-orientated perspective is emphasized. It means that the comparative perspective in the class-room must be related to the legal systems the students are representing.

The Finnish comparatist Jaakko Husa has in a recent article argued for a quite now position of comparative law in the law curriculum, making it possible to develop a pluralistic legal mind among the students.[9] Instead of taking the

[9] Jaakko Husa, "Turning the Curriculum Upside down: Comparative Law as an Educational Tool for Constructing Pluralistic Legal Mind", *German Law Journal*, Vol. 10, No 7, 1 July 2009.

mother-system of the teacher as the normal perspective he takes the transnational and pluralistic perspective of the students as the normal. Husa argues for "a globalization of the mind" of the lawyers. The lawyers must be taught to "think like global lawyers".

Husa is pleading for going beyond McGill's famous transsystemic/bijural thinking in common law and civil law, towards a transsystemic/multijurial type of thinking, mixing legal systems in the education – just like the students are mixed and are representing a multijurial composition. Husa underlines the difficulties to change the whole law curriculum in that direction, due to the fact that "comparative law and foreign legal material have a very small role in the law curricula around the globe". So Husa is pleading for a visionary strategy: To reform the law curricula all over the place.

From my point of view Husa has a point if we apply his thesis on the field of European legal history. We have left the evolutionary perspective behind us, and are trying to demonstrate for the students how important legal history is for our current interpretation of the law. Modern European legal history is one way to demonstrate this for a class of mixed students. With help of the concept of modernity we can demonstrate our current late modern position in relation to modernity, but also to the pre-modern concepts of the law.

The war catastrophes in Europe, The Great War and World War II, are also related to new chapters in modern European legal history. Not least within public law, constitutional law and administrative law of the social welfare state the political events were related to the legal development. Interesting enough, comparative constitutional law is an expanding field both in the US and in Europe. Vicki C Jackson and Mark Tushnet have in an interesting way developed this field in the US – comparing the US Constitution with other constitutions of the world.[10] From a European perspective a comparative constitutional legal history would be a priority for European legal historians, even if this perspective, in my view, has to be different from the American one. We have to identify the European Constitutional history with help of a multijurial method.

6.

I have to conclude. The concepts of legal identity and legal culture have given European legal history a twofold perspective. On one hand are we emphasiz-

[10] Vicki C. Jackson & Mark Tushnet (eds.), *Defining the Field of Comparative Constitutional Law*. Westport, Connecticut: Praeger 2002.

ing the differences between national legal systems. On the other hand we are defining the European Unions as a construct with a common history with common threads back to Greek philosophy and Roman law. Education in comparative European Legal History has to reflect this part of the new romantic wave within law.

Comparative law has to a great extent adopted the contextual way to develop this discipline from a scientific position. Comparative legal history of today in that respect is an integrated part of the discipline legal history. But how to find the methods for comparative legal history in the multijurial classroom is the challenge we have to tackle not only at this workshop, but also in the future.

Maeva Marcus

European Legal History – From an American Perspective

One of the primary reasons for the convening of this workshop is to discuss the formation of a European legal history society, so I'd like to begin with a little history of the American Society for Legal History. The ASLH, as it is familiarly known, was founded in 1956 by law professors who had an interest in legal history (and note that it is *not* a society for *American* legal history). The society, as its first order of business, adopted the *American Journal of Legal History*, published by Temple University School of Law, as its official publication. In the introduction to the first issue, the editor noted that the journal would publish articles on the history of all legal systems, but it especially encouraged work in English law, Roman law, and canon law.

After this initial flurry, the American Society for Legal History languished. It wasn't until 1970, when a conference was held to reorganize the society, that interest in legal history began to increase. Meetings took place annually, attended by 100 or so people. The two-day program consisted of concurrent sessions in each time slot, one American legal history and one non-American. Harvard University Press agreed to publish a series of monographs, undertaken by the ASLH, known as Studies in Legal History. Within a few years, the society transferred the series to the University of North Carolina Press, where it remains today. The *American Journal of Legal History* continued as a society publication, but dissatisfaction with its quality grew. In 1982, a reinvigorated American Society for Legal History decided to sponsor its own journal, *Law and History Review.* The society chooses the editors, the press that will publish the journal, and makes all editorial policy, for example, deciding to include many articles on the legal history of countries other than the United States. Those of you who have read the journal or who have had an article published in it, or even won a prize for the best article in a given year, know that the journal is one of the best scholarly publications around. (The *American Journal of Legal History* continues to publish today, but it's years behind, and it's struggling.)

The ASLH's efforts to reach out to people other than law professors teaching legal history paid off, because the society today has more than 1,000 members

– 400 institutions and 600 individuals, including historians, political scientists, practicing lawyers, and judges. Three to four hundred people come to the annual meeting, and there are now five concurrent sessions in any given time slot and a lot of competition to get on the program. In the 1970s we had 8 sessions at a meeting; now we have 35, with panels on American, Canadian, British, continental European, Asian, Israeli, Islamic, and comparative legal history. All of this reflects a growing attention to legal history in scholarship. Tom Green, one of the editors of the ASLH's Studies in Legal History series, worked diligently over the years to attract manuscripts dealing with non-American subjects. He focused first on British legal history, but lately he has concentrated on continental European legal history. Books on German, French, and Catalan legal history have been published or will be in the next year or two, including one by Maria Ågren called *Domestic Secrets: Women and Property in Sweden 1600–1857,* due in the fall. None of these is a best-seller (nor are works on America), but Tom persuaded the University of North Carolina press that this scholarship deserves publication.

Studies that devote at least some pages to legal history proliferate, and these are published by a variety of other presses. This accounts for the many new faces seen on the American Society for Legal History programs. These professors and graduate students have developed an expertise in some specialized area of legal history that enables them to be valuable contributors to annual meeting sessions. But paradoxically, the growth of legal history scholarship has not resulted in an increasing number of legal history courses taught, whether the subject be American or non-American, either in law schools or in university departments. Law schools in the United States are to a large extent trade schools. They train students to be practicing lawyers. In recent years, the number of faculty members with dual degrees, a J.D. and a Ph.D. in a related discipline like history, political science, or economics, has risen, but with little effect on law school curricula. Most law school faculty members must teach a bread and butter, black letter law course, and then perhaps are permitted to teach a course of their choice as an elective. Thus, at law schools, we find courses in American legal history, English legal history, Roman law, canon law, and, more and more, comparative constitutional law and human rights law, but not in abundance. And very few are in European legal history per se.

On college campuses, these courses are even more rare. History and political science departments publicly proclaim their lack of interest in legal and constitutional history of any sort. Charles Donahue, of Harvard Law School, examines the reasons for this in an essay included in a festschrift for Morton Horwitz (*Transformations in American Legal History*, Hamilton and Brophy eds.,

Harvard U. Press), "Whither Legal History?" that I commend to you. There are many historians who have written in the field of legal history, and I'm sure you know their work, but they do not teach it in their home departments. As a result, we have very few graduate students in American legal history and even fewer in European. This means that in the next generation of university faculty few will be prepared to teach this subject. Those who obtain a legal history Ph.D. now, usually couple it with a J.D. and go to teach at a law school. American law schools do not train graduate students. Thus, while scholarship in legal history is flourishing, the subject has largely disappeared from humanities departments in universities and colleges across America.

I should enter a disclaimer here: these thoughts are not backed up by a scientific survey. They come from conversations with legal historians in a variety of law schools and universities.

Law schools in the U.S. have done better than universities in hiring people who can teach European legal history, but it's usually someone who specializes in comparative law. Some professors, like Mathias Reimann at the University of Michigan, the editor of the *American Journal of Comparative Law*, take a historical approach, but it's now global in reach, so there's very little taught about the legal history of nations. Law schools that don't have permanent faculty members who teach comparative law and possibly legal history, often import visitors from abroad to fill in the gaps. But these are usually the top law schools that can afford to do this.

Another barrier in the United States to the study and teaching of European legal history is the lack of knowledge of languages other than English. You all have learned English (and I am certainly the beneficiary of that today) and can take advantage of the interesting work that's being done by American scholars on European legal history. But most Americans cannot read the books and articles that you are publishing, unless you write them in English. Translations are few. (The Organization of American Historians once gave a prize for the best book on some topic in American history written in a foreign language. That lasted for a few years, but it was so difficult and expensive to get the books translated that the prize was eliminated.) Someone who wishes to teach a course on French legal history for undergraduates has a hard time finding enough reading material to assign to students, or so I'm told.

Another problem stemming from lack of knowledge of foreign languages is whether a primary document in European legal history can be translated into English without changing its meaning. For example, can a legal concept in Latin or French be adequately and accurately expressed in English?

I think the language barrier can be overcome, but the resistance in university departments across the United States to the subject of European legal history, and American legal history, too, is much harder to combat. I look forward to your papers today and tomorrow in the hope that I'll learn how to do that.

Miloš Vec

National and Transnational Legal Evolutions Teaching History of International Law

I. Introduction: Possible, Impossible and Detrimental Aims of this Workshop

It is obvious that this workshops issue – teaching – is not only of theoretical importance and intellectual charm but it also has a high practical relevance for all of us. How about changes and challenges for legal history and its agenda? The call for papers addressed these questions in a very open way and it could be read from many perspectives. Consequently, we found wide-ranged answers with different approaches in the abstracts which circulated before the opening of the workshop. Let me start with a thesis: Such a workshop should and could not lead to an agreement on one teaching model.

Methods, theoretical approaches and class material are currently different from one place to another and – more important – they will also be in future. Research-based teaching will work best in a wide-ranging cosmos of ideas and perspectives. Although legal historians may be considered as a community of researchers, our perspectives on law, on Europe and the World, on history differ – even if we read the same courses and often recommend the same books from the same heroes, dead or alive. We have to consider a permanent change of theories and interest in our field: From time to time and even from place to place. To put it simply: There are different cultures of thought ("Denkstile"[1]) and schools of thought. And that is a good thing: students and researchers know that they will learn something different about law and society at the London School of Economics than in Bologna or Vienna. They will meet different teachers with individual attributes, teaching methods, and fields of knowledge.

[1] This concept was coined by Ludwik Fleck, Entstehung und Entwicklung einer wissenschaftlichen Tatsache. Einführung in die Lehre vom Denkstil und Denkkollektiv. Mit einer Einleitung herausgegeben von Lothar Schäfer und Thomas Schnelle, Frankfurt am Main 1980 (first published in 1935). See: Rainer Egloff (ed.), Tatsache – Denkstil – Kontroverse: Auseinandersetzungen mit Ludwik Fleck, Zürich 2004 (Collegium Helveticum, book no. 1).

Therefore, I understand hat this workshop does not strive for standardization, but only for what is already named in the call for papers: "a common European *discourse* regarding teaching methods, theoretical approaches and class material". In light of this assumption it is necessary for our exchange to introduce our individual and varied teaching concepts of what we are doing in the classroom. Therefore, I will follow the model many colleagues have used and I will illustrate my point by arguing from concrete experiences. I am currently familiar with one particular subject of legal history: teaching history of international law. Let us then start with some first findings concerning the practical teaching of history of international law in our academic community.

II. Empirical Findings I: Interviews

These first findings are the result of the research I carried out after receiving the invitation to the workshop. Different from our general work, I did not conduct the usual massive reading of old printed books. Instead I referred to another method of empirical research that is familiar to the social sciences: interviews. For better transparency, let me quote precisely my transcripts.

Q: Martti,[2] Do you teach history of international law?

A: No. But I think, Ben[3] in New York does.

Q: Luigi,[4] Do you teach history of international law?

A: No.

Q: Matthew,[5] Do you teach history of international law?

A: No.

Q: Gaitán,[6] Do you teach history of international law?

A: No.

---

[2] Martti Koskenniemi, Director of the Eric Castrén Institute of International Law and Human Rights, University of Helsinki, Finland.

[3] Benedict W. Kingsbury, Murry and Ida Becker Professor of Law and Director of the Institute for International Law and Justice at New York University School of Law, USA, http://its.law.nyu.edu/facultyprofiles/profile.cfm?personID=20046. Courses: http://its.law.nyu.edu/courses/index.cfm?sortLabel=Semester&searchButton=1&keyword=&coursetitle=&viewFirstYear=&CourseInstructorId=20046&CourseCode=&CourseTerm=&ExactCode=&Block=&CourseCredits=&startTime=&endTime=&location=&pastSemesters=Y&page=2; (History and Theory of International Law; Fall, 2006) http://its.law.nyu.edu/courses/description.cfm?id=6021; http://its.law.nyu.edu/courses/description.cfm?id=4087; http://its.law.nyu.edu/courses/description.cfm?id=6805.

[4] Luigi Nuzzo, Professore aggregato per la storia del diritto medievale e moderno presso la Facoltà di giurisprudenza dell'Università del Salento, Lecce, Italy.

[5] Matthew Craven, Professor of International Law at the Faculty of Law and Social Sciences, University of London, GB.

[6] Julio Gaitán Bohórquez, Profesor de Historia del Derecho, Universidad Bogotà, Colombia.

Q: Santiago,[7] Do you teach history of international law?
A: No.
Q: Harata,[8] Do you teach history of international law?
A: No.
Q: Raymond,[9] Do you teach history of international law?
A: No, but I think Randall[10] and Laurens Winkel[11] do. And Roelofsen[12] also did before retiring.
Q: Matthias,[13] Do you teach history of international law?
A: No.
Q: Bardo,[14] Do you teach history of international law?
A: No.

Let me stop here. These were the unmistakable findings of nine interviews, held at the side of a conference on the history of international law in Lecce/ Italy in May 2009.[15] Maybe you can identify one or two of the persons I asked. This is of some importance, because then you will understand the quite representative character of this finding. All in all they are nine acknowledged researchers from nine different countries, all of them with different academic backgrounds. They come from legal history of civil or public law; from international law; from history of international relations or from legal theory.

All of them are currently interested in the history of international law; many contributed substantial works and some of them are – if I may say so – the

7 Santiago Legarre, Profesor de Derecho, Universidad Austral Buenos Aires, Argentina.

8 Hisahi Harata, Professor for International Private Law and Conflict of Laws at the University of Tokyo, Japan.

9 Raymond Kubben, Assistant Professor (UD), Expertise: History and Theory of International Law and International Relations at Tilburg University, Netherlands.

10 Randall Lesaffer, Professor of legal history and dean of the Tilburg Law School, Netherlands. Courses: http://www.tilburguniversity.nl/webwijs/show/?uid=r.c.h.lesaffer; http://rechten.uvt.nl/lesaffer/indexen.htm.

11 Laurens Winkel, Professor at the Erasmus University of Rotterdam, Netherlands. Courses: http://www.erasmus.org/index.cfm?fuseaction=site.show&CTX_ID=3035998D505693014B26667DCE65D491.

12 Cornelis Gerrit Roelofsen was extraordinary professor at the Department of Public International Law & Social and Economic Law – ISEP, part of the Utrecht School of Law and the Faculty of Law, Economics and Governance at Utrecht University, Netherlands; http://www.onderzoekinformatie.nl/en/oi/nod/organisatie/ORG1235801/#persoon. Courses: http://www.onderzoekinformatie.nl/en/oi/nod/onderzoeker/PRS1242532/.

13 Matthias Schulz, Professor für Geschichte der internationalen Beziehungen und transnationale Geschichte, Universität Genf, Switzerland.

14 Bardo Fassbender, Professor für Internationales Recht, Universität der Bundeswehr München, Germany.

15 Its title was „Storia teoria e diritto internazionale. La costruzione di una disciplina", organized by MPI für europäische Rechtsgeschichte in cooperation with the Università del Salento, Lecce & Copertino, 20.–22. May 2009.

eminent or leading figures in this field, which seems to have flourished in the recent past.[16] But none confessed or claimed he (a woman was not among them) actually *teaches* history of international law. As you see: Research and teaching sometimes do not go hand in hand.

III. Empirical Findings II: Research by Email, Internet and reading

I conducted a second series of empirical research. This time I used our principal research tool, which is the internet. Doing so, I am now able to add some evidence to the suspicion, that, nevertheless, classes on history of international law are of course taught. However, it is taught in a slightly different way than most other subjects of legal history. The following remarks are just a present snap-shot. This paper does not focus on the question of teaching history of international law during the 19th and 20th century at universities in the course of academic law or history lessons, this would be a particular subject for legal history.[17]

1. Few classes on history of international law

First of all, history of international law is less taught. In general history of international law appears academically not as separate course. One of a few exceptions I could identify was Heinhard Steiger, giving a lecture on "Geschichte des Völkerrechts" at Gießen university (Hesse, Germany) in 2003. At that time, he had already retired. Ben Kingsbury from NYU held a course on "History and Theory of International Law" in fall 2006. I do not know where Kingsbury laid the focus in this combination of history with another subject. Few other courses can be found on the web, too.[18]

---

[16] Alexandra Kemmerer, The Turning Aside. On International Law and Its History, in: Russell A. Miller, Rebecca M. Bratspies (eds.), Progress in International Law (Developments in International Law 60), Leiden 2008, pp.71–93.

[17] Legal history has interest in the history of teaching subjects, see e.g. Heinz Holzhauer, Familienrecht als universitäres Lehrfach. Geschichte und gegenwärtige Lage, in: Hans G. Hermann, Thomas Gutmann, Joachim Rückert, Mathias Schmoeckel, Harald Siems (eds.), Von den „leges barbarorum" bis zum „ius barbarum" des Nationalsozialismus. Festschrift für Hermann Nehlsen zum 70. Geburtstag, Köln 2008, pp.658–672, or the remarks on teaching of constitutional history at Ewald Grothe, Zwischen Geschichte und Recht. Deutsche Verfassungsgeschichtsschreibung, 1900–1970, München 2005, pp.103, 200.

[18] Norman Weiß (Universität Potsdam), Vorlesung Völkerrechtsgeschichte, Sommersemester 2008; Dominique Gaurier (Universite Nantes), Histoire du Droit International Public Cours de Licence 3 (online: http://www.droit.univ-nantes.fr/ressources/gaurier/Plan_Hist_DIP.pdf); Bertrand Ancel (Université Panthéon Assas = Paris 2), Histoire du droit international; Marcus Hanke (Universität Salzburg), Vorlesung Geschichte des Völkerrechts, Sommersemester 2009; Thilo Marauhn (Universität Gießen), Vorlesung Geschichtliche Einführung in das Völkerrecht, Wintersemester 2005/2006.

The other hits I had online came from University curricula where history of international law was taught as short introduction or appendix to another subject. These were in particular international law (often starting with a short overview on its history[19]) and international relations, sometimes history, too. In some cases, courses on legal history also deal with history of international law.[20] Then they claim to cover "The Origins of the International Legal Order and its Nature"[21]. Yet that is already all from a legal perspective.

My suspicion is that this shortcoming of my subject results from the traditional shape of teaching on the one hand and splitting legal history into separate subjects which are hardly to modify in the curricula on the other hand. History of international law does neither belong to history of private law[22] (Privatrechtsgeschichte) which embraces the major part of academic legal history (at least in Germany) nor to the minor part on history of constitutional law[23] (Verfassungsgeschichte). And it is definitely no part of criminal legal history;[24] however, as this subject plays hardly any role in teaching, this point is of least importance. And if you consider the traditional division of the Zeitschrift der Savigny-Stiftung für Rechtsgeschichte into the three sections "Germanistische Abteilung", "Kanonistische Abteilung", "Romanistische Abteilung" – where should you then localize history of international law? Let me put it radically: history of international law does not even have a place at the periphery of the discipline; but it is only a poor cousin of legal history.

---

[19] E.g. Alexander Proelß (Universität Kiel), Völkerrecht I, Wintersemester 2009/10, 1. Abschnitt, II.: „Völkerrechtsgeschichte und Völkerrechtswissenschaft" (online: http://www.internat-recht.uni-kiel.de/veranstaltungen/lehrveranstaltungen/archiv/ws0910/proelss/vr/materialien/Voelkerrecht%20I.pdf).

[20] Guido Pfeifer (Universität Regensburg), Gliederung zur Vorlesung Einführung in die Rechtsgeschichte, Wintersemester 2006/2007 (online: http://www.uni-regensburg.de/Fakultaeten/Jura/hofer/Einfuehrung%20RG/Gliederung11.pdf); Christian Baldus (Universität Heidelberg), Römisches Recht, Sommersemester 2010 (online: http://www.rechtsgeschichte.uni-hd.de/rom-gliederung-rr-ss10.pdf); Rainer Wahl (Universität Freiburg), Verfassungsgeschichte der Neuzeit, Sommersemester 2009 (online: http://www.jura.uni-freiburg.de/institute/ioeffr_5/de/downloads/verfgliederung.pdf).

[21] Bartram Brown (Kent College of Law Chicago), International Law, Fall 2007, Reading Assignments, Assignment 1: „The Origins of the International Legal Order and its Nature" (online: http://www.kentlaw.edu/faculty/bbrown/classes/IntlLawFall2007/CoursePages/Syllabus.htm).

[22] Hans-Peter Haferkamp, Wege der Historiographie zur Privatrechtsgeschichte der Neuzeit, in: Zeitschrift für Neuere Rechtsgeschichte 32 (2010), pp.61–81.

[23] Not mentioning it: Ewald Grothe, Zwischen Norm und Symbol. Tradition und Innovation in der deutschen Verfassungsgeschichtsschreibung nach 1945, in: Zeitschrift für Neuere Rechtsgeschichte 32 (2010), pp.19–36.

[24] Günter Jerouschek, Sunt hic leones? Zu Fortschritten in der Strafrechtsgeschichte und in der historischen Kriminalitätsforschung, in: Zeitschrift für Neuere Rechtsgeschichte 32 (2010), pp.52–60.

2. The specific interdisciplinary Character

This lack of genuine interest from the side of the traditional legal history leads to an uncommon presence of other disciplines in this field. Political science, sociology, history and international law are stronger present than in the history of private law or constitutional law. Therefore, legal history has a much broader interdisciplinary character. This is shown by the fact that many other disciplines and their students have interest in the genesis and decline of the Westphalian System;[25] the discourses on hegemony from the Ancient to modern times;[26] they investigate on international trade and other international economic relations,[27] on diplomatic immunities and pre-modern ceremonies,[28] in short: on the varying subjects of the international relations.

We have to take these different disciplinary perspectives into account – and moreover: we have to regard them as an intellectual enrichment. They often raise different or new questions; these disciplines widen our perspectives on law in its historical context. They introduce new concepts or challenge ours by their adoption and critique. The confrontation both with students from these other disciplines and researchers and their key concepts like "world-system" (Wallerstein) or "Weltgesellschaft" (Luhmann) bring us to comparable complexity.

My own teaching experience strongly emphasizes this point. In the next Semester I will conduct with my research group the fourth seminar on "History of International law" in a row at Frankfurt University. We do this because we have the impression that this form of teaching supports our own research. Yet as there were no lectures scheduled on this topic in the curricula, I had to move my interest to smaller forms of teaching to establish this as a subject in the law faculty and in academically neighboring faculties.

After a shattering experience at Bonn University in 2005, where not a single student showed up in the preparatory meeting,[29] I knew I had to make strong efforts to attract students. However, it already went better in the first Frankfurt Seminar and the number of students steadily increased since. In our last Seminar

---

[25] See „Internationale Konflikte und europäisches Mächtesystem 1648–1789" of the „Lehreinheit Geschichte des Fachbereichs Geschichte/Philosophie" on http://www.uni-muenster.de/FNZ-Online/politstrukturen/maechte/gliederung.htm.

[26] Martti Koskenniemi, International Law and Hegemony: A Reconfiguration, in: Cambridge Review of International Affairs, vol. 17, no. 2, July 2004, pp.197–218.

[27] Michael Zürn, Regieren jenseits des Nationalstaates. Globalisierung und Denationalisierung als Chance, Frankfurt am Main 1998, p.56.

[28] See Chapter „4. Rahmenbedingungen internationaler Politik, 4.2. Diplomatie" of „Lehreinheit Geschichte des Fachbereichs Geschichte/Philosophie" on http://www.uni-muenster.de/FNZ-Online/politstrukturen/rahmenbedingungen/unterpunkte/diplomatie.htm.

[29] Nevertheless, it took place as I could recruit some students in my civil law lectures.

in July 2009 we had 20 presentations, some external discussants joined in, too (PhD-students; guests of the Institute; colleagues from the Exzellenzcluster 243 "Formations of Normative Orders"). It was a paradigm of the international and interdisciplinary composition of the classrooms which the call for papers mentioned: I counted in our seminar participants not only from different faculties – which were the usual suspects: Law, sociology, political sciences and history – but from 17 different countries (including all migration backgrounds).

This composition was really fruitful for the issue! We discussed "structural discrimination in late 19th century international law". Classical Topics in the sources were – as you all know – Christendom, civilization and culture. Of course students from Turkey, Morocco or Belarus read some delicate sentences by the German Professor Karl Baron Kaltenborn von Stachau or St. Petersburg's Fedor Fedorowitch von Martens with quite a distance and intellectual and moral attention or even irritation. Concepts of "International community", highly emphasized in their doctrine by both authors, read quite different when going into details and suppositions. Martens focused on "civilized states" and "civilized peoples" ("civilisirte Staaten", "gesittete Völker") when making his idea of an international community explicit.[30] He excluded other peoples from participating in this system:

> "Demnach beschränkt sich das Geltungsgebiet des Völkerrechts auch nur auf diejenigen Völker, welche die elementaren Grundsätze der europäischen Cultur anerkennen und also des Namens gesitteter Nationen würdig sind. Die eigenthümlichen socialen und staatlichen Zustände, in denen sowohl die muhamedanischen Völkerschaften als auch die heidnischen und wilden Stämme leben, gewähren absolute keine Möglichkeit, beim Verkehr mit diesen uncultivirten oder halbcultivirten Nationalitäten das Völkerrecht in Anwendung zu bringen."[31]

Stories of evolution and progress, often told by 19th century authors like US-American Daniel Gardner[32] also have their irritating aspects considering that Gardner is linking progress[33] and foundation of international law not only to Christianity,[34] but to Gospel.[35] In this sense "Morality" in international law

---

[30] Friedrich von Martens, Völkerrecht. Das internationale Recht der civilisirten Nationen, German edition by Carl Bergbohm, 2 vol., Berlin 1883 and 1886, here: vol. I, § 39 (p. 177).
[31] Idem, § 41 (p. 181).
[32] Daniel Gardner, A treatise on International Law and a short Explanation of the Jurisdiction and Duty of the Government of the Republic of the United States, New York 1844.
[33] Idem, pp.14, 80.
[34] Idem, pp.67, 85.
[35] Idem, pp.80, 83, 92, 139.

has a quite narrow religious foundation, excluding not only other religions than Christianity, but also Catholicism. In other words: Gardner's rhetorics of "peace, equity and humanity"[36] in international relations is tied to a specific religious denomination.

This irritation is only a potential teaching result, not an automatism. The way to a successful seminar on history of international law is always long and it demands a lot of preparation. I assume that there is no or little difference to seminars in other fields of legal history. The standards and steps in their chronological order are very much the same: Fixing a general theme that covers not more than some decades in legal history; formulating around 20 single themes for students – these topics also include presentations on specific aspects in the work of single international lawyers in that period (e.g. his doctrine of sources). This composition enables the combination and comparison of detailed works (by single lawyers) and general overviews over international legal topics in the seminar; we even ask for papers on international lawyers to whom no secondary literature can be found (like British Richard Wildman[37]). After this preparation we fix a first meeting with students where we will explain the themes to our potential customers and applicants; we give hints on sources and secondary literature; we distribute introductory papers to be discussed in preparatory meetings; we also let students work with (primary and secondary) sources: we let them read a passage from Johann Ludwig Klüber's textbook from 1821[38] or a provoking paper by Anthony Anghie from 2009[39]. Then we conduct the two-day seminar on the basis of first draft-versions of the student's papers; we give them individual critique on oral presentations and written papers; we collect the final versions after another four weeks and make corrections and grades. Finally, we evaluate the seminar internally and we plan the next one. Continuity is a value.

As our research interests and themes change, there is no fixed class material which is recycled from term to term. We always take the sources and secondary literature we find currently most fascinating and which attracts our intellectual attention most. Therefore, the codification of a set of class material or theoretical approaches would bare the danger of a petrifaction of research and teaching. However, it is precisely the combination of the research and teaching process with our actual interests which produces the most vital and interesting results.

---

[36] Idem, pp.87.

[37] Richard Wildman, Institutes of international law, vol. I. International rights in time of peace, London 1849; vol. II. International rights in time of war, London 1850.

[38] Johann Ludwig Klüber, Europäisches Völkerrecht, 2 vol., Stuttgart 1821.

[39] Antony Anghie, Die Evolution des Völkerrechts: Koloniale und postkoloniale Realitäten, in: Kritische Justiz. Vierteljahresschrift für Recht und Politik 42 (2009), pp.49–63.

IV. Teaching what and why to compare?

I illustrated the challenge and the joy of teaching a subject located at the periphery of legal history. But the fact that history of international law is not a common subject in our classrooms does not mean it will not be one in the future. Curricula in (legal) history are never final: they will be modified not only by new subjects, approaches and methods but particularly through political and social circumstances. (The so-called) Bologna-Process, Internationalization and Globalization of law and society brought new challenges to our Universities. A recently published special issue of the German Law Journal is exclusively devoted to the subject "Transnationalizing Legal Education".[40] The contributors were aware of the fact that the rise of studies in comparative law in the past had positive effects on similar questions in legal history[41] and they claimed that with "the development of a New European Private Law" "there is no longer room for the traditional – nationally oriented – law school curriculum".[42] Others point to the increasing interest of (US-)universities to integrate comparative and international law courses in their regular curricula; this indicates the willingness to open up for international aspects.[43] For many reasons named in various contributions, I consider it quite likely that history of international law will gain more importance in the future.

But this is not the only and quite trivial insight one can achieve by regarding this field. The central and attracting word in the title of our workshop seems to be "comparative". It reflects both the wish and the will to leave behind the narrowing focus of national traditions and frameworks of legal history.[44] We should always bare in mind the alternatives of regulatory paths which other European countries took, their jurisdictions, their doctrines. Hence, the idea of comparison is a very good one[45]; I wish only to make two critical remarks.

---

[40] German Law Journal Vol. 10, Issue Number 7 (2009).

[41] Bram Akkermans, Challenges in Legal Education and the Development of a New European Private Law, in: German Law Journal 10 (2009), pp.803–814 (805).

[42] Idem, p.813.

[43] Helge Dedek, Armand de Mestral, *Born to be wild*: The „Trans-systemic" Programme at McGill and the De-Nationalization of Legal Education, in: German Law Journal 10 (2009), pp.889–911 (897 et seq.).

[44] Johannes Liebrecht is mentioning this function of comparison, see Art. Rechtsgeschichte, in Jürgen Basedow, Klaus J. Hopt, Reinhard Zimmermann (eds.), Handwörterbuch des Europäischen Privatrechts, vol. 2. Kauf – Zwingendes Recht, Tübingen 2009, pp.1245–1249.

[45] See also the paper from Martin Löhnig, Vergleichende Rechtsgeschichte: Bestandsaufnahme und Perspektiven, in: Zeitschrift für Neuere Rechtsgeschichte 32 (2010), pp.82–90.

1. Difficulties and challenges

First of all you should not underestimate the difficulties and challenges of a comparative approach in legal history – particularly when speaking about teaching. It is already hard to explain the complexity of pre-modern regulatory regimes or procedural law in one country or territory to students. Additionally, not all parts of legal history were investigated in the same intensity; particularly the link between legal history and comparative law seems to be a domain of civil law history.[46] Other fields are already of less interest, both from the perspective of legal history and from the one of comparative history; no or little research is done on them. Although I would really like to speak about it, I know too little about the different strategies of regulation technology in many European countries or even German territories during the industrial period.[47] And it gets even worse when trying to compare two or more regimes in classroom. Imagine briefly the necessary language abilities and required reading time, the often found lack of general historical knowledge and sometimes even the lack of interest in details and differentiations among students (universities are not able to compensate these deficits[48]) – now you will understand what heavy task it is to introduce a comparative perspective in legal history.

2. Beyond the European framework

Secondly, a European comparative approach is geographically too narrow. We live in a global normative order. A comparative legal history should widen its focus beyond Europe, "Weltgeschichte", "global history" would be a more appropriate perspective; not only, but particularly when speaking about the 19th century.[49] It should consider US-American legal history, as well as other parts of the world. In 2010 South America celebrates its autonomous constitution-

---

46 See the characteristic examples in: James Gordley, Comparative Law and Legal History, in: Mathias Reimann, Reinhard Zimmermann (ed.), The Oxford Handbook of Comparative Law, Oxford 2006, pp.753–773.

47 See the example of (international) steam engine regulation at Ina vom Feld, Staatsentlastung im Technikrecht. Dampfkesselgesetzgebung und -überwachung in Preußen 1831–1914 (Studien zur europäischen Rechtsgeschichte 216; Recht in der Industriellen Revolution 5), Frankfurt am Main 2007, pp.209 et seqq.

48 Miloš Vec, Bildung als Schnäppchenjagd. Erst hat sich's ein-, jetzt hat sich's ausgebildet: Wovon alle reden, worum sich aber niemand kümmert – über das Verschwinden einer Leitidee aus der deutschen Hochschulpraxis, in: Frankfurter Allgemeine Zeitung, 1. Juni 2010, p.31.

49 Jürgen Osterhammel, Die Verwandlung der Welt. Eine Geschichte des 19. Jahrhunderts, München 2009; Christopher A. Bayly, Die Geburt der modernen Welt. Eine Globalgeschichte 1780–1914, Frankfurt am Main 2006.

alization.[50] Other parts of the world are very much aware of their reception of European legal models like Turkey or Japan. Researchers from these countries are in vital exchange with the ones from European countries.[51] To achieve a global reciprocity we should include their legal history in our narrations, and if possible also that of other parts of the world; although I must admit to know little about many regions in the world and their historical law regimes. Yet the international composition in our classrooms would support such a widened focus.

3. Modified comparative approaches

Thirdly, a comparative approach gives testimony of our focus on entities which are comparable. National and territorial regulation can be compared synchronical and diachronical, even whole "legal cultures", "legal systems" or "legal families" can be the object of comparison.[52]

Yet, how do we deal with the issue of comparability in the history of international law? I do not want to claim that comparing does not make any sense here. However, it is obviously different. International law bears an international component in its subject. Nevertheless, it also can be compared. I will name three possibilities:

a) You can compare different national approaches to International law, *inter alia* the English tradition with the Baltic one. Comparing these doctrines or diplomatic practices would reveal the usual scheme of commons and differences.

b) You can also try to compare on a higher level "our" ius publicum europaeum[53] – that means international law founded and developed in Europe and designed mainly for the purpose of regulating relations within this geographical and political frame – with efforts to establish a regional international law in the Americas. This was forwarded by South American lawyers like Andres Bello[54]

---

[50] See Rechtsgeschichte. Zeitschrift des Max-Planck-Instituts für europäische Rechtsgeschichte 16 (2010) with numerous contributions to „Verfassung und Verfassungsrecht in Lateinamerika im Licht des bicentenario", pp.16–130.

[51] E.g. Masasuke Ishibe, Neuere deutsche Rechtsgeschichte in Japan, 1. Teil: Von 1880 bis 1890, in: Zeitschrift für Neuere Rechtsgeschichte 27 (2005), pp.62–76; Kenichi Moriya, Neuere deutsche Rechtsgeschichte in Japan, 2. Teil: Von 1890 bis zur Gegenwart, in: Zeitschrift für Neuere Rechtsgeschichte 31 (2009), pp.95–131.

[52] Ralf Michaels, Art. Rechtsvergleichung, in: Jürgen Basedow, Klaus J. Hopt, Reinhard Zimmermann (eds.), Handwörterbuch des Europäischen Privatrechts, vol. 2. Kauf – Zwingendes Recht, Tübingen 2009, pp.1265–1269.

[53] Heinhard Steiger, Art. „Ius Publicum Europaeum", Friedrich Jaeger (ed.), Enzyklopädie der Neuzeit, vol.5, Stuttgart 2007, column 1148–1153.

[54] A[ndres] B[ello], Principios de Derecho de Jentes, (*no place, no date*) [Santiago de Chile 1832].

and Alejandro Alvarez[55] in the 19th century. Political independency was brought to juridical constructions of international law and its principles after 1810.

c) Finally, you can compare the European pre-modern system of international relations with those autonomous pre-modern systems established in the Far East where China's hegemony lasted for centuries. Was this law or did it only constitute rules and customs? How about the European system of diplomacy: Did its rules (e.g. on immunity or precedency) constitute legal or (only) social norms?[56] Contemporary early modern legal theory had some observations on that.[57] Thus, what is the right concept of law?

We all know from current research that all of the three approaches are very interesting. The point I want to make is that in this particular field the comparative approach is not needed to introduce internationalism as the history of international law is already international in its subject-matter and perspective.

To be clear, comparison is still fruitful but it will be a particular challenge for the classroom: For a third year law student it is hard to understand the genuine characteristics of August von Bulmerincq's international law system[58] – a person they have never heard of before and probably they will never again, even if they specialize in international law and even given the fact that he was founder of the Institut de Droit International in 1873.[59] Anyhow, it is even

---

[55] Alejandro Alvarez, Le droit international amèricain, Paris 1910; idem, International Law and related subjects from the point of view of the American continent. A Report on Lectures delivered in the Universities of the United States, 1916–1918, under the auspices of the Carnegie Endowment for International Peace, including a Comparative Study of the Universities of Latin America and the United States (Pamphlet Series of the Carnegie Endowment for International Peace. Division of International Law 48), Washington 1922.

[56] Some observations on international relations too at Barbara Stollberg-Rilinger, Des Kaisers alte Kleider. Verfassungsgeschichte und Symbolsprache des Alten Reiches, München 2008, pp.106, 150 et seqq., 259 et seqq.

[57] Miloš Vec, Juristische Normen des Anstands. Zur Ausdifferenzierung und Konvergenz von Recht und Sitte bei Christian Thomasius, in: Reiner Schulze (ed.), Rechtssymbolik und Wertevermittlung (Schriften zur europäischen Rechts- und Verfassungsgeschichte 47), Berlin 2004, pp.69–100; idem, Höflichkeit als Selbstgesetzgebung. Beobachtungen zu einer spezifischen Normativität im Natur-, Staats- und Völkerrecht der Aufklärung, in: Gisela Engel, Brita Rang, Susanne Scholz, Johannes Süßmann (ed.), Konjunkturen der Höflichkeit in der Frühen Neuzeit (=Zeitsprünge. Forschungen zur Frühen Neuzeit, vol. 13, book no. 3/4), Frankfurt am Main 2009, pp.510–530.

[58] His main works: August von Bulmerincq, Die Systematik des Völkerrechts, Erster Theil: Kritik der Ausführung und Forschungen zu Gunsten der Systematisirung des positiven Völkerrechts, Dorpat 1858; idem, Praxis, Theorie und Kodifikation des Voelkerrechts, Leipzig 1874; idem, Völkerrecht, in: Heinrich Marquardsen (ed.), Handbuch des Öffentlichen Rechts, Band 1, Allgemeiner Teil, Zweiter Halbband, Tübingen 1884, pp.177–384; on Bulmerincq see: Lauri Mälksoo, The Context of International Legal Arguments. "Positivist" International Law Scholar August von Bulmerincq (1822–1890) and his Concept of Politics, in: Journal of the History of International Law 7 (2005), pp.181–209.

[59] See Martti Koskenniemi, The Gentle Civilizer of Nations. The Rise and Fall of International Law 1870–1960, Cambridge 2001, pp.39 et seqq.

more challenging trying to compare Bulmerincq's system of international law from the second half of the 19th century with those of his contemporaries, *inter alia* James Lorimer[60] or H.W. Halleck[61]. My group did so in our last seminar at Frankfurt University. This comparison was based on student's individual presentations on each of those lawyers. However, it only took place on the final stage and those students who knew neither of them (Bulmerincq or Halleck) felt maybe excluded from discussion.

V. Transnational developments and the charm of national perspectives

Analyzing teaching of history of international law you understand that there is more than the dichotomy of national legal history on the one and comparative legal history on the other hand. There are transnational developments which demand our attention. We all know Philip Jessup's terminological invention of 1956: "Transnational law"[62]. These transnational developments show better than others the relativity of epochs, cesura and geographical frontiers.

They show that our cultures were never fixed but existed in processes of exchange, adoption and reception. Maybe the focus on comparison holds up the illusion of principally autonomous regulatory entities. By the way: The investigation of the processes of exchange, adoption and reception are one example of the influence of different disciplinary perspectives in the research of history of international law I mentioned earlier in this paper. While legal historians focus their methodological discourses on the comparative approach, sociologists and political scientists develop new fields of research by investigating the interdependencies of research units.

On the other hand, national frameworks of legal history are more than atavisms. Our legal histories will always be told differently, depending on the perspectives we have and the geographical and political positions belonging – among many other categories – to these perspectives. These perspectives shape both the interests and the focus of our research; they lead us to different and new subjects. Therefore, we should take them and their implications seriously. However, this does not mean we should not be critical towards them.

---

60 James Lorimer, The institutes of the law of nations: a treatise of the jural relations of separate political communities, 2 vol., Edinburgh and London 1883 and 1884.

61 H[enry] W[ager] Halleck, International Law or Rules regulating the Intercourse of States in Peace and War, San Francisco 1861.

62 Philip Jessup, Transnational law, 1956; Peer Zumbansen, Art. Transnational Law, in: Jan Smits, Edward Elgar (ed.), Encyclopedia of Comparative Law, Cheltenham 2006, pp.738–754.

VI. Conclusions

1. European comparative legal history is hard to achieve, not only but particularly in the classroom. Its requirements are high.
2. European comparative legal history is not enough. We should strive for a global comparative legal history. The international composition of the students in our classrooms goes already beyond European citizenships; hence, it strongly supports a broader focus.
3. There are international subjects and transnational legal evolutions which are beyond the dichotomy of national legal history and comparative legal history.
4. National traditions are more than atavisms; we should handle them seriously and critically in our classrooms.
5. Standardization of teaching approaches and practices can hinder progress; we should not use this discourse and exchange on topics, aims and methods for a convergence of our work.
6. Plurality, exchange and competition are vital elements to improve teaching and research on legal history.

Heikki Pihlajamäki

When Small is Beautiful: Teaching Comparative Legal History in the Periphery

Introduction

A few years back, Charles Donahue wrote an article on comparative legal history in North America, starting with an observation that he actually had hardly anything to write about. In fact, the predominantly national orientation has plagued legal history for as long as it has existed as an independent discipline.[1] In big countries, which have produced great history, comparative outlook has been rare, although it had to be admitted that things have been changing since Donahue wrote his piece. Exceptions apart, it can safely be said that legal history not only in the United States but also in Germany, France and England is predominantly nationally oriented. Small countries have followed the bigger ones, and because university education is based on research, legal history teaching is traditionally very nationally oriented.

James Gordley has said that we can no longer "accept the premise from which comparative law began [in the nineteenth century]: that one is comparing a domestic law contained in domestic sources with foreign law. This is because domestic law contains elements, "formants" (as Rodolfo Sacco would have it), taken from abroad. What are frequently portrayed as national legal systems are not system in the strict sense but rather "amalgams of solutions developed over time".[2]

If comparative legal history thrives somewhere today, it does in small countries. A few examples will have to suffice in this short abstract. This conference is organized by a Valencian, a Belgian, a Dutch and two Swedes. Much of legal history teaching in Sweden is comparative by nature these days, and in Helsinki the Law Faculty has recently founded a chair in comparative legal history. The papers at this conference offer a wide range of other examples.

---

[1] Charles Dohahue, Comparative Legal History in North America, 65 *Tijdschrift voor Rechtsgeschiedenis* (1997) 1–17.

[2] James Gordley, "Comparative Law and Legal History", in Mathias Reimann – Reinhard Zimmermann (eds.), *The Oxford Handbook of Comparative Law* (Oxford, 2008) 762–764.

Quite obviously, little countries need other aspects on their legal past more desperately than big countries.

In our presentations, we intend to approach the teaching of comparative legal history from the point of view of a small nation, which in some respects differs from that of a larger country. We will first explain why the legal history of small country always needs to be viewed in comparative context. Then we will attempt to lay out a scheme of how these theoretical ponderings could be translated into classroom work on the general level. Lastly, we will present a model of course in comparative legal history which, according to our understandings fulfils well these needs.

We take periphery as an unproblematic concept, meaning any country that does not belong to the legal historical core area of Europe or North America. Finland, as well as all other Nordic countries, is definitely to be considered periphery for the purposes. We also embrace a very wide concept of comparative legal history: comparative legal history is simply the opposite of purely national legal history. Thus, comparative legal history does not need to involve classical comparisons of legal historical cases. Comparative framework for national history will count as comparative legal history, as will any supra-national legal historical work.

The Need for Comparative Legal History

According to F. C. von Savigny, law grows organically, much in the same way as language or poetry. Innovations and adaptations are made, and they travel to other regions and countries. The phenomenon of legal transfers is thus clearly one reason to understand the development of foreign law. The law of a nation state is never pure anything, just like any language or the population of any nation is ever racially pure. National legal orders develop in continuous interaction with those of other nations. This goes for all levels of law: academic legal writing, legislation, and even court practice frequently receive impulses from the outside. The impulses go many different ways, but they do not traverse borders in a balanced way. As Ugo Mattei has explained, the hegemony of legal science has shifted during the course of modern Western legal history: from the nineteenth-century German hegemony, the scales tipped in favour of the United States in the post-war period and have remained so.[3]

Generally speaking, legal history teaching includes always a comparative

---

[3] See Ugo Mattei, " "Why the Wind Changed: Intellectual Leadership in Western Law", The American Journal of Comparative Law 42 (1994).

perspective, either temporal or spatial. To understand current legal developments, one needs to know history of law. – And to understand one's own legal culture, one needs to understand those of other countries as well. However, the phenomenon of legal transfer, when looked at from narrow perspective of the development of one legal system, for instance, the Finnish one, does not put foreign legal orders at an equal footing. A Finnish law student will have to gain knowledge of German and American law, in particular, but does not have to be equally aware of the particularities of Chinese law codes during Han Dynasty or the complexities of Spanish colonial law in Latin America.

However, this is only a narrow national perspective. Any theoretical or more advanced understanding of legal history will need to abandon the narrow national perspective completely, if legal history is to offer anything valuable to the understanding of law. It is impossible to grasp any of the particularities of Western law without it with non-Western legal systems, such as Chinese or Islamic law. In this sense, any legal history is comparative legal history as well.

And finally, a global understanding of law requires at least a basic understanding of world's major legal systems. An understanding of systems other than the domestic one is becoming a practical necessity for at least part of the legal professionals.

In today's world, deeper understanding of legal history cannot be gained anywhere without some understanding of comparative issues. This is, however, particularly evident in small countries. An easy way to provoke Finnish law students is claiming that, as far as law is concerned, nothing or next to nothing was ever invented in Finland. Not that Finns are particularly non-innovative, obviously the same can be said about other small nations. Students of legal history of small countries, however, unavoidably run into comparative legal history, if they are to understand any significant feature of their legal past other than superficially or to do anything more than purely descriptive work. Nor does this observation excuse legal historians of large countries from the comparative perspective. Clearly, the differences between small and large countries are only quantitative not qualitative.

Local Legal History in Large Context

As is well-known, traditional legal history is a product of the nineteenth-century national state. By focusing on the national state, and by concentrating on backing up and legitimizing the national state's statutory law, its prime legal source, national legal histories have not only neglected larger comparisons but also smaller local histories. The latter will, however, now be neglected. Purely national legal history thus can hardly exist.

Two recent German text-books masterfully combine the local and the comparative: Knut Nörr's[4] and Mathias Schmoeckel's [5] books both start at a regional level – Nordhein-Westfalen and Rheinland, respectively – and then link the regional legal history to German and European developments, thus avoiding the national trap. This comes, however, more naturally in Germany than in Finland, where the national level was dominant from early on and where there never existed such an abundance of legal sources competing with it as in Germany. The supra-national level, however, comes naturally. Finland was part of the Kingdom of Sweden until 1809, which makes Swedish legal history before that ours as well.

The links of the Finnish-Swedish legal history with German law extend the need for comparative perspective to wider European circles. After 1809, when Finland became a Grand-Duchy within the Russian Empire, the links with Sweden and other Nordic countries continued because of the legislative cooperation; on the contrary, little influence was received from the Russian side. In fact too little, as Finnish research, perhaps for nationalistic reasons, has traditionally largely avoided the Russian context, consequently receiving little attention in the teaching of legal history. On the other hand, even Russians themselves are yet to update the history of their legal past, which could help the neighbouring countries such as Finland to construct their own histories. This missing link is what bothers me the most in our teaching.

It should also be mentioned that a domestic/Nordic perspective for a long time dominated the teaching in law, and in legal history as well. At the beginning of the 1990s – when it became clear that Finland would become a member of the European Union – the curriculum in law faculties was reformed, and since 1993 courses in European legal history have been taught. For the past six years seminars in global legal history have been offered as well.

The Course: Finnish Legal History in Global Context

This course description is not a complete one, meaning that I will not go into the pedagogical details, sticking instead to contents. A few words as to the legal education, the system of teaching law and legal history are nevertheless in place.

In Finland, the law faculties train and examine future legal professionals. The

---

4 Karl Kroeschell, recht unde unrecht der sassen. Rechtsgeschichte Niedersachsens (Göttingen 2005).

5 Mathias Schmoeckel, *Auf der Suche nach der verlorenen Ordnung* (Böhlau 2005).

access to the faculties is restricted by a numerus clausus system (admission test), and even the fresh first year students have some knowledge in law and a high motivation to the studies. After students have finished their university studies they are qualified for working as judges, advocates, civil servants, or university teachers. Thus, the curriculum of a Finnish law student includes, except legal theory and legal history, all possible fields (ca. 20) of positive law. The expressed goal of the studies is to "train students in legal thinking – to be able to identify, which problems are legal and to solve them".

Legal history is currently, according to the (semi)compulsory curriculum, the first subject to be studied during the first semester, after General Introduction to Law. The compulsory course can either be taken as book exam consisting of three books, or instead of each book a lecture course can be taken. Few end up reading any books, instead taking part in teaching. This means that the student-teacher-ratio is not particularly favourable as far as the first year introductory course is concerned.

Contents-wise the course, for the past few years, has consisted of the following elements: Roman law and its historical development, European legal history and Finnish legal history. In teaching the first two have been practically merged into two courses of European legal history, the first ranging from antiquity roughly until the French Revolution and the second encompassing the nineteenth and twentieth centuries. The domestic legal history remains a course of its own, building on the two lecture courses on European legal history. The lecture courses have their own exams, and the teaching methods vary according to the teacher. Some teachers use text materials, for instance, while others most rely on traditional, straight lecturing. The audience of 200 students sets its natural limits to the teaching methodology.

This is thus the compulsory first-year course that we have described above. After the compulsory legal history offers several optional courses, the topics ranging from legal historical theatre courses to different kinds of text courses and more traditional seminar courses. The optional courses or the specialization year are not a huge challenge to the discipline. Being optional, both teachers and students tend to be highly motivated to participate. These courses are flexible and, by nature, research-oriented.

The challenge, however, is first-year teaching. To be sure, the courses have changed considerably over the last few years. Modern teaching methods have been introduced, although given the (what we would call excessive) freedom of teachers to plan their own teaching, the three courses hardly form a coherent whole. It is not that the teaching of legal history in our faculty would be in any grave crisis. On the contrary, legal history has a stable, self evident status in the curriculum, it regularly receives outstanding feedback from the students and is, it is fair to stay, considered one of the most ambitious subjects as far as developing teaching is considered. However, much remains to be done, and our basic course has not yet been fully adjusted to the changed thinking about legal history as an academic endeavour. That is, to the notion of constantly viewing the national within the comparative context.

In this presentation, we would like to introduce a model to integrate the three teaching courses – the two courses of European legal history and the one on Finnish legal history – into a coherent whole, "Finnish legal history in comparative context". The description is, naturally enough, not complete. We must limit this presentation to a few examples of what the course could look like. Combining the three courses would give us a slot of 60 lecture hours (à 45 minutes). Because of the rigid positioning of the different subjects within the academic year, all of these 60 hours have to be fitted within the three first weeks of November. This means four hours per day. The tight schedule places constraints on the teaching methodology. However, the students are expected to spend (theoretically) four hours studying each day after the lectures. This allows for distributing teaching materials and home assignments.

The basic structure of the course is chronological. It consists of three parts: 1) The origins of Western law, 2) Western law before modernity, and 3) the development of Western law in modernity. Each section will be allotted 20 teaching ours.

1. We start from the Roman antiquity, on to the early middle ages, and the birth of law as an academic enterprise in the middle ages. Much emphasis is placed on the particularity of Western law in the global context. This requires that an understanding on the findings of legal anthropology on the role of law in primitive societies and the "birth of law" will need to be given. To speak of Western law is meaningless, unless we contrast it other major global systems of law. Thus, a brief introduction to the specific features of Islamic and Chinese law is in place (law as a separate norm system from morals and religion; the university; Roman law as heritage of private law; legal positivism etc.; human rights etc.).

The early history is important, if we want the students to understand what is specific and what is typical of Western law. In order to understand our own, modern national or European law, we need transcend it, go outside of it both temporally and spatially.

2. This section begins in the 11th and 12th centuries, and the rebirth of the Roman law. An emphasis is placed on the interplay of academic law with legal practise. Canon law, Roman law, etc. The written versions of local customary

laws European-wide is especially important, because of the correspondent phenomenon in Sweden (county laws, *landskapslagar*).

The effect of Canon law, and Roman law from the 16. century onwards. The founding of the Swedish High Courts in the seventeenth century against the background of European high courts (the French parliaments, German imperial high courts, etc). The link of the high courts to political power.

3. The third section deals with modernity, 19th and 20th centuries. The history of codification, the historical school, and positivism as the background. German legal history is of primary comparative interest here, but also the Nordic context. The national versions of the international themes, the birth of modern Finnish law towards the late 19th century: rule of law, legal positivism, constitutionalism, procedure, criminal law etc. Critical schools of law, shifting the comparative emphasis to the US. The importance of the US after the Second World War. EU etc.

The whole idea is to depart from the international (European or global) level, which is represented by the dominant legal cultures of each period, then transcending to the national level to see what became of these influences in Finland, what kind of national versions of the international themes of law developed. In what ways Finland was similar, in what ways not and what was the social and political context for those nationally adopted versions.

Jørn Øyrehagen Sunde

Legal Cultural Changes in Europe – Teaching Future Prospects on the Basis of Legal History and Comparative Law

Preliminary discourse

I do not teach comparative legal history. I teach Legal History and Comparative Law under the overreaching title "Legal cultural changes in Europe".[1] I do not teach legal history to teach my students history of law, and I do not teach comparative law to teach my students how to compare law. I teach them legal history and comparative law to be able to analyse and comprehend the basic features of the legal cultural changes taking place in Europe today.

The European Human Rights and EU law are today part of Norwegian internal law, as is the case in other European nations. This supranational law has to be applied with the legal method of the place of their origin, and/or of the place of their authoritative appliance. Legal method is, as we shall see, one of the major legal cultural elements, and hence is not merely a technique to find law, but a vital part of how law is perceived. Applying the European Human Rights and EU law as internal law implies a major legal cultural change in the everyday life of Norwegian law, and thus legal cultural knowledge has to be passed on to those studying law.

Legal culture might seem a very academic approach to law. And it used to be. But the interest for legal culture is at least in Norway more intense among practitioners and students than academics. This is due to the fact that they every day face the need for legal cultural knowledge as an instrument to analyse and comprehend the European Human Rights and the EU law and the manner in which they are to be applied. To send law students into society today without legal cultural knowledge would simply be to lower the degree of legal certainty of the citizens.

[1] The title of the subject in Norwegian is "Rettskultur i eit Europa i endring".

The naked facts

Legal History and Comparative Law is taught as the last course at the third year of law study at the Faculty of Law at the University of Bergen, on the west coast of Norway. This has been done since 2005. Legal history has long been taught in Norway, while comparative law had never been taught before. Comparative law is still only taught in Norway at the Faculty of Law in Bergen.[2] All students at year three to five of the law study can take the exam. Usually about 450 students sign up for the subject every year, while about 350 actually sit the exam.[3]

In Bergen, lectures in Legal History and Comparative Law begin every year in the very last days of April or the first days of May. At this time the lecture disposition and all subjects for group discussions and seminars are made public. The teaching is done by the professor with a duty to teach legal history in Bergen, who is also in charge of the subject, and four assistants.[4]

The first two weeks the students are offered 16 lecturing hours of lectures,[5] and are encouraged to spend the extra time reading the curriculum. They then have one week off to study on their own before the last, tough three weeks of preparations for the exam. On the Monday of these three weeks they meet in groups of twelve students, with both a right and duty to participate, to discuss a subject. Within Wednesday morning they have to write a paper of more then 700 words on the same subject.[6] The paper is put on the web and made available for their fellow students in the group. By midday Thursday at least two students have written comments to each paper, which is also made available to the other members of the group. From mid-Thursday till Friday morning one of the five persons in the teaching team comments on one of the papers in each group, and these comments are available to the members of the three discussion groups that make up each seminar.

Friday is seminar day, and ten seminars are held during the day. Each seminar lasts for two lecturing hours, each have 36 students with a right and duty to turn

---

[2] The other Faculties of Law are at the University of Oslo and at the University of Tromsø. Legal history and comparative law is also taught at the bachelor study of law at the College at Lillehammer, which has applied the study model used in Bergen since 2008

[3] At Lillehammer 100 students will take an exam in legal history and comparative law from 2012 when their bachelor study in law is fully operational.

[4] The system of professor chairs was abolished in Norway in 1967, and professors are today employed with a duty to teach certain subjects.

[5] At Norwegian universities, one lecturing hour covers a time period of 45 minutes. The lectures are held in pairs with a fifteen minutes break in between. The lectures in this subject are held between 8.15 and 10 a.m.

[6] The papers are usually between 1200 and 1800 words.

up, and each is taught by one of the five teachers in the subject. The seminar opens with the teacher commenting on the written papers for 20 to 30 minutes. Then follows a discussion on a subject related to the one dealt with in the group discussion and the paper, but the subject is wider and more complex. During the seminar the teacher will deal with both the subject itself and how to present it in a paper. This is done in dialogue with the students. If the students do not participate, the teacher has a standing order to leave the seminar.

After three weeks of exam preparations we have reached June, and the students are offered a four lecturing hours repetition lecture on the Monday of the last week of the course. On Tuesday morning a document containing all questions asked and answers given on e-mail during the course are made available to all students. And on the Thursday the same week the students take a four-hour exam in Legal History and Comparative Law.[7] Five weeks later they receive their grade on the commonly ten to twelve pages paper written during the exam. They then have three weeks to decide if they will demand a new reading and grading of their exam. Those who failed, and those who fell ill at the day of the exam, can take an exam in mid August. Those who want to improve their grade can retake the exam the next year in June.

The literature and making a coherent curriculum for an incoherent subject

In general Norwegian law students are very open to study almost any branch of law if the literature on the subject is found comprehensible and readable. When basing a subject on several independent pieces of literature coherence is yet another crucial factor. The first years of teaching Legal History and Comparative Law in Bergen suffered from the lack of coherent literature, and hence of student interest. Only in 2008 a radical change in the reading material for the subject put it on the road towards increased student interest. In 2010 the students at the Faculty of Law in Bergen voted the lecturer of the subject the lecturer of the year, a token of the interest the subject had gained since 2008.

In 2005 a book on the history of the Norwegian legal culture entitled *Speculum legale* was published as the first comprehensive treaty on Norwegian legal history since 1972.[8] The book was written to be used when teaching Legal History and Comparative Law at the Faculty of Law in Tromsø, but comparative law was

---

[7] Only those who have participated at 75% of the teaching offered have a right to take the exam.

[8] Jørn Øyrehagen Sunde, *Speculum Legale – Rettsspegelen: Ein introduksjon til den norske rettskulturen si historie i eit europeisk perspektiv* (Bergen: Fagbokforlaget, 2005).

taken off the schedule even before the first lecture was held in 2006. This book was used in Bergen from 2008, and suited the subject well since it was aimed at being used as a parallel to literature on comparative law.

It has been a problem to find suitable literature in comparative law. The choice fell on the book by Michael Bogdan, since it was updated and provided hard core pre-millennium comparative law in the tradition of Konrad Zweigert and Hein Kötz.[9] This book is the supplemented by *Rendezvous of European legal Cultures*, first made available to the students in 2009, and finally published in 2010.[10] This book is an anthology with articles on legal culture and reception of law in past and present, where articles on the contributions to a European legal culture through the practice of the European court of Human Rights and the European Court of Justice play a central role. Together with hardcore pre-millennium knowledge of English, French, German and American law, this post-millennium approach makes up the comparative law part of the literature.

The students do not have to read the three books in their entirety, and all together the curriculum is only 449 pages. Even though each of the three books making up the literature in the subject Legal History and Comparative Law are comprehensible and readable, it does not make up a coherent body of knowledge, despite the relationship explained above. This problem is partly reduced, as has already been stated, by the fact that the teaching subject is not really legal history and comparative law in itself. Instead the subject is defined as "Legal cultural changes in Europe". To be able to study these changes the lectures are divided into six different, overreaching themes: Conflict resolution, norm production, idea of justice, legal method, professionalisation and internationalisation.

Each theme is taught by first lecturing on the Norwegian legal history from about year 1000 till today. When lecturing on Norwegian law today, the question posed is what has happened and what will happen to the Norwegian legal cultures after the European Human Rights and EU law have become part of Norwegian law in 1999 and 1994. Then the question posed is what is the state of affairs on this theme in the English, French, German and American legal culture today, and what challenges are English, French and German law faced with after the European Human Rights and EU law became part of their internal law. Thus each part of the literature is interwoven, even though it is not completely intervened.

---

9 Michael Bogdan: *Komparativ rättskunskap* (Stockholm: Norstedts Juridik, 2003).

10 *Rendezvous of Europen Legal Cultures*, ed. by Jørn Øyrehagen Sunde and Knut Einar Skodvin (Bergen: Fagbokforlaget, 2010).

The structure from the lectures is also applied on the group discussions, the papers, the seminars and the exams. Hence, a 154-page disposition for the lectures is made available for the students electronically. The disposition is the very intellectual glue in the subject Legal History and Comparative Law as taught at the Faculty of Law in Bergen, and might be regarded as the fourth and last part of the literature.

How legal culture is defined and explained

Legal culture, and the legal cultural changes taking place in Europe today, is what brings the different part of Legal History and Comparative Law together when taught at the Faculty of Law in Bergen. The problem is of course that legal culture is much like champagne: The first sip tastes wonderful, but the more you get of it the more nonsense is likely to be the outcome. To avoid the nonsense that follow when abuse replaces use, an approach must be found that delimits the set of relevant factors when moving outside the boundaries of positive law. The most crucial part of the teaching material is hence the article "Champagne at the Funeral – an Introduction to Legal Culture", which is the first article in *Rendezvous of European Legal Cultures* and the first part of the literature dealt with in the lectures. Because, to quote Charles Dickens, if this concept is not perfectly understood, "nothing wonderful can come of the story" to be revealed.[11] This also applies for this article, and hence an outline of legal culture as taught in Bergen will be given in the following.

To make the concept of legal culture more manageable it is defined as ideas and expectations of law that are made operational by institutional (-like) practices.[12] But legal culture is still a concept that is difficult to manage even when it is defined. To obtain a larger degree of clarity among the students the structures that determine the *style* of a legal culture, to apply a term used by Zweigert

---

[11] Charles Dickens, *The Christmas Books*, volume 1: A Christmas Carol/The Chimes (Harmondsworth: Penguin Classics, 1985) p. 45.

[12] Jørn Øyrehagen Sunde, "Champagne at the Funeral – an Introduction to Legal Culture", *Rendezvous of Europen Legal Cultures*, ed. by Jørn Øyrehagen Sunde and Knut Einar Skodvin (Bergen: Fagbokforlaget, 2010).p. 11. This definition is not wholly original, and is in debt to two other definitions: Lawrence Meir Friedman, 'Some Thoughts on Comparative Legal Culture', in *Comparative and Private International Law – Essays in Honor of John Henry Merryman on His Seventieth Birthday*, ed. by David S. Clark and John Henry Merryman (Berlin: Duncker & Humblot, 1995) p. 53, and See John Bell, 'Comparative Law and Legal Theory', in *Prescriptive Formality and Normative Rationality in Modern Legal Systems*, ed. by W. Krawietz, N. MacCormick and G.H. von Wright (Berlin: Duncker & Humblot, 1994) p. 25 (partly quoting van Canegem) and p. 29.

and Kötz in their *An introduction to comparative law*,[13] are displayed.[14] As a starting point, the students are told that the body and soul of a legal culture is its institutional and intellectual structures.

The institutional structure of a legal culture is, in short, made up of institutions that shape law through their practices. Law is separated from other spheres of life by some form of institutionalising. In non-state societies these institutions are extremely weak, but might still, with terminological generosity, be called institutions. To illustrate this, the students are presented with an early medieval Norwegian law dealing with the case when a man kills another man whom he found in bed with his wife. After the killing the husband had to announce his deed to his neighbours, and to take the bloody sheet to the public assembly when repeating the announcement there, to make it a legal killing.[15] There is not much separating this killing from any other, except the condition – in bed with his wife – and the actions – the announcement and presentation of the sheet. The condition and action required are still stamp marks of law, and signalises that a first institutionalising of law has taken place.

There are several kinds of institutions shaping law. Only two major institutions are presented to the students: Conflict resolving and norm producing institutions. The most basic institutions are those settling conflicts, since the only reason law exists is that it resolves conflicts in a manner that limits the use of non-state violence. When law does not resolve conflicts, the will of the strongest replaces law. In non-state societies such conflict-resolution institutions will simply be limits on the use of violence, or *ad hoc* mediation organs. With the emergence of a state-like power the use of violence as a legitimate way of resolving conflicts will cease, and the mediating organs will by and by meet regularly, be more professionalised and finally turn into courts with presiding judges. These courts will then, in short, be organised in a hierarchy with appeals regulating access from lower to higher court levels.

This basic perspective is a surprising one to the students, since they are used to thinking of norm production in general, and lawmaking more specifically, at the core of law. But norm production is originally only a by-product of conflict resolution – historically each time a case was settled a norm was produced. By

---

[13] Konrad Zweigert, and Hein Kötz, *Introduction to Comparative Law* (Oxford: Clarendon Press, 1998) pp. 67–72. In German Zweigert and Kötz speak of *der Stil*.

[14] This is also done by Mark van Hoecke, and Mark Warrington, 'Legal Culture, Legal Paradigms and Legal Doctrine: Towards a New Model for Comparative Law', *The International and Comparative Law Quarterly*, 47 (1998) pp. 514–5. They end up with six structural elements as well, but only legal methodology is a structural element in both their theory of legal culture and this one.

[15] The Frostating Compilation IV-39, seen in relation with The Gulating Compilation X-11.

and by these norms were reused in similar cases, and case law appeared. The case law was systematised and developed by a lawmaker, and at this time conflict resolution and norm production had become the affairs of two distinctly different institutions within the institutional structure of a legal culture. However, the students are told to keep in mind that courts have never ceased to create norms, even when this has formally been the exclusive domain of the lawmaker. The reason is the limitation on human fantasy: it is impossible to foresee and prescribe a solution to all possible conflicts.[16]

Somewhat simplified, the students are told that the institutional structure of law is a question of who – who settles conflicts and who produces legal norms? The intellectual structure of a legal culture is a question of what – what is the idea of justice, the legal method, the degree of professionalisation and character of internationalisation dictating the resolution of conflicts and the production of legal norms?[17] The students are told to keep in mind that these are not the only structural elements of a legal culture, but they are major ones.

The production and application of legal norms do not take place in an intellectual vacuum. Rather, there are several intellectual factors that dictate how norms are made and applied. The most basic is the idea of justice. Just like conflict resolution, justice is a basic demand directed towards law. That is, if law to some extent does not settle conflicts, it loses all legitimacy, and just solutions have a much higher degree of legitimacy than those experienced as unjust. The students are told to keep in mind that what is considered just is not constant, but vary from place to place and from time to time.

To make an idea of justice operative – that is, to solve a specific case in accordance with an idea of justice – a method is of great assistance. A legal method is simply the manner in which ideas of justice, values, principles or laws are turned into legal rules used to settle a conflict. While an idea of justice might be shared by lawyers and non-lawyers alike, legal method appears, and is more and more specialised, with an increased professionalisation of law. The reason is that it is not legal knowledge, but methodological knowledge, that separates lawyers from laymen.

---

[16] It must be kept in mind that there are other norm producers than courts and lawmakers. Customary law is for example produced through the intricate interplay between the practice of legal subjects and the recognition of the courts, while systems of law, principles and legal rules are created by legal science, etc.

[17] This is evident when asking which idea of justice and which legal method, because they are both obvious mental constructs with no parallels in the physical world. But professionalisation and internationalisation might be regarded as facts rather than ideas. The point is that the degree of professionalisation and character of internationalisation influences how law is viewed and understood, and is therefore, as far as legal culture is concerned, part of the intellectual structure.

Firstly, professionalisation means that the persons handling law on behalf of a society spend more and more of their time on legal issues. Secondly, it means that there are special criteria to fulfil for those to be entrusted with the position of handling law. The students are taught that such criteria will, in short, often at first be a good reputation, later practical legal experience, and in the end a legal education. But all kinds of professionalisation has the same effect – it makes lawyers obtain an internal view of law. This implies that good law in the eyes of the professional becomes more and more a question of internal correlations, while good law for the unprofessional is still more a question of justice in each individual case.

Internationalisation is not possible before there are nations producing national law that might be internationalised. However, internationalisation is in this context used on all kinds of influence of norms produced outside jurisdictional boundaries, since norms from outside such boundaries might change how law is perceived inside those same boundaries. The power to change is much dependent on both quality and authority.[18]

In short, the students are taught that the intellectual structure of law is ideas and expectations of law that set up the framework for how law is shaped within the institutional structure, while the institutional structure is the framework for how law is imagined within the intellectual structure. In other words, the institutional and intellectual structures exist in a symbiosis. Just as we cannot do without institutions making and applying law, we cannot do without ideas of how law ought to be. Their relationship is dialectic in the way that it is not one that shapes the other, but they influence each other in a continuous process. One cannot do without the other, and together they make up the style of a legal culture.

How the historical dimension of legal culture is used to create an awareness of complexity

It is a challenge that the term structure is easily associated with a static framework around which a building is erected. In such a context a structure cannot be changed without the building falling down. Speaking of the institutional and intellectual structures of a legal culture with this image in mind, a legal culture becomes a static unit that cannot be altered without fatal consequences. This

[18] But see Eirik Holmøyvik, A little Bit of This and a little Bit of That – The Complexity of Legal reception", *Rendezvous of Europen Legal Cultures*, ed. by Jørn Øyrehagen Sunde and Knut Einar Skodvin (Bergen: Fagbokforlaget, 2010) pp. 45–59.

is all false, since a legal culture is both dynamic and static. Hence, the students are presented the image of an atom, where the neutrons are structured around a proton by electricity. These structures are firm, but might change very fast through fusion or fission. New structures are then created, and might again change by expansion or reduction. This is also the case with a legal culture – it has firm structures, but the structures are highly changeable, and thus are at the same time both dynamic and static.

With the display of the different structural elements in the institutional and intellectual structure of a legal culture, we have seen that they are not historical constants, but change over time. This acknowledgement is stressed, since it keeps the students from subscribing to the idea of a constant and unchangeable essence of legal cultures. This is best explained to the students by applying the terms and analytical tools *Erfahrungsraum* (Space of Experience) and *Erwartungshorizont* (Horizon of Expectations), developed by Reinhard Koselleck.[19] His point is that you cannot have expectations beyond what might be deduced from your experience. Experience in this context includes both the conscious and unconscious, and it embraces what has been read, heard, observed, discussed and done. In this context we might conclude that a legal culture is shaped by different kinds of historical events in a society. Together they form the legal cultural base that gives it a static character. But since new experiences are continuously made, a legal culture will be ever changing, and this is what gives it its dynamic character.

A legal culture is in constant flux, but does not change at a constant rate. In general, we might say that each particular part of a legal culture often goes through changes, that each section more rarely changes, and that change in the entire legal culture takes place only in exceptional periods of profound legal cultural disturbance. Such exceptional periods might be regarded as equivalent to what Koselleck refers to as *Sattelzeit*.

The ideas of distinct legal cultural historical periods are presented by Franz Wieacker in his lecture on *Foundations of European legal culture*, first held in 1983. In this lecture he split the European legal culture into four different phases – Early Middle Ages, High and Late Middle Ages, Early Modern Age, and Modern Age – due to the major changes that took place at the transmission from one period to another.[20] In a Norwegian context at least, it is more useful

---

[19] Reinhart Koselleck, Futures Past : *On the Semantics of Historical Time* (New York: Columbia University Press, 2004).

[20] Franz Wieacker, 'Foundations of European Legal Culture', *The American Journal of Comparative Law*, 38 (1990) pp. 1–29.

to define only three phases: the first phase until 1260 with none or only weak legal institutions and a case-by-case approach to all aspects of law, a second phase from 1260 to 1590 with independently ordered legal institutions and a sectional approach to all aspects of law, and a final phase from 1590 until the present day with strengthening ties between the different institutions and a systematic approach to all aspects of law.

Based on the characteristics of each period, they might be named Pre Legal Order, Legal Order and Legal System. The transformation from one period to another is caused by a radical change in the institutional and intellectual structure of the legal culture. Despite that, a single event might be seen as the very Archimedes fulcrum, the students are told to keep in mind that the event will still be one in a chain of events leading up to and continuing after the turning point.

Scaling down complexity, achieving awareness

The historical dimension makes legal culture more complex, and hence more incomprehensible. That is why a legal culture is put into a model that displays on one hand the relationship between legal culture, its institutional and intellectual structures and structural elements, and the historical periods and development on the other. This model is drawn on the blackboard at the beginning of every lecture, and is used as a map as each of the six overreaching themes, which are the structural elements, are dealt with. These are, the legal history of the Norwegian legal culture from about year 1000 till today, a depiction of the legal culture of England, France, Germany and the USA, and the situation facing different European legal cultures today.

Legal historical period	**Legal cultural structures and structural elements**					
	Institutional structure		**Intellectual structure**			
	Conflict resolution	Norm production	Idea of justice	Legal method	Degree of profession-alisation	Character of internationalisation
Legal System (ca. 1590 to the present)	Court hierarchy	Lawmaking	Predictability	Deduction	High	Systems of law
Legal Order (ca. 1260 to ca. 1590)	Courts	Lawmaking and court rulings	Equity	Differentiation	Some	Chunks of law
Pre Legal Order (prior to ca. 1260)	Mediating organs and violence	Through conflict resolution	Equivalence	Analogy	None	Bits and pieces of law

Just as the model does not display the total complexity and interrelations of a legal culture, nor does the subject Legal History and Comparative Law, as taught at the Faculty of Law in Bergen.. But this is the case for any subject on the schedule of a law school, just like no map can reflect the landscape 1:1. The scale of a subject dealing with the legal cultural changes in Europe has to be fairly large. Still,.the subject is suitable to raise awareness among the students of the complexity of law that comes with the intense internationalisation we experience today. This awareness can serve as a compass to them when practicing law, venturing into the legal landscape. This alone will increase the legal certainty of the citizens.

Mats Kumlien

The History of Law Does Not Write Itself

1 Mission impossible?

Teaching comparative legal history raises questions on delimitations and definitions.

The task demands good knowledge about the national law in force and its background. Moreover, it calls for knowledge about legal traditions in other countries, since internationalisation of law is now much stronger than ever before. At the same time, a multicultural society calls for orientation about cultures like the Muslim world.

From a Swedish view, the membership in the EU, and the influence of pluralistic doctrines on legal sources, has increased the significance of discussing legal method. In addition, influenced by American currents, many European legal historians want to add feministic theory, religion and a bunch of "law ands". The points of contact between legal history, jurisprudence and comparative law have become more evident.

"History" means travelling in time. But how far? It can stretch at least 2.500 years back. And what does "legal" mean? We know that a lot of areas could be discussed; private law, law of obligations, law of succession, matrimonial law, constitutional law, criminal law, procedural law, labour law, social law, environmental law, etc.? Why not space law? "Comparison" means travelling in space. How far? What systems ought to be compared? Europe? Balkan? Post Soviet countries? Why not going global?

In total: the potential of teaching legal history has expanded and become more complex. However, the resources of time and money have not expanded. On the contrary, the span of time for legal history courses has been shortened. Consequently, teaching legal history is to a great degree a matter of selecting information and taking a position, of choosing a perspective.

2 Why legal history?

The starting point is the fact that teaching legal history in general takes places at a law faculty. In Sweden, the position of legal history within the law schools' curriculum has been a tricky issue for more than 60 years. Christian Häthén has pointed out that during the 20th century there was a striking continuance in the structure and content of Swedish legal education. Legal history remained – and remains – firmly within that framework of being a "vocational training" and of catering the needs of the so called "legal sector" ("*rättslivet*"). Legal history is placed in a pragmatic, utilitarian light. Students should be raised to be good professional lawyers.[1]

But, what is a good lawyer? And what is the role of comparative legal history within the law curricula? Why is it necessary to look back and outside one's own country? There are a great number of opinions on this issue.[2] I want to mention three currents.

The *outside perspective* aims at implanting a certain understanding of contemporary law by understanding the past or "the other". According to this approach, an historical perspective could function as a radical alternative to a purely pragmatic approach. Thus, the students should gain a critical attitude to the norms and their applicability.

The *inside perspective* aims at promoting the students' ability to apply the prevailing law in force. Legal history is considered as a complement to methodological training and education. The quality of it as a teaching subject has to be fundamentally legal, jurisprudential, and relevant to the practice of the positive law. Consequently, legal historians ought to mark their position as lawyers, as jurists.

The *in-between perspective* aims at providing a certain cultural understanding of the past in order to promote purposes of a European future. This "neo-pandectist" approach departs from the view that legal history can be used to solve the current political issues in Europe.

3 The Uppsala model

In Uppsala, we have not solved the problems sketched above. But we have launched an English-language course called *Comparative Legal History*, which

1 C. Häthén, "Legal education reform in the emerging Swedish welfare-state. The discourse of legal theory vs. legal practice in Swedish legal education during the 1940s and 1950s. An outline", in *Juristische Fakultäten und Juristenausbildung im Ostseeraum*. Stockholm 2004.

2 See for example K.Å. Modéer, "Rättshistorieämnets uppgifter. Reflektioner inför ett rätts- och forskningspolitiskt paradigmskifte" in *Svensk Juristtidning* 1996; R. Nygren, "Rättshistoria och samhällsförändring. Ett pedagogiskt perspektiv", and C. Peterson, "'Genom rättshistorien, utöver rättshistorien' Ett inlägg i diskussionen om rättshistorieämnets uppgift i juristutbildningen", both in Modéer (ed.), *Rättshistoria i förändring*. Lund 2002.

lies close to the first model – understanding contemporary law by understanding the past. Nevertheless, it demands knowledge of law in force, and consequently it is placed at the advanced level, the seventh semester out of totally nine.

The course is open for exchange students, and they are coming from every continent except the Antarctic. Furthermore, it is open for students from the law school in Uppsala, who are allowed to take it as an alternative to the mandatory course of legal history. This mixture of students from different legal systems is one of the course's most important resources.

3.1 Some theoretical points of departure

We and the other

The course aims at developing the students' knowledge of fundamental features of Western legal history, and to facilitate orientation about other legal traditions. Special attention is paid to the interaction between domestic traditions and foreign influences. Knowledge from previous courses shall be placed in historical, comparative and theoretical perspectives.

Constitutional law is fundamental

While *research* within Nordic legal history often has focused on public law, legal history as a *teaching* subject has to a far extent been linked to private law. Public law has been placed in the background. We, however, agree with Ditlev Tamm's thesis that studying constitutional law is an important component to promote understanding of law as a cultural phenomenon.[3] Furthermore, the history of private law has its political dimensions, which becomes obvious to the students when discussing, for example, the emergence of *Code Civil*, *Bürgerliches Gesetzbuch*, the Swedish draft of a Civil Code from 1826, the Nordic co-operation around the turn of the century 1900, and the project on a European Civil Code.

Legal history does not write itself

One ambition is to pay attention to the role of legal actors. In doing so, we try to get the students to question so-called universal trends. Such deterministic perspectives are to be found not only in Marxism, but also in theories about general shifts from status to contract or about the "inner relationship" between

[3] D. Tamm, *Global retskultur, en indføring i komparativ ret på historisk grundlag*. Frederiksberg 2009

different legal systems, as well as in functional ideas, which claim that even if different countries may use different legal methods, they will eventually reach the same address. Those kinds of theories seem to imply that history follows a linear, evolutionary process. We do not agree.

Changes of legal systems are in general products of factors which are neither "natural" nor "necessary". Furthermore, it is far from self-evident that hard modernisation, like industrialisation, infrastructural changes, etc., must walk hand in hand with soft modernisation, such as values, constitutionalism and democracy. One task during the course is to look for the specific features of different countries, to make specific historical comparisons rather than to fit phenomena into traditional families or traditions.

Since legal history is a result of power, and legal history teaching, as well as research, has ideological implications, we have reason to ask ourselves: What role does our teaching play in maintaining established positions of power?

Legal history ideal models are constructed ex post facto

Knowledge about the world is always marked by the cultural and historical context in which it is produced. Categories, groupings, concepts, etc., are abstractions which are used to survey a muddling input of data from "the reality". This approach, of course, is in opposition to a more positivistic view on science, which considers knowledge as a passive reflection of reality.[4]

Historical knowledge is produced, and it is not a reflection of reality; accordingly, it does not tell us "wie es eigentlich gewesen". When analysing the legal past, the use of meta-concepts, like "legal families", "modernity" etc. is unavoidable. However, we try to keep in mind that the "reality" of a structured past lies in the reality of the legal historian's interpretation of the historical material that she has chosen to study – and nothing else.[5]

3.2 Some pedagogical points of departure

A thematic approach

Legal history requires *diachronic* order, examining developments in stages or periods. Legal comparison requires *synchronic* order, that is a cross-evaluation

---

4 D. Edwards & J. Potter, *Discoursive psychology*. London 1992; N. Fairclough, *Critical discourse analysis*. London 1995; E. Laclau & C. Mouffe, *Hegemony and socialist strategy. Towards a radical democratic politics*. London 1985.

5 D. Michalsen, "The nominalistic argument in interpreting past legal texts", in *Reading past legal texts*. Oslo 2006.

between countries and their institutions in the same period. Comparative legal history requires both diachronic and synchronic orders. Within these orders, we have chosen to discuss developments thematically. This approach lends itself more readily to a comparative analysis of specific aspects of the subject than a straightforward historical narrative does.

Some central themes could be mentioned: Why is Roman law relevant today?; The significance of codification projects; The role of the Swedish Code of 1734; To which legal tradition does Sweden belong?; What do we mean by a common law/*ius commune*? Human rights in an historical perspective; Law and gender; *La bouche de la loi* v. *Professorenrecht*; What do we mean by legal sources? Why did not Sweden get a Civil code?; Law and religion; What's the best: East or West?; The role of lawyers and the emergence of totalitarian regimes; Centre and periphery.

Course material

The literature consists of Zweigert's and Kötz' *An introduction to comparative law* and van Caenegem's *Judges, legislators and professors*. Besides that the students use an extensive amount of articles (by, among others, Patrick Glenn, Mary Ann Glendon, Jamilla Husain, Thijmen Koopmanns, Reinhard Zimmermann, Pierre Legrand, Ingo Müller, Simone de Beauvoir), as well as primary sources and excerpts from Magna Carta, The law of Uppland, Habeas Corpus, national constitutions and codes and international conventions on human rights. The students are also encouraged to use the Internet.

Student activity

The methodological point of departure is self-directed and problem-based learning. The structural foundation is a series of 5-6 seminars, with groups of 12-15 students. Different assignments are analysed in sub-groups, in which around five students prepare and perform presentations, as well as initiate and govern discussions. During the presentations the students shall use key words on the white board, transparencies, power-point presentations, etc. In addition to make presentations, every student is expected to participate in the discussions that are initiated by the other subgroups.

One central aim is to develop the students' capacity of solving a problem by cultivating information from a lot of sources. Thus, even if the students are expected to report essential facts, the seminars aim at problemising the issues in order to reach a deeper understanding of the complexity of legal history.

Another one is to promote team work and good oral presentations. Thus, the most important resource is the students themselves. It has already been mentioned that the course involves interaction between Swedish students and a "smorgasbord" of exchange students from all over the globe. Consequently, theoretical comparative issues can be analysed on a practical level: "What is really the difference between a French lawyer and a Swedish lawyer?" "Is Legrand's picture of the deep gap between English jurists and German jurists correct?" Well, let the English and the Germans initiate a discussion! Or why not ask our colleagues from Perth and Wuhan?

Non-Swedish students, who have never heard about problem-based and self-directed learning, in general quite smoothly adapt to our system. On the other hand, Swedish students, who take many parallel courses (which they are not allowed to do) often face problems when it comes to prepare group-presentations. Thus, the outcome of different forms of teaching is influenced by the surrounding social context.

Every teacher has her or his own model. I myself try to get the student to get active as soon as possible. During the seminars I want them to talk two thirds of the time. This, however, does not mean that the teacher is stepping backwards in the sense that content and structure is delegated to the students. On the contrary, this approach is probably more demanding than traditional lectures and classes. The tutor's task is to govern the exercise in a way that certain specific stations are passed, certain facts observed, and discussions and issues are brought to the forefront. Thus it demands a meta-capacity, and the teacher governs the discussion on the level of matters of fact, and at the same time observes this process on a higher level.

It could be problematic to start with a series of introductory lectures, since it might establish notions of one-way communication rather than dialogue. However, an experienced lecturer can always promote an open atmosphere by getting the students involved through questions and discussions. Thus, lectures are good, or even necessary, complements to the student-active teaching in seminars and classes.

Take-home exam

The examination has shifted from just measuring the students' ability to memorise facts towards testing their methodological skills and independent thinking. At present we are using take-home exams: during 30 hours the students are directed to write an essay in comparative legal history containing about 5 pages.

The general exam requirements are the same as for the seminars, namely to show the ability 1) to compare in an independent and competent way, 2) to identify and concentrate on facts that are relevant, to make a digest from an extensive mass of material and texts, and 3) to make a balanced division between different parts of the essay.

When grading the essays, the teacher has a difficult task in articulating what parameters that should be important.

Some examples of exam questions can be given. The students have been assigned to analyse the Preface to *Institutiones*, guided by questions on what kind of document it is, its historical context, its relevance today, etc. Other issues have concerned "A new ius commune?", "How to make a good judge", and "Reception of foreign law is not so much a 'question of quality' as a 'question of power' "

In 2007 the assignment was: "A travel organizer asks you to arrange a study tour to a place which you consider to be of importance from the perspective of comparative legal history. You decide to choose Istanbul. State the reasons for your choice". The exam comment on that question is attached to this paper.

3.3 Some shortcomings

Prerequisites

Of course there are shortcomings. In Uppsala we have noticed that even if students in general are familiar with current national and international law, their knowledge on history and chronology is less solid. It is also worth noting that our issues and texts are of a different character than the ones that the students are used to.

Biased literature

There is a lack of texts in English on Swedish and Nordic legal history. It is slowly getting better, but here is plenty of room for joint ventures. Some of the used literature is outdated (refers to Yugoslavia, the significance of Muslim law is said to be decreasing, etc.). Moreover, they often are Eurocentric, implying the assumption that the West is progressive, rational and democratic, and thus legitimates a specific colonial relationship between West and East, or even that intervention from the West is necessary to remedy oriental destitution.[6]

Many authors deal with meta-concepts like legal families, traditions etc. These kinds of simplifications are useful as pedagogical instruments: they should be considered as ideal types and as tools for analysing and understanding legal

6 Said, E., *Orientalism. Western conceptions of the Orient*. London 1978.

history rather than descriptions of the reality. Thus the simplifications make our picture of society more comprehensible.

At the same time, classification into groups can be starting points for discussing differences within the groups (do black women have more in common with white women than with black men?). Classifications can also promote discussion on the emergence of lawyers' self-images. You become something by distinguishing yourself from something or someone else. Who are "we", who are "the other"?

Generalisations

There might be a tendency to generalise. Legal history teaching pays much attention to central power and supreme courts, which might risk losing the significance of diversity, pluralism and local variations. In medieval times legal life was in essential aspects concentrated to the local society. Royal, central power and local law existed side by side, which is of special interest today, when globalisation, centralisation and harmonisation walk parallel with regionalism, nationalism and separatism.[7]

What is comparison?

According to Zweigert and Kötz, comparison means something more than listing similarities and differences. It means building a system, which in turn demands a special syntax and concepts that are large enough to embrace the quite heterogeneous legal institutions which are functionally comparable. One can ask whether the authors apply this method themselves, but that is another story. What is important for our students is to analyse what parameters that could be considered as fundamental for making comparisons.

Shallowness

Since the course lasts only six weeks, one consequence is that issues are observed from a bird's-eye view, rather than from the perspective of close reading. Accordingly, there is always a risk that a course like this runs the gauntlet through the history of law" (*gatlopp genom rättens historia*").[8]

---

[7] D. Heirbaut, "A tale of two legal histories" in Michalsen (ed.) 2006 (fn 3 above). P. Letto-Vanamo, "Synpunkter på straffrättskipningens historia", in P. Asp, (ed.), *Eftersyn och eftertanke*. Uppsala 2007.

[8] C. Peterson in Modéer 2002 (fn 2 above).

4 Some final words

We are heading for greater variety of pedagogical models in legal history, not only between different universities, but also within each institution. That's good. The predominant Swedish legal method is a pluralistic one, in which different legal *sources* complement rather than compete with each other.[9] Likewise different *courses* in legal history can complement, rather than compete with each other.

[9] M. Sandström, "Den svenska modellen – en juridisk metodlära i tre platta paket", in *Norden, rätten, historia. Festskrift till Lars Björne*. Helsinki 2004.

UPPSALA UNIVERSITY
Juridicum
Comparative legal history

Exam
Commentary
2007-02-22/23

The question was:

> A travel organizer asks you to arrange a study tour to a place which you consider to be of importance from the perspective of comparative legal history. You decide to choose Istanbul. Write an essay in which you state the reasons for your choice.

1 First of all we would like to call your attention to the general academic requirements for the seminars as well as for the exam, namely the ability
– to compare in an independent and competent way,
– to identify and to concentrate on the relevant question, and
– to make a balanced division between different parts of the question.

2 The essay ought to start from the perspective of *legal history*, which means that it should be based on specific legal historical references. Moreover, it ought to be *comparative*, which means that references should be picked from several different legal traditions and compared in a way that implies something more than just simply describing the two systems separately and then listing the similarities and differences.

3 A good essay ought to pay attention to at least three aspects of legal history, which easily can be picked from the literature, the seminars and the lectures of the course.

1) Istanbul, which has been called Constantinople, once was the centre of the Eastern Roman Empire and thus influenced by Roman law and Christianity. Around 530 A.C., the emperor Justinian introduced Corpus Iuris Civilis, which is considered to be one of the most important documents in Western legal history.
2) In 1453 the city was incorporated in the Ottoman Empire, which has been described as a multicultural society, dominated by Islamic religion and Islamic law.
3) When the Ottoman Empire eroded during the 1920s, Turkey emerged. It has been marked by a tension between on the one hand secularisation and ambitions to connect to the Occident, and on the other hand aspirations for

consolidate Muslim and Eastern traditions. A discussion on the reception of the Swiss civil code (ZGB) as well as the current debate on Turkey's membership of the European Union can elucidate this conflict.

4 These three essential aspects of comparative legal history may function as points of departure for general lines of reasoning concerning a number of issues, for example:

- Roman law, Bologna, universities, canon law, legal revolutions, "holy books" (Corpus Iuris Civilis, The Bible, the Koran, the Constitution, ECHR, etc.).
- Codification projects, different types of codes.
- A European civil code, believers and non-believers, argument pro et contra.
- Legislation v. judge-made law.
- civil law v. common law.
- Legal actors, legislators, professors, judges.
- Empires, multicultural societies, protection of minorities.
- Reception, legal transplants, facts and notions, examples (Sweden, your own country).
- Spreading, different colonial strategies.
- parallels, Japan, India, Egypt, etc.
- East/West.
- Istanbul: Eastern outpost of the Roman Empire and Western outpost of the Ottoman Empire.
- Law and religion.
- The legal position of women and children in different legal and historical cultures.
- Is law eternal or changeable?
- The origin, purpose and scope of law?
- A flexible law: different schools of interpretation, legal tricks, general clauses, gaps.
- EU.
- The rule of law, human rights, freedom of expression (Botolf).
- The war against terrorism.

5 The author of the essay ought to demonstrate that she or he has digested the literature, the seminars and the lectures of the course. Decisive for the grading has been the author's ability to (a) demonstrate knowledge about basic facts from comparative legal history, (b) meet the formal academic requirements, and (c) in an independent way put legal historical details in relation to comprehensive themes.

Martin Sunnqvist

Competing Sources of Law and the Adjudicative Power
Advantages of Nordic Law in a European Context and the Need of Comparative and Historical Research and Teaching

A little more than 10 years ago, Pierre Legrand wrote the well known article in the *International and Comparative Law Quarterly:* "European Legal Systems are not Converging".[1] Under the subtitle "Two Epistemological Trajectories", he identified some characteristics which distinguished common law and civil law from each other. R. C. van Caenegem has in his recent book *European Law in the Past and the Future. Unity and Diversity under Two Millennia,*[2] discussed a similar topic. He has also identified this type of characteristics. What I want to add to the discussion is a Nordic perspective. Where does Nordic legal culture, seen as a whole, fit into the picture?

Konrad Zweigert and Hein Kötz have described the legal systems of the Nordic countries as a specific legal family, within civil law but outside common law. The countries have, according to Zweigert and Kötz, the same structure of mediaeval laws which during the late 17th and early 18th century were replaced by codifications, which later have been amended but never replaced by new codifications. Roman law has only affected the Nordic legal systems slightly, and the legal scientific attitude is characterised by realism and common sense.[3]

The rather scarce observations that Zweigert and Kötz have made regarding the Nordic legal orders are mainly correct. I will – in spite of the clear differences between the Danish, Finnish, Norwegian and Swedish legal cultures

---

1 Pierre Legrand, "European Legal Systems are not Converging" in *International and Comparative Law Quarterly*, vol. 45, January 1996, 52–81.

2 Raoul Charles van Caenegem, *European Law in the Past and the Future. Unity and Diversity under Two Millennia*. Cambridge 2002, 38–53.

3 Konrad Zweigert and Hein Kötz, *An Introduction to Comparative Law*, 2nd ed. Oxford 1987, 286–295. Cf. also Jacob W. F. Sundberg, "Civil Law, Common Law and the Scandinavians" in *Scandinavian Studies in Law*, vol. 13, 1969, 179–205.

– for the purpose of this text treat them as a unity. What could be challenged, however, is on the one hand that the Nordic legal orders are arranged within civil law and on the other hand that civil law and common law are considered as the two only relevant European legal families. Of course, also the notion of legal families as such is open to criticism,[4] but still, in this text, I will try to characterise Nordic law, and in order to do this I will contrast Nordic law against some main features of civil law and common law, as they have been analysed by Legrand and van Caenegem. I will, eventually, argue that there might be some attitudes in Nordic legal theory and practice, that we might not always think of ourselves but which might be useful for other legal orders to consider.

Let me first consider how Nordic law can be defined using one of the characteristics commonly used to contrast civil law and common law against each other. I will concentrate on the approach of lawyers toward the law. Legrand has claimed that common law lawyers use an inductive way of legal reasoning, where new cases are decided with the help of analogies from older cases. Civil law, according to Legrand, uses a deductive way of legal reasoning with the help of an institutional legal scheme. Thus, common law focuses on the resolution of the single case and the interpretation of law in that context, while civil law is systematised and should – at least in theory – give the answer beforehand.[5] Caenegem has made similar reflections but focussed on the actors. In common law, the judge is paramount and practise is the way to learn the law while in civil law the professor, with his systematising abilities, is paramount.[6]

Apparently, these attitudes are important. In the Nordic Countries, neither the professor nor the judge is paramount, but the legislator is – or has been seen to be – paramount. The judge should be loyal to the legislator, is a common view.[7] This view has been applied in the Nordic courts during most of the 20th century, which can be seen through an analysis of the use of judicial review in the Nordic countries. In Norway, judicial review of legislation was well established

---

[4] See e.g. Mark van Hoecke and Mark Warrington, "Legal Cultures and Legal Paradigms: Towards a New Model for Comparative Law", in *International and Comparative Law Quarterly*, vol. 47, July 1998, 495–536, and Jaakko Husa, "Classification of Legal Families Today: Is It Time for a Memorial Hymn?" in *Revue Internationale de Droit Comparé*, 1-2004.

[5] Legrand op.cit. 64–67.

[6] van Caenegem op.cit. 44–48. See also R. C. van Caenegem, *Judges, Legislators and Professors. Chapters in European Legal History*. Cambridge 1987.

[7] See e.g. the analysis by Aleksander Peczenik, "Lagstiftningen, domstolarna, rättsmedvetandet och rättsvetenskapen" in *Löser juridiken demokratins problem? Demokratiutredningens skrift nr 23,* SOU 1999:58, 11–17. The argument is e.g. to be found in Göran Lambertz, "Normprövning och demokrati" in *Svensk juristtidning*, 2007, 809–826, esp. 817.

in the early 19th century but declined in the 1930's only to rise again in 1976 and thereafter. In Finland, judicial review was not applied during the time after the constitution of 1919 except for governmental ordinances. In Sweden and Denmark the constitutionality of governmental ordinances and statutes from the parliament could be assessed by the courts according to case law from the 1920's to the 1960's, but – which is most important here – no enacted rules were declared unconstitutional.[8] The judges were loyal to the legislator.

The change started in Norway in 1976, when the Supreme Court set a statute aside as unconstitutional and identified different margins of appreciation for the legislator depending on which type of right or freedom the alleged unconstitutionality concerned.[9] In the 1990's, the same court applied The European Convention on Human Rights and the case-law of the European Court of Human Rights in order to interpret Norwegian law in the light of the human rights according to the convention.[10] In Denmark, the Supreme Court in 1999 declared a law unconstitutional.[11] The statute was, according to the Supreme Court, in reality a judgment and was as such contrary to the separation of powers. In 1996, the Danish Supreme Court allowed ten citizens to get the issue whether the Maastricht treaty was constitutional tried.[12] This judgment should be seen in the context of the German *Solange*-cases.[13] In Sweden, it has been made clear by some Supreme Court cases from 2005 onwards that statutes and ordinances should be interpreted in conformity with the constitution.[14] This is an extension of the judicial review according to the constitution, which requires, if a law is to be set aside as unconstitutional, that it is *obviously* contrary to the constitution.[15] Furthermore, the Swedish Supreme Court has made clear that Swedish law should be interpreted in conformity with the European Convention on Human Rights and the case-law of the European Court of Human Rights.[16] In Finland, the Parliamentary Constitutional Committee, which is the foremost

---

8 See Martin Sunnqvist, "From Deference to Difference. Nordic Judiciaries and Judicial Jurisprudence", forthcoming in Kjell Å Modéer and Martin Sunnqvist (eds.), *Beyond Nordic Legal Modernity* København 2010.

9 Rt. 1976, 1.

10 Rt. 1997, 1821.

11 UfR 1999, 841.

12 UfR 1996, 1300, cf. UfR 1998, 800.

13 Henning Koch, "Dansk forfatningsret i transnational belysning" in *Juristen* 6 1999, 213–227.

14 NJA 2005, 33; NJA 2006, 293 I–II; NJA 2007, 918 and NJA 2008, 567.

15 Instrument of Government, Ch. 11 § 14. This rule will, if the proposal is accepted a second time by parliament, be altered with effect from 2011. The requirement that the law has to be *obviously* contrary to the constitution to be set aside is to be abolished. Instead, the courts will be reminded that the parliament is the premier representation of the people and that the constitution is above the laws. Prop. 2009/10:80.

16 NJA 2005, 805; NJA 2006, 467 and NJA 2007, 805 I–II.

guardian of the constitution, has used the European Convention on Human Rights as a tool when interpreting the Finnish Constitution.[17]

This brief overview suggests that the Nordic Supreme Courts during the last twenty years have been surprisingly keen to use other legal sources than the traditional – such as case-law from the European Court of Human Rights –, other methods than the traditional – such as the far-reaching interpretation of statutes in order to maintain rights and freedoms, and other sources of inspiration than the traditional, such as the German *Solange*-cases. Loyalty to the single national legislator is lost, and a new loyalty to the law of rights and freedoms and the common European legal order is emerging.[18]

This is not a self-evident development, which will be clear from a short comparison with the main common law and civil law countries. According to the United Kingdom Human Rights Act, which came into force in 2000,[19] judges should as far as possible apply the European Convention on Human Rights and the case-law of the Strasbourg Court, but, if interpretation of a statute in conformity with the convention is not possible, the court can declare the statute unconstitutional. The statute is, however, still valid and is to be applied until parliament decides otherwise. In this way, the sovereignty of parliament is retained. In Germany, the *Bundesverfassungsgericht* has had a difficult task defining the position of the European Convention of Human Rights and the judgments of the Strasbourg court. On the one hand, the courts should, as far as possible, interpret German law in the light of the convention and the cases of the Strasbourg court but on the other, the *Bundesverfassungsgericht* emphasises that the convention is an ordinary German law below the *Grundgesetz*.[20] In this way, the supremacy of the *Grundgesetz* is protected. In the Nordic countries, there was no such strong principle as the sovereignty of parliament or the supremacy of the *Grundgesetz* that had to be circumvented. The mere existence

---

[17] Veli-Pekka Hautamäki, "Authoritative Interpretation of the Constitution: A Comparison of Argumentation in Finland and Norway", *Electronic Journal of Comparative Law*, vol. 6.3, October 2002, http://www.ejcl.org/63/art63-1.html.

[18] After the time when this speech was held, the Swedish Supreme Administrative Court (judgment September 17th, 2009, case 8133-08) and the Swedish Supreme Court (decisions March 31st, 2010, cases B 5498-09 and B 2509-09) have, in the issue whether tax surcharges and criminal proceedings for tax crime are subject to the principle *ne bis in idem*, been less keen to apply the ECHR generously towards the citizen. A thorough discussion about this matter would be too far-reaching for this article. It should be noted, however, that there is a clear difference in attitude between the two supreme courts, the Supreme Administrative Court being – in this context – much more reluctant towards the judgments of the European Court of Human Rights than the Supreme Court.

[19] Human Rights Act 1998 (c. 42).

[20] BVerfG 2 BvR 1481/04, October 14th 2004 (Görgülü), www.bundesverfassungsgericht.de. Cf. Clemens Höpfner, *Die systemkonforme Auslegung*. Tübingen 2008, 360, 365–369.

of a plurality of legislators and the case-law of the Strasbourg court mean by itself that the legislator is no longer paramount, and the lack of a theoretical sovereignty of parliament or supremacy of the *Grundgesetz* means that the courts are left to themselves balancing the enactments of different legislators.

If this development is to be compared with the distinctions of reasoning by analogy and reasoning with the help of institutions and of seeing disputes as problems to be solved or as single cases to be fitted into the system, I think we come to the following conclusion. In Nordic law, the point of departure for a judge is to find the right place in the system for the legal question at hand. But the judges are not at all unfamiliar with the method of comparing cases with each other in order to find similarities and differences between them. This is clear from the way the Norwegian and Swedish courts, in the above mentioned human rights related cases, have compared the cases at hand with earlier national cases and cases from the Strasbourg Court. Increasingly, cases are about finding the balance between different rights and freedoms that should govern the specific case,[21] so the notion of the pre-existence of a system into which the case could be fitted is weakening.

What is then the historical explanation for this? Probably that we are used to taking what we have, when it comes to legal sources. The Dano-Norwegian codifications of the 1680's and the Swedish codification of 1734 were not complete from the beginning and have only partially been updated. In some areas of law case-law has been important, and in some areas legal doctrine. One good example is Swedish property law, "sakrätt" (cf. *Sachenrecht*), where law is a conglomerate of statutes on detail issues, Supreme Court cases and legal doctrine. Case-law lacks a theory of the interpretation of precedents, and statute law has had a theory of statutory interpretation built on the intent of the legislator according to the *travaux preparatoires,* but to what extent it is still valid is an open issue. It has been common in legal doctrine to refer to the law of other countries, Nordic and beyond. This open-mindedness in relation to legal sources has been in full effect during the 20th century but it has been concealed – in theory – by the reverence for the legislator.

The lack of a theoretical sovereignty of parliament or supremacy of the *Grundgesetz*, combined with open-mindedness towards the legal sources, means that the European human rights law has access to and a possibility to easily influence Nordic law. If the advocates take the opportunity to argue for the rights of the citizen, the judges do not face any theoretical obstacles giving the citizen these

---

[21] E.g. Rt. 1997, 1821, NJA 2005, 805.

rights. There are, thus, great advantages attached to Nordic law. When competing legal rules emerge from different sources and it is impossible to arrange these sources hierarchically or according to some fundamental principle, the judges will have to weigh interests, principles and rights against each other and find the balance that used to be defined and enacted by one single legislator.

However, there are also risks. Judges have, during history, not always chosen the alternatives that have been to the benefit for the citizen. Not always could balancing of interests be done by help of the principle that rights and freedoms should be interpreted generously toward the citizen,[22] because different rights and freedoms can also be in conflict with each other. The assessment of these rights and freedoms and finding the right balance is an extremely different task.[23] Sometimes, the interest of safety in society has to be balanced against the rights of an individual.[24] Still, it is difficult to see that other institutions than the courts could do this assessment, since it needs to be done in particular cases and since there is no single legislator that can do the assessment in a final binding way.

When rights, interests and freedoms should be interpreted and balanced by the courts, an approach that is both theoretical and practical will be needed. We need some reference to the system of law but also some reference to the similarities and differences between cases. In my view, a Comparative European Legal History focussing on different attitudes of lawyers toward the law in our time and the history of dealing with competing laws is needed to give the emerging case-law the necessary theoretical strength. Without understanding the historical reasons for the different approaches toward law in Europe, we cannot foresee the impact in different countries of the common European legal development. And if we do not compare our present legal situation with the law of earlier generations, we may fail to use useful experiences already made.

---

[22] NJA 2005, 33.

[23] Cf. the European Court of Human Rights judgments May 26th, 2004, case *Görgülü* v. *Germany*, and June 24th, 2005, case von Hannover v. Germany.

[24] Cf. the European Court of Justice judgment September 3rd, 2008, cases C-402/05 P and C-415/05 P, *Kadi* and *Al Barakaat* v. *Council of the European Union and Commission of the European Communities*.

Sanita Osipova

Europäische Rechtsgeschichte: Geopolitisch, kulturell oder historisch gebildete Wissenschaft

Die Rechtsgeschichte bildet eine Grundlage für die Rechtswissenschaft, aber wir haben nicht *eine* Rechtsgeschichte, sondern die Rechtsgeschichten sind zahllos. Zuerst ist da die römische Rechtsgeschichte, dann die nationale Rechtsgeschichte jedes einzelnen Landes, regionale Rechtsgeschichten (unsere Studenten haben baltische Regionalrechtsgeschichte gelernt) und natürlich die globale Rechtsgeschichte, die zum Beispiel die sowjetischen Jurastudenten studiert haben.[1] Damit man mit der Forschung in dem konkreten Wissenschaftszweig anfangen kann, muss man das zu erforschende Objekt näher bezeichnen, es von anderen Objekten abgrenzen und bestimmte Untersuchungsmethoden auswählen. Jedes Forschungsobjekt hat bestimmte Grenzen.

Wenn wir über die römische Rechtsgeschichte sprechen, ist das eine Wissenschaft mit klaren Grenzen hinsichtlich Zeit und Raum[2]. Dies zeigt uns zum Beispiel das Buch von Mario Bretone "*Geschichte des römischen Rechts von den Anfängen bis zu Justinian*".[3] Auch die nationalen Rechtsgeschichten sind hinreichend konkretisierte Wissenschaften bezüglich Zeit und Raum sowie im Hinblick auf den Rahmen der zu untersuchenden Rechtsquellen. Europäische Rechtsgeschichte ist ein relativ neuer Zweig der Rechtswissenschaften, eine regionale Rechtsgeschichte mit heute unklaren Grenzen. Schon Paul Koschaker fragte 1966: „Was ist Europa?" und antwortete:

> „Es gibt keine Sparte der Rechtswissenschaft, die so ausgesprochen europäischen Charakter trägt wie die Privatrechtswissenschaft, aus dem

---

[1] Osipova S. *Voldemāra Kalniņa ieguldījums Latvijas pilsētu tiesību zinātniskajā pētniecībā.* // Likums un Tiesības.-Jūnijs, 2008.- 10. sēj, Nr.6. (106).- S. 166. Kennzeichnende Beispiele für sowjetische Rechtsgeschichte: *История государства и права зарубежных стран.* Под ред. Галанзы П.Н. и Жидкова О.А. Ч. 2. Москва: Юридическая литература, 1969 und *Хрестоматия по истории государства и права. под ред. Корецкий*, В. М., Москва, 1958, S. 380, 381.

[2] Koschaker P. *Europa und das römischeRecht.* München und Berlin: C. H. Beck, 1966, S. 62, 63.

[3] Bretone M. *Geschichte des römischen Rechts von den Anfängen bis zu Justinian.*München: C. H. Beck, 1998.

> einfache Grunde, weil sie, als sie in strahlendem Glanze vor rund 850 Jahre in der Rechtsschule der Glossatoren zu Bologna sich erhob, in dieser langen Zeit einen nicht unwesentlichen Baustein zu dem Aufbau des Gebildes geliefert hat, das wir heute Europa nennen.“[4]

Europäische Rechtsgeschichte hat ihre Bedeutung in der zweiten Hälfte des 20. Jahrhunderts gewonnen, als bald nach dem zweiten Weltkrieg das Zusammenrücken Europas begann. Aufgrund dieses Prozesses hat sich die Europäische Union gebildet als eine regionale Organisation mit der Tendenz, ihre Grenzen zu erweitern. In den letzten sechs Jahren hat die Zahl der Mitgliedstaaten bedeutend zugenommen und auch heutzutage werden Gespräche mit potenziellen Kandidaten geführt, so zum Beispiel mit der Türkei.

Wenn man das Lehrfach europäische Rechtsgeschichte als einen Zweig der Rechtswissenschaften vorbereitet, muss man die Frage über die Grenzen der Wissenschaftsforschung konzeptionell beantworten. Es muss eine zeitliche Grenze (wann beginnt die Europäische Rechtsgeschichte) und eine räumliche Grenze (welche Staaten und Völker bilden historisch gesehen Europa) bestimmt werden. Die Frage ist wesentlich und nicht so leicht zu beantworten, wenn wir historisch auf Europas Kultur schauen, die sich auf die griechisch-römische Kultur und das Christentum stützt. In dieser Kultur ist auch das Recht verwurzelt. Eine hochinteressante Untersuchung auf diesem Forschungsgebiet bildet Norbert Roulands Buch *Introduction historique au droit.* [5]

Es ist nicht so einfach, wie esd klingen mag. Die Wurzeln des Christentums und die in der Bibel eingefassten Rechtsnormen legen die Pflicht auf, die geografischen Grenzen Europas zu überschreiten. Das liegt daran, dass die Grenzen Europas nicht mit den Grenzen des Römischen Imperiums direkt übereinstimmen. Das altägyptische und babylonische Recht hat das althebräische Rechtsverständnis des alten Testaments bedeutend beeinflusst.[6] Also ist meine erste Schlussfolgerung, dass der Anfang der europäischen Rechtsgeschichte beim Studieren des altägyptischen, sumärischen, babylonischen und althebräischen Rechts zu suchen ist, deren Normen einen Grundpfeiler für das Rechtsverständnis der Bibel gebildet haben (wie es Erich Anner in seinem Buch über die europäische Rechtsgeschichte geschrieben hat). Zudem hat das altägyptische Recht eine besonders große Bedeutung.[7] Dessen Einfluss ist nicht

---

[4] Koschaker P. *Europa und das römischeRecht.* München und Berlin: C. H. Beck, 1966, S. 1.

[5] Рулан Н. Историческое введение в право. Москва: Nota Bene, 2005,S. 13, 14.

[6] Assmann J. *Das kulturelle Gedächnes. Schrift, Erinnerung und politische Identität in frühen Hochkulturen.* 4. Auflage, München: C. H. Beck, 2002, S. 196–200.

[7] Osipova, S. *Hamurapi kodekss Latvijas zinātnieku darbos par cilvēktiesībām.*// Latvijas Universitātes raksti 740. sējums Juridiskā zinātne. Rīga: Latvijas Universitāte, 2008. S. 27–41.

nur im Rechtsverständnis des Alten Testaments zu finden, sondern auch in der altgriechischen Rechtswissenschaft, weil die altgriechischen Philosophen, wie Pythagoras und Platon, zum Studieren nach Ägypten gefahren sind.

Aus dem Blickwinkel betrachtend, dass Europa die griechisch-römische Rechtskultur übernommen hat, muss man den historischen Fakten folgen, dass das Römische Imperium in Ostrom respektive das Byzantinische Reich und Westrom respektive Rom aufgeteilt worden ist. Die daraus folgende Spaltung der christlichen Kirche[8] und die Rezeption des klassischen römischen Rechts nach dem *Corpus iuris civilis* verbreitete sich von Italien über Kontinentaleuropa.[9] Die Rezeption des byzantinisch römischen Rechts verbreitete sich seinerseits in Osteuropa.[10] So ist Westeuropa das Gebiet, das im Mittelalter den katholischen Glauben angenommen hat und das römische Recht nach dem Corpus iuris civilis rezipiert hat. Hingegen ist Osteuropa der Teil Europas, der das römische Recht und das Christentum aus Ostrom-Byzanz übernommen hat.

Wie beeinflusst das die Europäische Rechtsgeschichte? Um eine vollständige Vorstellung über die Europäische Rechtsgeschichte gewinnen zu können, muss man diese umfassend untersuchen. Die Untersuchung fängt mit den Gemeinsamkeiten an. Nach der Alten Welt, d.h., nach dem altägyptischen, mesopotamischen und althebräischen Recht, wird die griechische und römische Rechtsgeschichte bis zum Jahre 395 analysiert. Nach dem Jahr 395 könnte die europäische Rechtsgeschichte in zwei Blöcke unterteilt werden: die Teritorialgeschichte Roms oder Westroms und die Rechtsgeschichte Ostroms oder des Byzantinischen Reichs. Nach dem Fall Westroms muss man zudem im Rahmen des ersten Teils die Gebiete erforschen, in denen während des Mittelalters das Christentum und das römische Recht aus Rom hereingekommen sind oder zumindest das Katholische Christentum. Der christliche Glaube ist wichtig, weil es nicht nur eine Werteskala für die Gesellschaft Europas darstellt, sondern auch das kanonische Recht mithilfe der Kirche eingeführt und angepasst hat.

Den zweiten Block würden die byzantinische Rechtsgeschichte und die Rechtsgeschichte derer Staaten bilden, die sich als christliche Staaten auf den Ruinen des Byzantinischen Reichs gebildet haben oder die die den orthodoxen Glauben und die Rechtstraditionen des Byzantinischen Reichs übernommen haben.

---

[8] Цыпин В. А. Церковное право. http://lib.eparhia-saratov.ru/books/22c/cipin/eccllaw/5.html [12.12.2009].

[9] Koschaker P. *Europa und das römischeRecht.* München und Berlin: C. H. Beck, 1966, S. 67.

[10] Византийское право как источник Уложения 1648 года и новоуказных статей: Опыт историко-сравнительного исследования / Тиктин Н.И. Одесса: Тип. Штаба окр. 1898, S. 22–32.

Für Lettland bedeutet das, dass es nach der Rechtsrezeption bis zum Ende des 19. Jahrhunderts eindeutig dem Gebiet Westeuropas zuzuordnen ist. Obwohl Lettland im 18. Jahrhundert dem Imperium Russlands einverleibt war, haben die Regierenden das vor Ort geltende Recht und den dort herrschenden Glauben anerkannt.

Also lautet die zweite These: Um die europäische Rechtsgeschichte gänzlich verstehen zu können, muss man nicht nur die Rechtswurzeln erforschen, die für ganz Europa gelten, sondern auch die zwei verschiedenen Wege in Bezug auf das Übernehmen des Christentums und des Römischen Rechts – der eine Weg wird von der Rechtskultur des Westroms und vom Katholizismus geprägt, der andere basiert auf dems Byzantinischen Imperium und demn orthodoxen Glauben.

Der nächste Gedanke ist, meiner Meinung nach, ein wenig ketzerisch. Es betrifft die Frage bezüglich der Rechtskultur der Muslime und dessen Zugehörigkeit oder Nichtzugehörigkeit zur europäischen Kultur.

Offen ist die Frage hinsichtlich der Muslime, weil der Islam sowohl Ideen des Alten Testaments über die Erschaffung der Welt übernommen hat, als auch das Christentum teilweise integriert hat, mit der Begründung Mohameds, dass Moses und Christus Propheten Gottes seien, aber Mohammed selbst sein letzter Prophet sei.[11] Im Koran sind Auszüge aus dem Alten Testament über die Entstehung der Welt und den ersten Menschen wiederzuerkennen, und der wichtigste arabische heilige Ort ist *Kaaba*, und nach den alten arabischen Legenden wurde dieser Ort von dem ersten Menschen gegründet, den Gott geschaffen hat, von Adam, aber der Ort wurde von *Ibrahim* (in der Bibel Abraham) und seinem Sohn *Ismael* erneuert.

Der Urvater Abraham (*Ibrahim*), der den hebräischen Glauben an einen Gott begründet hat, wird nach arabischen Legenden auch als arabischer Stammesvater durch seinen Sohn von Sklavin *Ismail* angesehen.[12] Im dritten und vierten Jahrhundert ist das Christentum von zwei Seiten in Arabien angekommen, und zwar aus Syrien und aus Äthiopien.

Noch früher haben die Araber das Judentum kennengelernt. Die Vertreter dieser Religionen haben zusammengelebt. Sie waren durch den gemeinsamen Handel verbunden.[13] Deswegen muss man sich nicht über den Kulturaustausch wundern, aus dem die Araber das Geschichtsverständnis und die mythologi-

---

[11] Элиаде М. История веры и религиозных идей- от Магомета до Реформации. Москва: Академический проект, 2008, S.99–103.

[12] Максуд Р. Ислам. Москва: Торговый дом ГРАНД, 2000, S. 13.

[13] Watt M.T., Welch A.T. Der Islam. Berlin: Verlag W. Kohlhammer, 1980, S. 118, 119.

schen Ahnen von den Juden übernommen haben. Demnach sind sowohl der Islam als auch das Christentum teilweise auf dem Alten Testament aufgebaut.

Die Araber haben im Mittelalter auch die griechisch-römische Kultur kennengelernt, hat man doch sowohl Aristoteles als auch Platon und viele andere Philosophen der Antike auf Arabisch studiert. So hat der berühmte arabische Wissenschaftler, Philosoph und Politiker *Abu Nasir al Farabi* (870–950) seine Philosophie auf der Basis der Philosophie der Antike ausgearbeitet. Dies spiegelt sich deutlich wieder in seiner Arbeit *„Platons ‚Gesetze' Wesen"*.[14] Die arabische Sprache wurde im Mittelalter im Süden Europas eine Sprache der Gebildeten, weil man mit dieser Sprache in den Schulen der Muslime eine gute Ausbildung erlangen konnte. Man konnte sowohl die Arbeiten der arabischen Philosophen und Wissenschaftler (*Ibn Sina, Al Biruni* und andere) als auch die Arbeiten antiker Klassiker in arabischer Übersetzung lesen. Bedeutet das, dass wir die arabische Kultur als einen Zweig, der die griechisch-römische Kultur übernommen hat, zur europäischen Rechtsgeschichte hinzufügen können? Man muss die Bedeutung der Muslime in der europäischen Rechtsgeschichte beachten, weil es im Süden Europas das ganze Mittelalter über muslimische Staaten gegeben hat. Wenn auch wegen der viel bedeutenderen andere Einflüsse die Möglichkeit zweifelhaft erscheint, die muslimische Rechtskultur als eine Alternative zu der griechisch-römischen Kulturezeption zu sehen, muss man doch eindeutig den Einfluss des muslimischen Rechts auf den Süden Europas feststellen, den die Muslime im frühen Mittelalter teilweise bewohnten und in dem muslimische Reiche existierten. „Für Europa und sein Recht hat die Eroberung Spaniens und Siziliens durch den Islam bleibende Spuren hinterlassen."[15]

Das muslimische Spanien von Jahr 750 war ein unabhängiges Staat bis zum Fall der Umayyaden-Verwaltung im Jahre 1031 und der *Reconquista* (angefangen im Jahr 1085, als *Alfonso* VI aus Kastilien *Toledo* eroberte, es hat vier Jahrhunderte gedauert, bis die Christen die Iberische Halbinsel von den Muslimen zurückerobert hatten)[16] war ein Teil Spaniens ein vereinigtes Muslimenreich. In Granada hat ein kleines islamisches Reich bis zum Jahre 1492 bestanden, als das *Vereinigte* Königreich Aragon-Kastilien dieses zerschlagen hat.[17]

Die nächste These: Muslimische Rechtsgeschichte ist ein Teil der Rechts-

---

[14] *Антология мировой правовой мысли* в пяти томах, I том:, рук.проекта Г.Ю.Семигин, Москва, 2000, Sc. 701–704.

[15] Hattenhauer H. *Europäische Rechtsgeschichte*. 3. erweiterte Auflage. Heidelberg: C. F. Müller Verlag, 1999. S. 161.

[16] Варьяш О.И. *Пиренейские тетради*. Москва: Наука, 2006, S. 46, 47.

[17] *Viduslaiku vēsture*. akad. S. Skazkina zin. red. Rīga: Zvaigzne, 1977., S. 161.

geschichte Europas, wie das Hans *Hattenhauer* in seinem Buch „Europäische Rechtsgeschichte" beschreibt. *Hattenhauer* beweisst überzeugend den muslimischen Rechtseinfluss auf das Recht Südeuropas.[18]

Zum Abschluss möchte ich die Aufmerksamkeit auf das Problem des zeitlichen Periodensystems lenken. Jede Wissenschaft muss eine innere Struktur schaffen. Für die Geschichte ist eine solche Schaffung hinsichtlich der zeitlichen Perioden – Epochen – wesentlich. Dabei sehe ich zwei Probleme:

– die Benennung der Zeitabschnitte der Geschichte;

– die Frage, ob die Perioden der Rechtsgeschichte den allgemeinen Perioden der Geschichte gleichzusetzen sind.

Wie bereits ausgeführt, wird in der Rechtsgeschichte und in der Geschichte allgemein die Einteilung in zeitlichen Perioden aktualisiert, weil die bestehende Teilung nicht erlaubt, den nächsten Abschnitt in der Geschichtsentwicklung zu bilden. Die Einteilung ist veraltet, weil sie während der Renaissance vorgenommen wurde, als Historiker zwischen den Kulturzeiten und den Nichtkulturzeiten unterschieden haben. Als Kulturzeit hat man die griechisch-römische Kultur betrachtet, der in der Zeit der Renaissance zum alten Glanz verholfen worden ist, aber das Mittelalter ist als ein dunkler Abschnitt zwischen dem früheren und späteren Aufblühen der Kulturen betrachtet worden. Historiker, auch die Rechtshistoriker, sehen das Mittelalter schon lange nicht mehr als „Nichtkulturzeit" an, aber die Einteilung der Geschichte in solche Perioden ist erhalten geblieben.[19] Wir gestalten die neue Zeit, dann die neuere Zeit, aber was kommt nach der neueren Zeit, wenn dieses veraltet ist? Noch eine wesentliche Frage: Inwieweit sind die Perioden der Rechtsgeschichte den der Allgemeingeschichte anzupassen? So ist Corpus iuris civilis erst im Jahre 1900 in Deutschland außer Kraft getreten, und mittelalterliche Landrechte haben ihre Anwendung noch im 19. Jhd. gefunden. Wie verhält es sich dann mit der neuen Zeit in der Rechtsgeschichte? Im Übrigen: Verläuft die Entwicklung des Privatrechts und des Öffentlichen Rechts gleichmäßig?

Kann es eine Sicht der europäischen Rechtsgeschichte geben, die sowohl die Entwicklung des Zivilrechts als auch die des Öffentlichen Rechts umfasst? In der UdSSR wurde die Rechtsgeschichte basierend auf marxistischen und leninistischen Dogmen als ein einheitlicher globaler Prozess gelehrt, mit Betonung auf

---

[18] Hattenhauer H. *Europäische Rechtsgeschichte*. 3. erweiterte Auflage. Heidelberg: C. F. Müller Verlag, 1999, S. 162.

[19] Osipova, S. *Feodālo tiesību jēdziena dinamika.// Latvijas Universitātes raksti. 652. Juridiskā zinātne.* Rīga: Zinātne, 2003., S. 105–116.

die Entwicklung des Öffentlichen Rechts.[20] In vielen postsowjetischen Staaten wurden bei der Abschiednahme von dieser Ideologie die Grundprinzipien in den Sozialwissenschaften beibehalten, so auch in der Rechtsgeschichte.

Auf diese Fragen müssen wir noch gemeinsam Antworten finden.

20 *История государства и права зарубежных стран*. Под ред. Галанзы П.Н. и Жидкова О.А. Ч. 2. Москва: Юридическая литература, 1969, S. 4–5.

Jānis Lazdiņš

Europäische Rechtsgeschichte: Gewohnheitsrecht oder Geschichte der Rechtsphilosophie?

Das Studium der Rechtsgeschichte bleibt unvollständig, wenn nicht wichtige Grunderkenntnise der Rechtsphilosophie darin eingegliedert sind. Das Studium der Rechtsphilosophie deckt den Geist der entsprechenden Epoche auf. Der Geist der Zeit oder das Rechtsbewusstsein erklärt uns seinerseits, warum der jeweilige Rechtssatz oder das jeweilige Gesetz so ist und nicht anders. Das bedeutet, dass das Verständnis der Evolution des Rechts unvollständig ist, wenn man die Bedeutung der Ideen der Epoche bei der Entwicklung des Rechts missachtet hat.

Dementsprechend ist das Studium der Rechtsgeschichte undenkbar, wenn man nicht wichtige Elemente der Ideengeschichte einbezieht wie z.B. die Pflichtenlehre von Samuel Pufendorf (1632–1694)[1], den Gesellschaftvertrag von John Locke (1632–1704)[2], den Geist der Gesetze und die klassische Gewaltenteilungslehre von Charles de Secondat, baron de la Brède et de

[1] Siehe z.B. Braun, J. Einführung in die Rechtsphilosophie. Der Gedanken des Rechts. Tübingen: Mohr Siebeck, 2006 – S. 279–285; Broks, J. Tiesības. Filozofija. Doktrīnas, koncepcijas, diskursi. Rīga: Turība Biznesa Augstskola, 2004. – S. 83, 84; Schlosser, H. Grundzüge der neueren Privatrechtsgeschichte. Rechtsentwicklungen im europäischen Kontext. 9. Auflage. Heidelberg: C.F. Müller Verlag, Hüthig GmbH&Co KG, 2001 – S. 100; История политических и правовых учений. Учебник для вузов. Под общей редакцией академика РАН, доктора юридических наук профессора В.С. Нерсесянца. Издание третье, стереотипное. Москва: издательство НОРМА, 2003 – S. 317–319 u.a.

[2] Siehe z.B. Gumplowicz, L. Geschichte der Staatstheorien. Innsbruck: Verlag der Wagner'schen Universitäts-Buchhandlung, 1905 – S. 226–234; Хайек фон, Ф.А. Право, законодательство и свобода. Современное понимание либеральных принципов справедливости и политики. Перевод с английского. / Hayek, Friedrich A. Law, legislation and liberty. A new statement of the liberal principles of justice and political economy. Москва: ИРИСЭН, 2006 – S. 126, 221; Исторія философіи права (новой). Профессора Университета Св. Владиміра князя Е.Н. Трубецкого. Кіевъ: Товарищество „Печатня С.П. Яковлева", 1898 – S. 59–69; Омельченко, О.А. История политических и правовых учений. История учений о государстве и праве. Учебник для вузов. Москва: Eksmo education, 2006 – S. 272–284 u.a.

Montesquieu (1689–1755)[3], die Souveränitätslehre von Jean-Jacques Rousseau (1712–1778)[4], die Vorstellung der Weltgeschichte als Weltgericht von Georg Wilhelm Friedrich Hegel (1770–1831)[5], das Verständnis der Geschichte als Geschichte von Klassenkämpfen und die Vision einer kommunistischen Gesellschaftsordnung von Karl Marx (1818–1883) und Friedrich Engels (1820 –1895)[6] und Lehren zu anderen Problemen, welche eng mit der Rechtsphilosophie verbunden sind[7]. Das bedeutet, dass das Studium der Rechtsgeschichte ohne Studium der Rechtsphilosophie unvollständig ist.

Der Uranfang der europäischen Rechtsgeschichte liegt in der antiken, griechischen Philosophie und im römischen Recht. Obwohl im Jahr 476 nach Christus das Weströmische Reich zusammenbrach[8], schwand nicht die Idee des europäischen Rechts dahin. Hier müsste man betonen, dass das Oströmische Reich noch ungefähr 1000 Jahre bis zum Jahr 1453 bestand, als die Türken Konstantinopol eroberten. Auch die Idee des Oströmischen Reiches ist nicht verschwunden. Die Gelehrten, Künstler und viele andere ausgebildete Leute flohen vor den Türken nach Westeuropa, und mit ihnen auch die Idee und

---

[3] Siehe z.B. Braun, J. Einführung in die Rechtsphilosophie ... – S. 303–316; Kaufmann, A., Hassemer, W., Neumann, U. (Hrsg.) Einführung in Rechtsphilosophie und Rechtstheorie der Gegenwart (mit Beiträgen von Alfred Büllesbach, Günter Ellscheid, Wilfried Hassemer, Arthur Kaufmann†, Ulfrid Neumann, Lothar Philipps, Jochen Schneider, Ulrich Schroth). 7., neu bearbeitete und erweiterte Auflage. Heidelberg: C.F. Müller Verlag, 2004 – S. 74, 261; Нерсесянц, В.С. Философия права. Учебник для вузов. 2-е издание, переработанное и дополненное. Москва: Издательство НОРМА, 2006 – S. 603–610; История политических и правовых учений. Учебник для вузов. Под общей редакцией академика РАН, доктора юридических наукб профессора В.С. Нерсесянца. Издание третье, стереотипное. Москва: издательство, 2006 – S. 367–376 u.a.

[4] Siehe z.B. Adomait, K. Rechts- und Staatsphilosophie II. Rechtsdenker der Neuzeit. 2., neubearbeitete und erweiterte Auflage. Heidelberg: C.F. Müller Verlag, 2002 – S. 81–87; Gumplowicz, L. Geschichte der Staatstheorien ... – S. 246–258; Омельченко, О.А. История политических и правовых учений. История учений о государстве и праве ... – 365–385; Рассел, Б. История западной философии. Высшее образование. Издание второе. Ростов-на-Дону: Феникс, 2002 – S. 773–791 u.a.

[5] Siehe z.B. Adomait, K. Rechts- und Staatsphilosophie II ... – S. 109–120; Braun, J. Einführung in die Rechtsphilosophie ... – S. 329–342; Broks, J. Tiesības. Filozofija ... – S. 162–170; Kūle, M., Kūlis, R. Filosofija. 2. izdevums. Rīga: Apgāds „Burtnieks", 1996. – S. 314–322; Нерсесянц, В.С. Философия права Гегеля. Москва: Юристъ, 1998 u.a.

[6] Siehe z.B: Markss, K., Engelss, Fr. Komunistiskās partijas manifests. / Marx, K., Engels, Fr. Das Manifest der Kommunistischen Partei. [O.O.]: Apgāds Zvaigzne ABC, 2008; Engelss, Fr. Ģimenes privātīpašums un valsts izcelšanās. Rīga: Izdevniecība „Liesma", 1970. Mehr zu dieser Problematik bei Markss, K., Engelss, Fr. Darbu izlase. Rīga: Latvijas Valsts izdevniecība, 1950. – I–II sēj.; Engelss, Fr. Dabas dialektika. Rīga: Latvijas Valsts izdevniecība, 1952; Маркс, К. Биография. Издание третье, дополненное и исправленное. Москва: Издательство политической литературы, 1989 u.a.

[7] Siehe z.B. Markss, K., Engelss, Fr., Ļeņins, V.I. Par sieviešu jautājumu. Rīga: Liema, 1980; Seelmann, K. Rechtsphilosophie. 2., überarbeitete Auflage. München: Verlag C.H. Beck, 2001 – S. 14; Бартенев, С.А. История экономических учений. Москва: экономистъ, 2005 – S. 125–137; Афанасьев, В.С. Первые системы политической экономии. (Метод экономической двойственности). Москва: ИНФРА-М, 2005 – S. 206–303 u.a.

[8] Hattenhauer, H. Europäische Rechtsgeschichte. Heidelberg: C.F. Müller Juristischer Verlag, 1992 – S. 86.

die Rechtskultur des Oströmischen Reichs[9]. Bis heute ist die Bedeutung des Russischen Reichs für die Übernahme des Rechts des Oströmischen Reichs mit der Hilfe der Griechisch-Orthodoxen Kirche ungenügend ausgewertet.[10]

Jetzt kehre ich zum römischen Recht in der katholischen Welt zurück, zu welcher das Territorium des heutigen Lettlands bis zur Verbreitung der Lehre Martin Luthers gehörte.

Nach dem Zusammenbruch des weströmischen Reiches blieb das römische Recht in den früheren Territorien des weströmischen Reichs teilweise in Kraft. In der Praxis erwarb jedoch so genanntes barbarisches Recht wie z.B. die Lex Salica[11], die Русская правда[12], der Sachsenspiegel[13], die Lībiešu – igauņu tiesības[14] u.a. eine viel größere Bedeutung. Demzufolge könnte man die Europäische Rechtsgeschichte bis zum Anfang der Renaissance in vielerlei Hinsicht als eine Geschichte das Gewohnheitsrechts betrachten.

Die Situation veränderte sich grundlegend gleichzeitig mit den großen geographischen Entdeckungen. Obgleich das römische Recht schon vorher mehrere Jahrhunderte studiert wurde, begann in der Realität die Rechtsphilosophie die Entwicklung des Rechts in Europa ernst ab der Zeit der Aufklärung zu beein-

---

9 Robinson, O.F., Fergus, T.D., Gordon, W.M. European legal history. London, Edinburg, Dublin: Butterworths, 2000 – S. 228; Osipova, S. Viduslaiku tiesību spogulis. [O.O.]: Tiesu Namu Aģentūra, 2004 – S. 269.

10 Vergleiche z.B. den Entwurf des russischen Zivilgesetzbuchs mit dem römischen Recht. Siehe z.B. Гражданское уложение. Проект. Высочайше учрежденной Редакционной комиссии по составлению Гражданского уложения (с объяснениями, извлеченными из трудов Редакционной комиссии) под редакцией И.М. Тютрюмова Обер-Прокурора 2-го Департамента Правительствующего Сената. Составил А.Л. Саатчиан. Книга первая. Положения общие. Москва: Волтерс Клувер, 2007; Гражданское уложение. Проект. Высочайше учрежденной Редакционной комиссии по составлению Гражданского уложения (с объяснениями, извлеченными из трудов Редакционной комиссии) под редакцией И.М. Тютрюмова Обер-Прокурора 2-го Департамента Правительствующего Сената. Составил А.Л. Саатчиан. Книга вторая. Семейственное право. Положения общие. Москва: Волтерс Клувер, 2008. Mehr zu dieser Problematik bei Синайский, В.И. Русское гражданское право. Классика Российской цивилистики. Москва: кафедра Гражданского права Юридического факультета МГУ им. М.В. Ломоносова, Статут, 2002; Неволин, К.А. История Российских гражданских законов. Часть первая – часть третья. Москва: кафедра Гражданского права Юридического факультета МГУ им. М.В. Ломоносова, Статут, 2005–2006; Пахман, С.В. История кодификации гражданскоого права. Русское юридическое наследие. Под редакцией и с предисловием доктора юридических наук, профессора В.А. Томсинова. Москва: Издательство „Зерцало", 2004 u.a.

11 Hattenhauer, H. Europäische Rechtsgeschichte ... – S. 34, 95, 102.

12 Тихомиров, М.Н. Пособие для изучения Русской правды. Под редакцией профессора Б.А. Рыбакова. [O.O.]: Издательство Московского университета, 1953 – S. 75–86. Siehe auch Момотов, В.В. Формирование русского средневекового права в IX–XIV вв. Москва: ЗЕРЦАЛО-М, 2003 – S. 320; Графский, И.Г. Всеобщая история права и государства. Учебник для вузов. Москва: Издательство НОРМА, 2007 – S. 246–250 u.a.

13 Der Sachsenspiegel. Übersetzt und eingeleitet von Paul Kaller. München: Verlag C.H. Beck, 2002.

14 Latvijas tiesību avoti. Teksti un komentāri. I. sējums. Seno paražu un Livonijas tiesību avoti 10. gs. – 16. gs. Prof. E. Meļķiša redakcijā. Autori: Jānis Lazdiņš, Valdis Blūzma, Sanita Osipova. Rīga: LU žurnāla „Latvijas Vēsture" fonds, 1998. – S. 30, 31.

flussen. Eine Ausnahme bildete selbstverständlich das kanonische Recht, weil die Kirche auch in Mittelalter nach dem römischen Recht lebte (z.B. *ecclesia vivit lege Romana* sagt die Lex Ribuaria 633/34[15]).

Beachtliche Bedeutung gewann die Idee der Erneuerung des römischen Rechts durch die Glossatoren und Postglossatoren, deren Tätigkeit in vielem die deutsche Historische Schule im Rahmen der römisch-germanischen Rechtsfamilie abgeschlossen (fortgesetzt?) hat.

Obgleich die Idee des Rechts in Europa die Entwicklung mehrerer Jahrtausende in sich verkörpert, ist bislang die Aufmerksamkeit der Rechtsphilosophie hauptsächlich auf die Fragen konzentriert, welche zum größten Teil unmittelbar oder mittelbar mit dem öffentlichen Recht verbunden sind. Eine Ausnahme bildet vielleicht nur die Historische Schule der Rechtswissenschaft (von Friedrich Carl von Savigny [1779–1861], Georg Friedrich Puchta [1798–1846], Otto von Gierke [1841–1921] u.a.)[16]. Hierin zeigt sich, dass das Lehren der Rechtsgeschichte bislang (mindestens in Lettland) einseitig war. Seinerseits folgt daraus für die Rechtsgeschichte das Ziel: die Forschungen auf dem Gebiet des Privatrechts als untrennbarem Teil der Rechtsgeschichte zu aktualisieren (intensivieren).

In der Rechtswissenschaft – ich möchte nicht in der Entwicklung der Rechtswissenschaft sagen – nimmt das sowjetische Recht einen besonderen Platz ein. Das sowjetisches Recht entstand auf der Basis des Marxismus und des kontinentaleuropäischen Rechts. In diesem Zusammenhang muss man solche Begriffe wie Marxismus und Bolschewismus oder Kommunismus unterscheiden,

[15] Mitteis, H., Lieberich, H. Deutsche Rechtsgeschichte. Ein Studienbuch von DR. Heinrich Mitteis, Weiland O. Professor an der Universität München. Neubearbeitet von DR. Heinz Lieberich, Professor an der Universität München. 19., ergänzte Auflage. München: C.H. Beck'sche Verlagsbuchhandlung, 1992 – S. 161.

[16] Siehe z.B. Coing, H. Europäisches Privatrecht 1800 bis 1914. Band II. 19. Jahrhundert. Überblick über die Entwicklung des Privatrechts in den ehemals gemeinrechtlichen Ländern von Prof. Dr. Helmut Coing. München: C.H. Beck'sche Verlagsbuchhandlung, 1989 – S. 41–53; Lazdiņš, J. Vēsturiskā tiesību skola un Latvija. *In: Latvijas Universitātes Raksti. Acta Universitatis Latviensis. Juridiskā zinātne. Law.* – 2006 – Nr. 703 – S. 21–43; Schlosser, H. Grundzüge der neueren Privatrechtsgeschichte ... – S. 142–171; Eisenhart, U. Deutsche Rechtsgeschichte. 3. Auflage. München: C.H. Beck'sche Verlagsbuchhandlung, 1999 – S. 366–380 u.a.

weil es nicht identische Begriffe sind. Bolschewismus war die Anpassung des Marxismus am Bedürfnis Russlands.[17]

Ich möchte betonen, dass die Institute des römischen Rechts nicht fremd für das sowjetisches Recht waren. Doch entsprechend der Ideologie des Bolschewismus *wurde* oftmals der Gehalt der Institute des römischen Rechts verändert. So fand z.B. allmählich eine Löslösung vom Begriff des Privateigentums statt, aber es wurden zwei neue Begriffe geschaffen – sozialistisches Eigentum (oder Staatseigentum) und persönliches Eigemtum. Kennzeichnend war, dass das Arbeitseinkommen nur einzige Quelle für die Vermehrung des persönlichen Eigentums sein konnte. Das bedeutet, dass die Privatunternehmerschaft verboten war und grundsätzlich der Staat und die vom Staat beaufsichtigten Kooperativen zu den einzigen Arbeitgebern wurden.[18] Besondere Bedeutung in der Ausgestaltung des sowjetischen Rechts hatten der Lette Pēteris Stučka (1865–1932)[19] und der Litauer Jevgenij Pasukanis (Евгений Пашуканис, 1891–1937)[20]. Meiner Meinung nach ist das Studium des europäischen Rechts unvollständig ohne Verständnis für das sowjetische Recht. In diesem Zusammenhang ist es wichtig, nicht nur die schlechte, sondern auch die positive Seite des sowjetischen Rechts zu zeigen. Z.B. den verfassungsmäßig

---

[17] Siehe z.B. David, R., Grasmann, G. Einführung in die großen Rechtssysteme der Gegenwart. Bearbeitet von Prof. Dr. Günter Grasmann, Würzburg; Prof. Dr. Ernst Klingmüller, Köln; Dr. Christian Müller-Gutenberger, Stuttgart; Prof. Dr. Karl H. Neumayer, Würzburg; Dr. Sabine Stricker, Peking; Prof. Dr. Klaus Wähler, Berlin; Prof. Dr. Klaus Westen, Berlin; Prof. Dr. Michael Will, Saarbrücken. 2. deutsche Auflage auf der Grundlage „Les grands systèmes de droit contemporains", von René David und Camille Jauffret Spinosa, 8. aufl., Paris, 1982. München: C.H. Beck'sche Verlagsbuchhandlung, 1988 – S. 235–393; Гурвич, Г.Д. Философия и социология права. Избранные сочинения. Перевод с французского М.В. Антонова. Перевод с английского М.В. Антонова, Л.В. Ворониной. Санкт-Петербург: Издательство юридического факультета С.-Петербугского государственного университета, 2004 – S. 434–459 u.a. Vergleiche z.B. die Werke von K. Marx und Fr. Engels mit den Werken von Lenin. Siehe z.B.: Ļeņins, V.I. Rakstu izlase 10 sējumos. Rīga: Izdevniecība „Avots", 1985.–1989. – 1.–10. sēj. u.a. Vergleiche auch „Das Manifest der Kommunistischen Partei" von Karl Marx und Friedrich Engels mit der Satzung der Kommunistischen Partei der Sowjetunion (Устав Коммунистической партии Советского Союза. Политиздат. Утвержден XXVI съездом КПСС. Москва: Издательство политической литературы, 1986.).

[18] Siehe z.B. die Verfassung der Lettlandischen Sozialistischen Sowjetrepublik von 1940 (Paragraph 1–10), Latvijas Padomju Sociālistiskās Republikas Konstitūcija (Pamatlikums) 1.–10. pants. *In: Hronoloģiskais likumkrājums. Latvijas PSR likumi, Latvijas PSR Augstākās Padomes Prezidija dekrēti un Latvijas PSR valdības lēmumu hronoloģiskais krājums 1940. – 1959.* Rīga: Latvijas Valsts izdevniecība, 1960 – S. 10, 11. Mehr zu dieser Problematik bei Vēbers, J. Padomju civiltiesības. I. Vispārīgā daļa. Īpašuma tiesības. Rīga: Zvaigzne, 1979 – S. 150–242; Бетелл, Т. Собственность и процветание. / Bethell, T. The noblest triumph. Property and prosperity. Through the ages. Москва: Ирисэн, 2008 – S. 189–208; Булгаков, Н.С. История экономических и социальных учений. Москва: Астрель, 2007 – S. 849–853 u.a.

[19] Нерсесянц, В.С. Философия права. Учебник для вузов. Москва: Издательская группа НОРМА–ИНФРА М, 1998 – S. 170–198.

[20] Фуллер, Л. Мораль права. Перевод с английского. Издание переработанное и дополненное. / Fuller, Lon L. The morality of law. Москва: ИРИСЭН, 2007 – S. 36–38, 137.

garantierten Arbeitsplatz für jeden, die kostenlose Ausbildung und ärztliche Betreuung usw.

Allgemeine Geschichte und Rechtsgeschichte sind nicht dasselbe, aber sie sind auch nicht Gegensätze, denn die Rechtsgeschichte bezieht sich auf die allgemeine Geschichte wie das Besondere sich auf das Allgemeine bezieht. Obgleich die Aufgabe der Disziplin der Rechtsgeschichte nicht darin liegt, allgemeine Geschichte zu lehren ist, ist es ganz wichtig, auch das jeweilige Zeitgepräge zu erklären. Das Verständnis des Zeitgepräges erleichtert es den Studierenden, die Evolution des Rechts aufzufassen.

Damit sind wir bei der Struktur des Lehrens der Rechtsgeschichte angekommen:
- Allgemeine, geschichtliche Übersicht des Zeitgepräges;
- Analyse der wichtigsten Rechtsquellen und der Voraussetzungen der Entstehung der Rechtsquellen (der Aspekt der Rechtsphilosophie);
- Übersicht über das öffentliche Recht in dem jeweiligen Zeitabschnitt;
- Übersicht über das Privatrecht in dem jeweiligen Zeitabschnitt;
- Schlussfolgerungen über die wichtigste Fortentwicklung des Rechts oder gerade umgekehrt über den Rückgang des Rechts;
- Unterrichtung der Studenten über die Fragen für die Lehrveranstaltung des Seminars.

National Experiences

Dirk Heirbaut

European Comparative Legal History as a Necessity: the Belgian Experience[1]

1. The impossibility of a national legal history in Belgium

Even if one studies legal history in a European context, it is impossible completely to break free of one's own national origins. One way or another every legal historian looks at European legal history through the glasses of his own national legal system and its history. Yet, some patterns may be found in the different national ways of looking at European legal history. In another article in this volume Heikki Pihlajamäki makes a distinction between small and big countries. The latter already have a great history of their own and thus there is less need of looking beyond the borders. In smaller countries, however, the situation is the opposite. The Belgian situation does not contradict Heikki Pihlajamäki at all, as it is a small country with legal historians who are very interested in European legal history. The latest example of that is a new handbook by a Belgian law Randall Lesaffer (who is, currently, the dean of the Law Faculty of Tilburg University in the Netherlands). Its title *European legal history. A cultural and political perspective*[2] leaves no doubt at all about Lesaffer's views. He is not unique, as other Belgian professors also use Europe and not Belgium as the theatre of their description of legal history. For example, R.C. Van Caenegem's *Historical introduction to private law*[3] comes to mind, as well as many other books of the grand old man of legal history in Belgium.[4]

---

[1] This article has been realised with the support of the research programme Interuniversity Attraction Pole P6/01 "Justice and Society: sociopolitical history of justice administration in Belgium (1795–2005)", *Interuniversity Attraction Poles Programme – Belgian State – Belgian Science Policy.* I would like to thank P. Carson, G. Sinnaeve, B. Van Dael and B. Debaenst for their comments. I would also like to express my special gratitude to R.C. Van Caenegem for the discussion we had about this article and for the many other discussions we have had over the years. Needless to say any remaining errors are my own.

[2] Cambridge 2009; the original handbook in Dutch is: R. LESAFFER, *Inleiding tot de Europese rechtsgeschiedenis*. Leuven 2004.

[3] Cambridge 1992.

[4] See especially, R. VAN CAENEGEM, *Judges, legislators and professors: chapters in European legal history*. Cambridge 1987; R. VAN CAENEGEM, *An historical introduction to western constitutional law*. Cambridge, 1995; R. VAN CAENEGEM, *European law in the past and the future. Unity and diversity over two milennia*. Cambridge 2002.

Strange as it may sound, whereas there is no problem finding a European legal history by a Belgian author, it is hard to find a truly Belgian counterpart. In 1999 I was commissioned to write the first, historical, chapter for an *Introduction to Belgian law*.[5] Although a lot of literature was available, there was no modern article or book which dealt exclusively with Belgian legal history and which also covered the subject from the early Middle Ages until the present. Thus, there is a strange contradiction. On the one hand, Belgium has many fine legal historians, but on the other there is no great national legal history. Some books may deal with it, but national legal history is then only seen as part of a greater story, as in John Gilissen's *Introduction historique au droit*.[6] In some fields the absence of nationalism is keenly felt. Thus, until a few years ago, Belgian legal historians had no books dealing with their legal history in the modern era, but had to turn to the chapters (actually books in themselves) written by Ernst Holthöfer in Coing's *Handbuch* and in other publications by the Max Planck Institute for European legal history in Frankfurt.[7]

Given the relatively high number of legal historians in the country and the presence of at least one obligatory course on legal history in the study programs of all Belgian law schools,[8] the absence of a great national legal history begs for an explanation. It can already be found by a comparison with Belgian history in general, which is not a popular subject either. True, there are some good books on Belgian history[9] and a new history of Belgium has recently been published,[10] but it is remarkable that great books on Belgian history are few, that their main audience sometimes seems to be political scientists (or law students) rather than historians,[11] and most of all that books on Belgian history only concern the modern era. Anyone starting with the Romans or the Middle Ages prefers another context. Thus, when I studied history at Ghent University in the 1980's I did not have to study Belgian history. Instead, the program had a course on

---

5 D. HEIRBAUT, "The Belgian legal tradition: does it exist?", in H. Bocken and W. De Bondt, *Introduction to Belgian law*. Kluwer 2001 (2000), 1–22.

6 Brussels 1979; Dutch version: *Historische inleiding tot het recht*. Brussels 1981.

7 E. Holthöfer, "Privatrecht. Belgien", in H. Coing (ed.), *Handbuch der Quellen und Literatur der neueren Europäischen Privatrechtsgeschichte*, III/1. Munich 1982, 1069–1165; E. HOLTHÖFER, "Handels- und Gesellschaftsrecht. Belgien", in Coing, *Handbuch*. Munich, III/3, 3276–3395; E. HOLTHÖFER, "Belgien", in P. Ranieri (ed.), *Gedruckte Quellen der Rechtsprechung in Europa (1800–1945)*. Frankfurt 1992, 3–94; E. HOLTHÖFER, *Beiträge zur Justizgeschichte der Niederlande, Belgiens und Luxemburgs im 19. und 20. Jahrhundert*. Frankfurt 1993, 54–87; 150–189.

8 See for the position of legal history in the curricula of law schools in Belgium, D. HEIRBAUT, *Legal history in Belgium*. Clio@Thémis, 2008 (http://www.ens.fr/droit/spip/spip.php?article12).

9 E.g. E. WITTE, J. CRAEYBECKX and A. MEYNEN, *Politieke geschiedenis van België*. Antwerp 2005.

10 DUJARDIN, V. e.a. (ed.), *Nieuwe geschiedenis van België*. Tielt 2005–2009.

11 E.g. the classic T. LUYKX en M. PLATEL, *Politieke geschiedenis van België*. Antwerp 1985, 2 vol.

the history of the Low Countries, i.e. Belgium and the Netherlands. Moreover, the greatest historical works Belgian historians ever produced, both in terms of quantity and in terms of quality, the twelve volume *Algemene Geschiedenis der Nederlanden*, published between 1949 and 1958,[12] and a fifteen volume work with the same title which appeared a generation later[13] and which involved hundreds of historians, were the product of a cooperation with Dutch colleagues and concerned the Low Countries as a whole.

Given the history of Belgium and the Netherlands it seems logical to study them together. After Charlemagne's great empire had broken up under his successors, France and Germany appeared and between them a patchwork of small principalities, some of them with names which still resonate today, like Flanders or Holland. From the end of the fourteenth century on French princes, the dukes of Burgundy, started to bring the territories between France and Germany under their rule. Final unification had to wait for their Habsburg successors in the sixteenth century, and even then two ecclesiastic principalities, Liège and the smaller Stavelot-Malmédy, remained independent. Apart from them, however, today's Belgium and the Netherlands formed one state. However, almost as soon as unification ended, the newfound unity broke up again, though along new fault lines. In the second half of the sixteenth century the Low Countries, which had become infected by Protestantism revolted against their catholic overlord, the Habsburg king of Spain. He managed to hold on to the South, but the North, the so-called United Provinces, became independent.[14] Nevertheless, ties were not completely broken and a few centuries later North and South were even reunited again, though only for a short period (1815–1830) and this shared history is still visible in their names. The Burgundian state in the Low Countries was called Belgium in Latin and in Dutch, the vernacular of most of its population, Nederlanden (Netherlands). After the split-up at the end of the sixteenth century, the South, which also had a large French-speaking population, kept the Latin name Belgium, whereas in the North almost everyone spoke Dutch (apart from a small minority which used Frisian), so that it took the Dutch name Nederland (Netherlands). Thus, Belgium and the Netherlands both mean the same thing, Low Countries, a common name which reveals a common heritage.[15] Given this shared past, a history of Belgium only makes sense from 1830 when Belgium was on its own

[12] Zeist 1949–1958.

[13] Haarlem 1977–1983.

[14] J. ISRAEL, *The Dutch republic: its rise, greatness and fall.* Oxford 1998.

[15] Cf. J. STENGERS, "Le vocabulaire national dans le royaume des Pays-Bas", in *Colloquium over de geschiedenis van de Belgisch-Nederlandse betrekkingen tussen 1815 en 1945*. Gent 1982, 9–28.

again, though even today many links remain, like in the Benelux, the cooperation between Belgium, the Netherlands and Luxemburg.[16]

Needless to say, legal historians are aware of this and if, studying the *Ancien régime*, they deal only with Belgium, they will scrupulously call it the Southern Netherlands (which may be a bit confusing to some foreign colleagues who will think that the South of today's Netherlands is meant). Even then, the author will be attacked because many critics are convinced that it is not possible to use a Belgian context before 1830. Thus, Philippe Godding's magnum opus *Le droit privé dans les Pays-Bas méridionaux du 12e au 18e siècle*[17] came under attack as the geographical limits the author used where those of a somewhat enlarged Belgium and he had to defend his choice in later publications. In one of these, he has to admit at the end that he could just as well have used a larger geographical context, more in particular that of the Low Countries.[18] However, one may in that case just as well blame some Dutch authors who have dealt with their part of the Low Countries only,[19] and, if one is fair, one has to admit that there were so many customary legal systems in the Low Countries that even studying them in either North or South is a challenge only 'giants of legal history' can hope to survive. Moreover, Belgium's greatest historian Henri Pirenne wrote a national history of his country from the Middle Ages onwards,[20] so a legal historian cannot be completely wrong if he follows in his footsteps. True, Pirenne's approach is nowadays criticised, but it is not completely unjustified.

However, legal history sometimes has its own characteristics which distinguish it from general history and the peculiarities of Belgium's legal history actually make it irrelevant for the period before independence. It may make some sense to a historian to study Belgian history before Belgium, but, for a lawyer its old legal history has no value. In 1795 the armies of the French Revolution annexed the Southern Netherlands. The French abolished its existing laws and replaced them with their own.[21] When Napoleon promulgated his great codifications (Civil

---

[16] See about the Benelux, J. Wouters, L. Van Langenhove, M. Vidal, P. De Lombaerde and W. De Vriendt, *De Benelux: tijd voor een wedergeboorte?* Antwerp 2006.

[17] Brussels 1987.

[18] P. GODDING, "Peut-on déceler un droit commun dans l'histoire du droit privé belge?", *Sartoniana*, XVI, 2003, 125–156. See also, P. GODDING, "Peut-on parler d'un droit privé « belge » avant 1830?", *Académie royale de Belgique. Bulletin de la Classe des lettres et des sciences morales et politiques*, 5th series, LXX, 1984, 262–281.

[19] S. ROES, *Het naaste bloed erfde het goed: de positie van de langstlevende echtgenoot in het Nederlandse erfrecht bij versterf. Deel 1 de periode van het oud-vaderlandse recht (tot 1809)*. Deventer 2006.

[20] H. PIRENNE, *Histoire de Belgique des origines à nos jours* (the edition I use is the posthumous Brussels 1948–1952, 4 vol.).

[21] F. STEVENS, "L'introduction de la législation révolutionnaire en Belgique" in *La Révolution et l'ordre juridique privé. Rationalité ou scandale*. Paris 1988, II, 485–493.

Code, Criminal Code, Code of Civil Procedure, Code of Criminal Procedure) 'Belgium' was just a part of France and Napoleonic law became the law of the land. In itself, this is not remarkable as many other countries in Europe received French law at that time, but Belgium is unique in that it is still today, as far as its legal system is concerned, a colony of France.[22] It still has the Napoleonic Civil Code and at the time of its bicentennial in 2004 Belgium had preserved more articles of the original than France itself. The Napoleonic Code of Criminal Procedure, abolished in France, has not yet been replaced by another Code in Belgium. Even if a Belgian code was written after independence, as happened with judicial law in 1967, the French model remained paramount.[23] Belgium has been so faithful towards France and Napoleon that until 1949 its Civil Code had its inhabitants living as Frenchmen in France under an emperor of Napoleon's dynasty.[24] Its Code of Criminal Procedure continued doing so until 1967,[25] and some statutes even until the 1980's.[26] In some cases, Belgium restored the principles of its pre-revolutionary indigenous law after 1830[27] – it even has a special royal commission for the edition of its old ordinances and customs –,[28] but in general the only relevant legal history of the Ancien Régime is that of France, not of Belgium itself. This shows in the handbooks of legal history. I put a picture of Napoleon on the cover of mine,[29] not because I particularly like this military dictator as some of my students wrongly assume, but because he is the pivotal figure of legal history for a Belgian lawyer. Napoleon is so

---

[22] J. GERKENS and D. HEIRBAUT, "In the shadow of France. Legal acculturation and legal transplants in the Southern Netherlands/Belgium" (forthcoming) and the references there.

[23] See D. HEIRBAUT, "Efficieny: the Holy Grail of Belgian Justice? Civil procedure in Belgium (1806–2008)" in A. Uzelac and C.H. Van Rhee (ed.), *Access to justice and the judiciary. Towards new European standards of affordability, quality and efficiency of civil adjudication* Antwerp-Oxford 2009, 89–117.

[24] Loi du 15 décembre 1949 corrigeant les termes périmés du texte français du Code civil et y constatant certaines abrogations tacites (*Moniteur belge*, 1–3 January 1950).

[25] Loi du 10 juillet 1967 1° corrigeant les termes périmés de la version francaise du Code d'instruction criminelle et y abrogeant certaines dispositions devenues sans objet et modifiant la loi du 20 avril 1874 relative à la détention préventive; 2° établissant la version néerlandaise du même Code et de la loi du 20 avril 1874 relative à la détention préventive (*Moniteur belge*, 6 September 1967).

[26] According to the 1803 Napoleonic statute organising the office of the notaries, Belgium was still ruled as late as 1980 by the *premier consul* and not by the king of the Belgians. It is also telling that this statute, following its original date according to the revolutionary calendar, is even today only known as the "Ventôse statute" (Ventôsewet, Loi de Ventôse) (for its history in Belgium, see F. Stevens, "La loi de Ventôse en Belgique" in *Destin d'un loi. Loi du 25 Ventôse an XI. Statut du notariat.* Paris 2003, 187–199).

[27] D. Heirbaut, *Hebben/hadden onze ministers van justitie een 'civiel' beleid?*, (Gandaius Thorbecke college, XXVII). Mechelen 2005, 31–32.

[28] G. VAN DIEVOET, "Geschiedenis van de Commissie", *Handelingen van de koninklijke commissie voor de uitgave van oude wetten en verordeningen van België*, 1996, 15–57.

[29] D. Heirbaut, *Privaatrechtsgeschiedenis van de Romeinen tot heden.* Gent 2005.

important for R.C. Van Caenegem that in his handbook the chapter on his codifications supersedes the normal chronological order. Whereas one would expect an author to slavishly follow the normal chronology, Van Caenegem kicks off with a chapter on Napoleon and his Civil Code and only thereafter the early Middle Ages and the other periods follow in the established order.

For a Belgian lawyer, legal history has to be about France, not about Belgium, but this is less of a problem than it may seem. 1795 was revolutionary in its abruptness as in one fell swoop French law replaced local law, but it was only the continuation of a trend which had been going on for centuries. Already in the thirteenth century France started to influence law in the South of the Low Countries and this would only grow stronger thereafter. Even the reception of Roman law to a large extent came via France. Thus, 1795 was not that much of a break with the past.[30]

2. A first alternative: universal legal history

France being so dominant in Belgium's legal history, a national legal history is not really an option and to some this means that they have to teach Franco-Belgian legal history,[31] to others it is a liberation. If one has to study the legal history of another country anyway, why not use this challenge as an opportunity to study many other legal systems? This approach is visible in two books written, or at least conceived, in the 1940's and 50's, which contain a universal legal history. John Gilissen's *Introduction historique au droit* was published in 1979 at the twilight of a very distinguished career and thus it was based on decades of teaching. Its second part is a survey of the sources of Franco-Belgian legal history, but its first is a world history of law, in which there is a place for inter alia Egyptian and socialist law.[32] In his universal approach Gilissen was surpassed by his colleague Dekkers's *Le droit privé des peuples*,[33] in which the reader encounters the most exotic systems he can imagine, their names in French adding even more mystery: *Aztèques, Bantous, Burgondes, Cochinchine, Dalmatie, Esclavonie, Frise, Gortyne, Hittites, Kabyles, Locres, Ossètes, Siam, Sumer* to name only a few. It is

---

[30] GERKENS and HEIRBAUT, "Shadow of France".

[31] In Gilissen's handbook (see note 5) part 2 deals with the sources of law since the thirteenth century. In the Dutch version "in de Belgische gewesten" ("in the Belgian territories") has been added. M. Magits published a revised and updated version of this part in Dutch (J. GILISSEN and M. MAGITS, *Historische inleiding tot het recht. 2: De bronnen van het recht in de Belgische gewesten sedert de dertiende eeuw*. Antwerp 1989).

[32] See note 5. This part was revised and updated in Dutch by F. Gorlé (*Historische inleiding tot het recht. 1: Ontstaan en evolutie van de belangrijkste rechtsstelsels*. Antwerp 1991).

[33] R. DEKKERS, *Le droit privé des peuples: caractères, destinées, dominantes*. Brussels 1953.

somewhat strange that these authors wrote or started to write universal legal histories when Koschaker had already published his *Europa und das römische Recht*, the great clarion call for a European legal history in 1947. One element which played a role is the character of the authors, both genuinely interested in universal legal history. Dekkers was a comparatist who specialised in Soviet law and who also became fascinated by China,[34] whereas Gilissen took the initiative for the congresses of the *Société Jean Bodin pour l'histoire comparative des institutions*, in which certain topics of legal history, ranging from the legal status of women to the great empires, were studied from a universal point of view, and for the *Introduction bibliographique à l'histoire du droit et à l'ethnologie juridique/Bibliographical introduction to legal history and ethnology*, a huge series of bibliographies of the legal history of the world's countries. Another element was chronology and availability. Both Gilissen and Dekkers formed their ideas before Koschaker's book was published and it was, at first hard for them to lay their hands on a copy. (When Raoul Van Caegenem heard that I had just bought a copy of 'Koschaker', he regaled me with a story of Gilissen's heroic and unsuccessful quest to find this book when it was first published.)

3. A second alternative: R.C. Van Caenegem's legal history

R.C. Van Caenegem, who started to teach the history of private law course in Ghent in the mid 1970's, is well-known for his *Historical introduction to private law*, published in 1992. The English translation, however, is somewhat misleading because it mentions the French 1988 edition[35] as the original, whereas that text was only the translation of a Dutch book published in 1981[36] based on the author's teaching in the 1970's. Van Caenegem had no problems with getting German literature. In fact, it is clear that he owes much to Wieacker's *Privatrechtsgeschichte der Neuzeit*.[37] Van Caenegem's choice for Europe was determined by his own personal interests (he is not as captivated by quaint exotic legal systems as Gilissen and Dekkers), but also by the change Belgium had undergone. Belgium had joined economic forces with Luxemburg after World War I in the Belgian-Luxemburg Economic Union. After World War II two became three in the Benelux, but the big leap ahead were the treaties establishing the European Communities in the 1950's. Because countries join-

[34] D. HEIRBAUT, "Rene Dekkers, rechtshistoricus – comparatist – civilist, 27 november 1909–22 oktober 1976", *Tijdschrift voor privaatrecht*, XXXVIII, 2001, 101–110.
[35] R. VAN CAENEGEM, *Introduction historique au droit privé*. Brussels 1988.
[36] R. VAN CAENGEM, *Geschiedkundige inleiding tot het privaatrecht*. Gent 1981.
[37] Göttingen 1967.

ing thereafter are only 'Johnny-come-latelies', to Belgians of Van Caenegem's generation and even to their children and grandchildren, Europe is to some extent born out of Belgium and to them it is no stranger. 'Brussels' may be a far-away mythical Eurocrat ivory tower to most Europeans, to most Belgians it is only a very short trip away. (If it takes more than two hours to drive to it from even the farthest place in Belgium, then one has been stuck in a traffic jam.) Needless to say, this sketch of the context of Van Caenegem's work is too short. Yet, the fact remains that his handbook is the product of a certain *Zeitgeist*.

By criticising his work I will now commit a very grave injustice towards my teacher, to whom I owe more than I can ever say. I do hope that the reader will understand that this criticism is only possible because the giant has picked up this dwarf and put him on his shoulders and that it should not be seen as ingratitude, but rather as an exploration of the chances I got by having a superb teacher of legal history. I will not offer here the often heard remark that Van Caenegem's book is too dense for students. When Van Caenegem was teaching, this was his book for first year law students and yet a few of us even memorised all the footnotes! A more justified remark is that for a work dealing with European legal history, it still puts an undeserved emphasis on Franco-Belgian topics. However, that can be explained by its origin in the Ghent course on the history of private law, which was called *Historical introduction to the Code civil* when Van Caenegem started his teaching. Thus, the special place awarded to Napoleon, which has already been mentioned. However, throughout the book some lesser gods in the pantheon of European law receive more attention than is their due. My personal favourite is William van der Tanerijen, a late fifteenth century author. Even well-read legal historians will never have heard of this person, unless they are Belgian or Dutch or have consulted Van Caenegem's book, as Van Caenegem himself condemns van der Tanerijen's work to obscurity: "*it remained virtually unknown*".[38] Why then mention him at all? The answer can be found in the *Historical introduction* and, more elaborately, in another Van Caenegem book, *Le droit Romain en Belgique*. Van der Tanerijen appears there as the first author from the Southern Netherlands who was really influenced by Roman law[39] and he marks the opening of the gate for a greater reception of it. On the European scene van der Tanerijen may not even be worth a footnote, he does not have an entry in the biographical dictionaries of

---

[38] VAN CAENEGEM, *Private law*, 43.

[39] R. VAN CAENEGEM, *Le droit Romain en Belgique* (Ius romanum medii aevi, V/5/b). Milan 1966, 41–43, 47–48.

legal historians,[40] he is not even mentioned in their indices, but for his corner of Europe he was important and given that Van Caenegem originally wrote for students living in that same corner of Europe, van der Tanerijen deserves to be mentioned. One might of course object that, even so, van der Tanerijen could have been left out in an English translation, but something would have been lost then. Like today's euro coins, law in Europe during the late Middle Ages and the early modern era always had two faces. On the one hand, there was the Europeanwide *ius commune*, on the other local *ius proprium*, specific to every individual city or region. Not mentioning elements of a local nature would give the wrong impression of a law in Europe which was as blandly uniform as a can of Coke today. It would then be great if Van Caenegem could also have covered completely all the local diversities which existed, but that is asking too much of an author. If legal historians from all over Europe, when writing a European legal history, also take care to put the local elements of their homeland in the picture, that should be sufficient. It is also necessary, because if the local specialists do not mention their lesser gods, they cannot expect others to know them. For example, Padoa Schioppa has written a wonderful *Storia del diritto in Europa*, but the Low Countries fare badly in his book. The blame there is also on other Belgians and Dutchmen than Van Caenegem for not better 'promoting' their own past.

Van Caenegem is 'typically Belgian' not just in his attention for local phenomena concerning his own country, but also in his view of Europe. At first glance, he seems to follow Koschaker and Wieacker in telling the 'myth of European legal history',[41] shortly and without much attention for detail summarised as follows: before 1100 Europe was primitive, so don't bother too much; then the *Corpus Iuris Civilis* is dusted off and for the rest of the Middle Ages the Italians dominate the scene; in the sixteenth century the French take over; in the seventeenth the Dutch replace them at the top of the legal hit-parade only to be in their turn ousted by the Germans (in the twentieth century 'the winds change'[42] in favour of the Americans, but that better remains unsaid). However, if one looks closer Van Caenegem's European legal history does not fit completely with the Koschaker-Wieacker view, as he pays a lot of attention to customary

[40] E.g. in M. STOLLEIS (ed.), *Juristen: ein biographisches Lexikon von der Antike bis zum 20. Jahrhundert*. Munich 1995, or in G. KLEINHEYER and J. SCHRÖDER (ed.), *Deutsche und Europäische Juristen aus neun Jahrhunderten*. Heidelberg 2008.
[41] D. OSLER, "The myth of European legal history", *Rechtshistorisches Journal* XVI, 1997, 393–410.
[42] U. MATTEI, "Why the wind changed: intellectual leadership in Western law", *American journal of comparative law*, XLII, 1994, 195–218.

law and also to England. Once again, personal interests play a role,[43] but also the Belgian perspective. Van Caenegem's Europe consists of Belgium and its neighbours, hence also England. Italy is a case apart. It was not a neighbour, but at least one of the six founding members of the EU. Moreover, it is impossible to ignore Italy when writing a European legal history and it is telling that as soon as Andre Alciato has been mentioned Italy falls off the map, as its history is no longer relevant to a Belgian. Spain is only mentioned four times and the school of Salamanca is conspicuous in its absence. Northern and Eastern Europe are written off as 'the periphery' and countries there are, at best, mentioned only once. The United States share that fate, though they and the late Soviet Union receive more attention in his book on constitutional history. In short, Van Caenegem's Europe is the Europe which existed for a Belgian when I was a kid. It was mostly about those countries which one could visit in a short trip by car or by boat. Other countries did not really exist, because of distance, but also because they were not democratic, either because they had their own dictators as in Spain, Portugal and Greece or because they were behind the Iron Curtain.

By now, the situation has changed, most of all, thanks to the enlargement of the European Union. When Europe expanded, so did the horizons of both ordinary Belgians and legal historians. Thus, I have in my handbook a paragraph about the school of Salamanca and Lesaffer ends his book with the entrance of the latest batch of member states into the European Union. I have also gone beyond that and added chapters on American and non-Western legal history, because in a globalising world, other continents also have an impact on the development of law in Europe. The focus may still be on Belgium and its neighbours, but this is because there is only so much one can put in a handbook and still call it a 'hand'-book. (I have never understood what possessed Coing to call the great multi-volume work on European legal history he edited, a *Handbuch*.) Another problem is that it is impossible to know all the languages of Europe.[44] Therefore, once again, a plea for more books of European comparative legal history which also leave some room for the local legal history of the author's country.[45]

---

[43] In fact, most Belgian intellectuals know Van Caenegem as a specialist of English history in general (R. VAN CAENEGEM, *Geschiedenis van Engeland*. Leuven 2003; see also R. VAN CAENEGEM, *Engeland. Wonderland*. Leuven 2005) and they are ignorant of his achievements as a legal historian. His English wife, Patricia Carson, also has become a household name in Belgium because she returned the love of her husband for her country by writing about his (P. CARSON, *The fair face of Flanders*. Tielt 2001). Actually, when I was in grammar school R.C. Van Caenegem was only known to me as Patricia Carson's husband.

[44] For a good try at it, see G. HAMZA, *Wege der Entwicklung des Privatrechts in Europa*, Passau 2007.

[45] See e.g. J. Øyrehagen Sunde, *Speculum legale – Rettsspegelen: ein introduksjon til den norske rettskulturen si historie i eit europeisk perspektiv*. Bergen 2005.

Whereas the normal succession of things is moving from national to European legal history, there are some indications that in Belgium national legal history is now gaining some ground. A first cause of this is the direct effect of the state's intervention with the study programme in law schools. Since 1849 the universities had to teach an obligatory course on the 'historical introduction to private law'.[46] The latter, significantly, is not called 'legal history' or 'history of private law'. A professor who wanted to be faithful to the statute, could only teach the history of the legal sources, not of legal institutions, like marriage or property. Some legal historians, like Gilissen,[47] disregarded this, others, like Van Caenegem, did not. However, when Belgium became a federal state and the linguistic communities became responsible for the universities, Flanders used this occasion to give the law schools freedom in organising their study program. Thus, Jos Monballyu teaches only legal institutions of family and criminal law.[48] The general tendency has been for those handbooks or parts of them which deal with legal institutions, to prefer a Belgian over a European context.

Another new element is the rise of 'post-French Revolution' legal history. For a long time, the line between legal history and contemporary law was clear. Legal history was only what had happened until the French Revolution and Napoleon. The history of Belgium thereafter was taught to law students, but not legal history. Only exceptionally was the modern era studied.[49] Even in the 1980's a legal historian was still expected to turn first and foremost to the Middle Ages. In the last two decades this had to change, if only for many Ph. D. students no longer knowing Latin. Modern legal history sees Belgium as its natural area.[50] This has also become necessary because courses of Belgian history have been abolished and had to be integrated into the history of public law.

A third factor is one which most foreigners will spontaneously link to Belgium: its linguistic strife. I was born in a unitary state and now live in a federal one. This process of regionalisation left its marks on the study of legal history, though in an unexpected way. Dutch- and French-speaking Belgian legal cultures may

---

46 R. VERSTEGEN, 'L'enseignement du droit en Belgique, évolution de la législation aux XIXe et XX siècles', in F. Stevens and D. Van den Auweele (ed.), *Houd voet bij stuk. Xenia iuris historiae G. Van Dievoet oblata*. Leuven 1990, 174.

47 See for that the third part of his handbook (note 6).

48 J. MONBALLYU, *Geschiedenis van het familierecht: van de late middeleeuwen tot heden*, Leuven 2006; MONBALLYU, *Zes eeuwen strafrecht: de geschiedenis van het Belgische strafrecht (1400–2000)*, Leuven 2006.

49 E.g. E. Van Dievoet, *Het burgerlijk recht in België en Nederland van 1800 tot 1940. De rechtsbronnen*. Antwerp 1943.

50 See e.g. D. Heirbaut, X. Rousseaux and K. Velle (ed.), *Politieke en sociale geschiedenis van jusititie in België van 1830 tot heden/Histoire socio-politique de la justice en Belgique*. Bruges 2004.

now be, slowly, but inexorably, drifting apart,[51] yet, one cannot see the same happening in legal history. Even in Flanders, the Flemish movement has not really inspired legal historians in their professional activities. There is only one Ph. D. thesis dealing with the position of Dutch in the courts between 1830 and 1935.[52] In fact, the most scathing condemnation of the arrogance of Belgium's French speaking lawyers is to be found in the recent doctoral thesis of Françoise Muller, who is herself French speaking.[53] On the other hand, many books and articles concern Flanders,[54] but this is the old county which is very distinct from today's Flanders (only two of the five actual Flemish provinces belonged to the old county, which, however, also encompassed the French *département du Nord* and part of what is now the Dutch province of Zeeland) and it is less Flemish nationalism than the riches of the old Flanders's history which inspires this.[55] Nevertheless, regionalisation has some influence. Belgian legal historians experience every day in their own country that European and regional identities and legal systems can go hand in hand. Hence, it is easier for them to see that in the past the common law of Europe was complemented by many regional legal systems.

4. Conclusion: the need for a history of law, not just of lawyers

Looking back, Van Caenegem's handbook still remains a masterpiece, new elements only complementing, not replacing it. However, its greatest lack is

---

[51] See D. Heirbaut and M.E. Storme, "The Belgian legal tradition: from a long quest for legal independence to a longing for independence", in E. Dirix en Y.-H. Leleu (ed.), *The Belgian reports at the congress of Utrecht of the International Academy of Comparative Law.* Brussels Bruylant 2006, 3–43; and add: E. DIRIX, *Privaatrecht en multiculturaliteit.* Antwerp-Oxford 2007; G. MARTYN, "The judge and the formal sources of law in the Low Countries (19th–20th centuries): from 'slave' to 'master'?", in W. Hamilton Bryson and S. Dauchy (ed.), *Ratio decidendi. Guiding principles of judicial decisions, I, Case law.* Berlin 2006, 206–207, 219–220.

[52] H. VAN GOETHEM, *De taaltoestanden in het Vlaams-Belgisch gerecht, 1795–1935.* Brussels 1990.

[53] F. MULLER, *La Cour de cassation belge à l'aune des rapports entre pouvoirs. De sa naissance dans le modèle classique de la séparation des pouvoirs à l'aube d'une extension de la fonction juridictionnelle, 1832–1914/1936.* Louvain-la-Neuve 2010 (unpublished doctoral thesis Université Catholique de Louvain).

[54] A good illustration of this is to be found in the bibliography accompanying D. LAMBRECHT and J. VAN ROMPAEY, "De staatsinstellingen in het Zuiden van de 11de tot de 14de eeuw", in *Algemene geschiedenis der Nederlanden,* III. Haarlem 1982, 470–472. D. Lambrecht points out the contrast between Flanders and the other principalities. The rule of thumb seems to be that whereas there are books about the legal and institutional history of Flanders, the others in general have to do with articles. However, thanks to the work of P. Godding (see e.g. his *Le Conseil de Brabant sous le règne de Philippe le Bon (1430–1467).* Brussels 1999) and others, Brabant is not doing so badly.

[55] For example, there is a general book in English about the history of medieval Flanders (D. NICHOLAS, *Medieval Flanders,* 1992), whereas the other principalities still wait for their historiographer in English.

common to all handbooks of European legal history. They chronicle the history of the great legislators, judges and professors, but not, with a few exceptions,[56] of the law these people made and developed. This is an enormous defect. After all, to a lawyer, the 'lords of the law' are not important in themselves, but only as law-makers. The study of the latter should only be a means to an end and not the sum of European legal history, as our students do not study lawyers, but law. Only in a few cases, is it possible to find literature about legal institutions in a European context, but almost always the same subjects will turn up, like constitutions, marriage, tort and contract. Going beyond that is impossible, because books on a European history of subjects like the law of succession or labour law are lacking. The *ius commune* had the *Corpus iuris*, today's specialists of European legal history still need to write many chapters of their *Corpus historiae iuris.*

---

[56] Most of all, H. COING, *Europäisches Privatrecht*. Munich 1985–1989, 2 vol.

Aniceto Masferrer

Spanish Legal History: A need for its Comparative Approach

1. An Introduction to the Legal History Teaching in Spain

Legal History teaching in Spain has a long tradition in the university *curricula*, more specifically in the Faculties of Law. The first legal history chair was set up in 1873.[1] Later on, other two Royal Decrees were issued establishing legal history as an independent discipline within the law curricula studies.[2] Although on several occasions legal history as a law curriculum discipline could have disappeared, fortunately this has never happened[3] Hence legal history has been taught in Spain for almost a century and a half.

In part because legislation enshrined a field called "History of Law and of the Institutions" thereby creating many chairs all over the country, particularly in the last forty years, Spanish legal historians have flourished and spread considerably. There therefore exist today in Spain many scholars who deal exclusively with legal history, both doing research and teaching.

Spanish history has witnessed a long legal development which goes from the period of its legal Romanization until today.[4] Interestingly enough, it has been

---

[1] Royal Decree on September 2, 1873 (on this matter, see VILLAPALOS G.: "Memoria de un maestro", *Homenaje al Profesor Alfonso García-Gallo*, vol. I, Madrid, 1996, p. 12).

[2] Royal Decrees on September 2, 1873, and on August 14, 1884 (on this matter, see AGUILERA BARCHET, A.: *Introducción jurídica a la Historia del Derecho*. Madrid, 1994, p. 23).

[3] In this regard, it is memorable that legal history was not abrogated in the context of the global reform process of the university curricula which took place in 1987, particularly considering the fact that in the Committee in charge of the legal reform there was no legal historian at all. Despite of it, the legislation which laid down the criteria to elaborate the law curriculum maintained the legal history as a compulsory course (see the Royal Decree 1497/1987, 27th September; see also the *Reforma de las enseñanzas universitarias. Título: Licenciado en Derecho*, Madrid, 1988, pp. 23–45). Later on, the legal reform concerning the law curriculum approved the compulsory character of the legal history course, granting to universities the possibility of introducing other optional courses dealing with legal history (see the Royal Decree 1424/1990, 26th October).

[4] An interesting question to pose is at what time Spanish legal history really begins. There are different views among legal historiography. Some state that it begins with the Roman conquest (218 B.C), others with the Visigothic period (476 or 568 AD), and others with the Constitution of Cadiz (1812). They give all different arguments to defend their own views. I think it is better to start from the beginning, that is, before the Romanization of the Iberian Peninsula, since it will enable us to cover the history of Roman law in Spain which constituted an important characteristic not only of Spanish legal tradition but also of civil law countries.

said – although not always recognized by non-Spanish scholars[5] – that Spanish legal history is one of the most instructive,[6] oldest[7] and richest[8] legal tradition which has ever existed, a statement which could have been hardly written by a Spanish scholar. Considering at least that Spanish legal history should cover all laws made and applied in the territories that have formed part of the current Spain throughout history, it is clear that Spanish legal history is quite long and rich, as will be seen.

One may ask what has been, is and will be the role of the European Comparative perspective in teaching Spanish legal history. In answering this question I will divide the paper into three parts. First, I will explain what has happened in the past; second, I will turn to what, in my view, should be done about it; and third, I will conclude by saying what I think will probably happen.

2. What Has Happened

In general terms, it could be said that Spanish legal historians have not paid much attention to the European context in which Spanish legal history was born and developed over the centuries. A brief look at the considerable number of Spanish legal history handbooks would be enough to realize that their authors

---

[5] This is, in my opinion, due to the fact that both not many non-Spanish legal historians can read Spanish and Spanish legal historians have made little effort to publish in other languages different from those used in Spain. This is, nonetheless, another matter that does not concern the topic of this paper.

[6] SCHMIDT, Gustavus: *The Civil Law of Spain and Mexico*. New Orleans, 1851, p. 9: "Few countries have experienced so many vicissitudes as Spain; and few, if any, present more varied and more instructive lessons in social sciences (...) the ancient history of Spain [referring to the period of Iberians, Celts and Phenicians], though obscure and by time and disfigured by fables, affords sufficient information to enable us to ascertain that it was at a very early period a rich and flourishing kingdom".

[7] PUTNAM, Herbert: "Preface" to PALMER, Thomas W. Jr.: *Guide to the Law and Legal Literature of Spain*. Washington, Government Printing Office, 1915, p. 4: "...Spain offers a fruitful field for study. It possesses one of the oldest developed systems of law–a composite of Roman, Germanic and Arabic elements, with a strong infusion of canon law; it is growing in industrial and commercial importance; it is participating actively in the legislative movement for social and economic reform; and – of particular interest to us – is the mother of the legal system of a large part of the world in which we have vital interests"; and later on, its author states that "the history of Spanish law assumes far more than a local importance. In the early Spanish codes and compilations may be traced some of the most lasting institutions of Roman law, and they were the medium through which Spain carried her law into the new world" (p. 26).

[8] KLEFFENS, E.N. van: *Hispanic Law until the end of the Middle Ages*. Edinburgh, 1968, pp. 27–28: "There is no doubt that the history of Spanish law in the middle Ages is exceptionally rich; it's study cannot but broaden the law-student's understanding, and open his eyes to his merits and demerits of a great many solutions for a great many problems which, through the ages, are basically and generally the same everywhere (...). Surely, a legal system of such unique magnitude would seem to deserve more attention than it has hitherto received beyond the frontiers of Spain".

were not very concerned with the European or comparative perspective.[9] Several reasons can explain this fact.

The most important one is that, with only a few exceptions Spanish legal historiography has barely explored Spanish legal history from a European or comparative perspective. Scholars have tended to teach the results of their research, and generally speaking, each scholar has been researching only teaching usually reflects the main research interests of the scholars who cultivate a specific scientific field.

When the first books containing the European perspective were written and published outside Spain,[10] Spanish legal historians' concerns mainly revolved around the medieval legal sources, particularly the local charters and customs or

---

[9] See, for example –and among others–, the following Spanish legal history handbooks written by CORONAS GONZÁLEZ, Santos M.: *Manuel de Historia del Derecho Español.* Valencia, 1999; ESCUDERO LOPÉZ, José Antonio: *Curso de Historia del Derecho. Fuentes e Instituciones Político-administrativas.* Madrid, 2003; FERNÁNDEZ ESPINAR, R.: *Manual de Historia del Derecho Español,* Madrid, 1989; FONT i RIUS, Josep Mª: *Apuntes de Historia del Derecho Español tomados de las explicaciones ordinarias de la cátedra: parte general: La evolución general del Derecho Español: lecciones 1–37 del programa de clases.* Barcelona: Universidad, D.L. 1974; GACTO FERNÁNDEZ, Enrique (et altri): *Derecho histórico de los pueblos de España.* Madrid, 1992; GARCIA GALLO, Alfonso: *Manual de Historia del Derecho.* Madrid, 1992; GIBERT Rafael, *Historia General del Derecho español.* Madrid, 1975; IGLESIA FERREIRÓS, Aquilino: *La creación del derecho. Una historia de la formación de un derecho estatal español.* 2 vols., Barcelona, 1992; LALINDE, *Jesús: Iniciación a la historia del Derecho español.* Madrid, 1989 MONTAGUT ESTRAGUÉS, Tomàs (coord.): *Història del dret espanyol.* Edicions de la Universitat Oberta de Catalunya, Barcelona, 1998; PESET, Mariano (y otros): *Historia del derecho.* Valencia, 1989; PÉREZ-BUSTAMANTE, Rogelio: *Historia del Derecho Español. Las fuentes del derecho,* Madrid: Dykinson, 1994; PEREZ PRENDES, Jose Manuel, *Curso de historia del derecho español,* Madrid, 1990; SANCHEZ, Galo: *Curso de Historia del Derecho español. Introducción y fuentes.* Valladolid, 1980; TOMÁS Y VALIENTE, Francisco: *Manual de Historia del Derecho Español.* Madrid, 1992.

[10] See, for example, WIEACKER, F.: *Privatrechtsgeschichte der Neuzeit.* Göttingen, 1967; BERETTA ANGUISOLA, P.: *L'Europa e il suo Diritto, I, Premessa romana,* Florencia 1967 (see its review written by E. Valiño in *Anuario de Historia del Derecho Español* –or *AHDE*– 39, 1969, pp. 779–780); COING, Helmut: "Die europäische Privatrechtsgeschichte der neueren Zeit als einheitlicher Forschungsgebiet", *Jus commune* 1 (1967), pp. 1–33; COING, Helmut: "Die Bedeutung der europäischen Rechtsgeschichte für die Rechtsvergleichung", *Rabels Zeitschrift für ausländisches und internationales Privatrecht* 32 (1968), pp. 1–23; CAVANNA, Adriano: *Storia del diritto moderno in Europa. Le fonti e il pensiero giuridico.* I. Milano, 1972; COING, Helmut: "Die historischen Grundlagen der europäischen Rechtseinheit", *Mitteilung aus der Max-Planck-Gesellschaft zur Förderung der Wissenschaft e. V.,* Jahrgang 1973, pp. 241–244; COING, Helmut: *Handbuch der Quellen und Literatur der neueren europäischen Privatrechtsgeschichte,* Munich 1973, 3 vols. (see its review written by A. García Gallo in *AHDE* 44, 1974, pp. 752–764 and 46, 1976); as known, Coing's *Handbook* remained unfinished: the 1st *Band* has one volume on the Middle Ages; the 2nd *Band* has two volumes; and the third *Band* has five volumes; later on, he published his *Europäisches Privatrecht,* Munich, 2 vols., 1985–1989 (which was translated into Spanish by Antonio Pérez Martín and published by the Fundación Cultural del Notariado, Madrid, 1996).

fueros. Many scholars devoted much interest to these medieval sources.[11] At the same time, it would be inaccurate to say that in the middle of the 20th Century Spanish legal historians were not aware of the emergence of the European perspective: papers written by foreign scholars, once translated into Spanish, were published in Spain,[12] and the celebrated legal historian A. García Gallo also wrote about it.[13] However, among the majority of Spanish legal historians, the national geographical context of interest prevailed,[14] considering the European legal history as a "ghost history", not a real legal history.[15]

The predominance of the study of the legal sources over the legal institutions was an important feature of the Spanish historiography of the second half of the 20th century (particularly in the 60s and 70s). This phenomenon was perfectly understandable since no real research on legal institutions could be done without a previous study of the main legal sources of the different Spanish legal traditions (Castile, Aragon, Catalonia, Valencia, Majorca, Navarre, etc.). In doing so, since much work had to be done, the European perspective was almost ignored or put it aside.

I said "almost" – and not completely – because there were some remarkable exceptions. Building on those exceptions, a European or comparative approach to Spanish legal history would emerge and progressively expand. Several legal historians should be mentioned, all of them focusing on the *ius commune*. The two most notable will be dealt with first: one dealt with the history of canon law (*Corpus iuris canonici*), Antonio García y García, another with the civil law (*Corpus iuris civilis*), Antonio Pérez Martín.

---

[11] It would be impossible to cite even a part of the Spanish legal historiography dealing with the *fueros*; for an exhaustive list of articles and books published between 1973 and 1998 dealing with it, see PUYOL MONTERO, José Mª: "Un balance de 25 años de historiografía histórico-jurídica en España (1973–1998)", *Cuadernos de Historia del Derecho* 5 (1998), pp. 283–409.

[12] THIEME, Hans: "Unidad y pluralidad en la Historia del Derecho europeo", RDP 49 (1965), pp. 689–700; WALL, Edward: "La unificación de Europa y el Derecho", *Cuadernos de Historia Económica de Cataluña* 21 (1969), pp. 185–190; see later on, in the 1990s, SCHULZE, R.: "De la aportación de la Historia del Derecho a una Ciencia del Derecho Privado Europeo", *AHDE* 66 (1996), pp. 1003–1013.

[13] GARCÍA-GALLO, Alfonso: "Cuestiones de Historiografía jurídica, I. La justificación de la Historia del Derecho; II. La Historia del Derecho Europeo", *AHDE* 44 (1974), pp. 741–764.

[14] On this matter, see CLAVERO, Bartolomé: "Leyes de la China. Orígenes y ficciones de una Historia del Derecho Español", *AHDE* 52, 193–221; PÉREZ MARTÍN, Antonio: "La 'Respublica christiana' medieval: Pontificado, Imperio y Reinos", *El Estado Español en su Dimensión Histórica* (ed. by Manuel J. Peláez). Barcelona, 1984, pp. 59–128; PÉREZ MARTÍN, Antonio: "Planteamiento y objetivos del Simposio Internacional 'España y Europa, un pasado jurídico común'", *España y Europa. Un pasado jurídico común* (ed. by A. Pérez Martín), Murcia, 1986, pp. 12–13; the same cannot be said regarding some historians like SUÁREZ FERNÁNDEZ, Luis: *Europa: una conciencia histórica en la encrucijada.* Valladolid, 1972.

[15] OTERO VARELA, A.: "La delimitación nacional de la historia del derecho. En torno a los orígenes de la nacionalidad española", *Boletín de la Universidad Compostelana* 78 (1971), p. 31.

Antonio García y García started an important task of editing and commenting canon law sources in 1973 in Spain and other European countries.[16] He also participated in many national and international conferences[17] and published in different canon law and legal history journals until the end of the last century.[18] In 1999 a selection of his scattered works dealing with the *ius commune* were collected and re-edited.[19]

Both the research and teaching of Antonio Pérez Martín, whose PhD supervisor had already showed interest in the European legal tradition,[20] were particularly focused on the *ius commune*'s legal sources and literature, taking the European perspective in mind from the very beginning. Working at the Institute Max-Planck for European Legal History (Frankfurt am Main, Germany) for ten years, he published several works in which legal development was approached within the European context.[21] Once back in Spain, as a professor of legal history at the University of Murcia, Pérez Martín's academic activity followed the same line. Regarding his research projects, he continued

---

16 See, for example, GARCÍA Y GARCÍA, A.: *Códices operum Bartoli de Saxoferrato recensit. Iter Hispanicum*, Instituto per la Storia dei Postglossatori e Commentatorim, Florencia, 1973.

17 See, among others, GARCÍA Y GARCÍA, A.: "Investigación y estudio del Derecho común medieval en España", *Atti del Convegno I Glossatori*, Pavia, 1974, pp. 21–41; "Del Derecho canónico visigodo al Derecho común medieval", *Estudios sobre Alfonso VI y la reconquista de Toledo. Actas del II Congreso Internacional de Estudios Mozárabes*, Toledo, 1987, pp. 165–185.

18 GARCÍA Y GARCÍA, A.: "El jurista catalán de Vallseca. Datos biográficos y tradición manuscrita de sus obras", *La investigación de la Historia hispánica del siglo XIV. Problemas y cuestiones*, Barcelona, 1973, pp. 677–708; *La canonística portuguesa medieval*, Madrid, 1976; "La canonística española postclásica", *Studia Gratiana*, 19 (1976), pp. 225–252; "Nuevos descubrimientos sobre la canonística salmantina del siglo XV", *AHDE* 50 (1980), pp. 363–374; "La canonística ibérica (1150–1250) en la investigación reciente", *Bulletin of Medieval Canon Law* 11 (1981), pp. 41–75; *Iglesia, sociedad y Derecho*, Salamanca, 1985; "La enseñanza universitaria en las Partidas", *Glossae. Revista de Historia del Derecho*, 2 (1989–1990), pp. 107–118; *Derecho común en España: los juristas y sus obras*, Murcia, 1991; "El derecho canónico medieval", *Dret Comú i Catalunya. Actes del II Simposi Internacional*, Barcelona, 1991; "El derecho canónico medieval", El Dret Comú i Catalunya, 1992, pp. 17–51; "Manuscritos de derecho común medieval en España: Acta et agenda", *El Dret Comú y Catalunya*, Barcelona, 1993, pp. 51–70; "De las colecciones gregorianas al derecho común medieval en Compostela", *Estudios de Historia del Derecho Europeo. Homenaje al Prof. G. Martínez Díez*, Madrid, 1994; "El derecho común en Castilla durante el siglo XIII", *Glossae*, 5–6 (1996), pp. 255 a 277.

19 GARCÍA y GARCÍA, A.: *En el entorno del Derecho común*. Madrid, Dykinson, 1999.

20 See, for example, GIBERT SÁNCHEZ DE LA VEGA, R.: *Elementos formativos del Derecho en Europa. Germánico. Románico. Canónico*, Madrid, 1982.

21 PÉREZ MARTÍN, A.: "Los colegiales de San Clemente de los Españoles en Bolonia (1368–1500)", *Salmanticensis*, XX-1, (1973); "Gesetzgebung in Spanien", *Handbuch der Quellen und Literatur der neueren europäischen Privatrechtsgeschichte*. München, 1976, pp. 228–281; "Los colegios de Doctores en Bolonia y su relación con España", *AHDE*, XLVIII (1978), "Büchergeschäfte in Bologneser Regesten aus den Jahren 1265–1350", *Veröffentlichungen des Max-Plank-Instituts für europäische Rechtsgeschichte*, VII (1978), pp. 7–49; (with SCHOLZ, J.M.), *Legislación y jurisprudencia en la España del Antiguo Régimen*, Valencia, 1978; *Proles Aegidiana*, 4 vols., Bolonia, 1979; "'Fori Aragonum' vom Codex von Huesca (1247) bis zur Reform Phillipps II (1547)", 8th volume of the *Mittelalterliche Gesetzbücher Europäischer Länder in Faksimileindrücken*, Vaduz-Liechtenstein, 1979.

publishing on the *ius commune* and its reception in the Spanish kingdoms,[22] organizing some conferences and joint projects in which he encouraged and involved other remarkable scholars from Spain and other European countries. Two conferences held in 1985 deserve to be mentioned: the 1st International Symposium of the *Ius-commune Institute* Pérez Martín held in Murcia on April 26-28,[23] and a Seminar J. Cerdá Ruíz-Funes and P. Salvador Coderch held in Barcelona, on the current developments of the study of the history of private law, in which Pérez Martín gave an interesting paper on the study of the reception of the *ius commune* in Spain.[24] Ten years later, in 1995, Pérez Martín held another conference in Murcia to celebrate the 7th Centennial of the death of Jacobo de las Leyes, who is – in Pérez Martín's view – the author of the Fuero Real and Siete Partidas.[25]

Perez Martín also created the *Instituto de Historia del Derecho Europeo*, along with a legal history journal called *Glossae: Revista de Historia del Derecho Europeo*, where several Spanish and non-Spanish legal historians published between 1988 and 1996 articles about the *ius commune*, European legal history and

---

22 PÉREZ MARTÍN, A.: "Importancia de las Universidades en la recepción del Derecho romano en la Península Ibérica", *Studi Sassaresi*, VIII, III (1980–81), pp. 255–332; "Estudiantes zamoranos en Bolonia", *Studia Zamorensia*, 2 (1981); "El *ordo iudiciarius 'Ad summarium notitiam'* y sus derivados. Contribución a la historia de la literatura procesal castellana (I. Estudio) y (II. Edición de textos)", H.I.D. 8 (1981), pp. 195–266; and 9 (1982), pp. 327–423; "Las glosas de Arias de Balboa al Ordenamiento de Alcalá. Su edición y estudio", *Aspekte europäischer Rechtsgeschichte. Festgabe für Helmut Coing zum 70. Geburtstag*, Frankfurt, 1982, pp. 245–292; "El Ordenamiento de Alcalá (1348) y las glosas de Vicente Arias de Balboa", *Ius Commune*, 11 (1984), pp. 55–215; "El Fuero Real y Murcia", *AHDE* 54 (1984), pp. 55–96; "La obra jurídica de Jacobo de las Leyes: las Flores del Derecho", *Cahiers de linguistique hispanique médiévale. De la variation linguistique et textuelle. En l'honeur de Jean Roudil*, n. 22, vol. 2, Paris.

23 The papers given in this symposium, organized to celebrate the 7th centennial anniversary of Alfonso El Sabio's death, were published in PÉREZ MARTÍN, A.: *España y Europa. Un pasado jurídico común*, Murcia, 1986; particularly interesting are, in this regard –and among others–, the following articles contained in this collective book: PÉREZ MARTÍN, A.: "Planteamiento y objetivos del Simposio Internacional 'España y Europa, un pasado jurídico común'", pp. 11–26; DOLEZALEK, G.: "Observancias sobre el desarrollo del Derecho común hasta la época de Alfonso X el Sabio", pp. 27–44; COING, Helmut: "La contribución de las naciones europeas al Derecho común", pp. 45–61; RANIERI, Filippo: "El estilo judicial español y su influencia en la Europa del Antiguo régimen", pp. 101–118; LALINDE ABADÍA, Jesús: "El Derecho común en los territorios de la Corona de Aragón", pp. 145–178; IGLESIA FERREIRÓS, Aquilino: "La obra legislativa de Alfonso X El Sabio", pp. 275–599.

24 PÉREZ MARTÍN, A.: "El estudio de la recepción del Derecho común en España", *I Seminario de Historia del Derecho y Derecho Privado: Nuevas técnicas de investigación*. Barcelona, 1985, pp. 241–325.

25 The papers presented in this conference were published in the volume 5–6 of *Glossae*.

Spanish legal history from a European perspective.[26] Concerning his teaching, Pérez Martín was most probably the first legal historian who taught European legal history as an optional course for some years. Furthermore, Pérez Martín's lectures on Spanish legal history clearly reflected his European or *ius-commune* approach to the history of Spanish law.

In addition to Antonio García y García and Antonio Pérez Martín, other legal historians who paid a considerable attention to either the *ius commune* or the European perspective should be mentioned.

Jesús Lalinde Abadía published in 1980s several works about the reception of the *ius commune* in the Iberian Peninsula,[27] the Spanish Monarchy from a European perspective,[28] as well as the Spanish and European legal historiography.[29] In 1992 he published a book on the history of criminal law looking from different cultural perspectives.[30] It is also worth mentioning his Spanish legal history handbooks,[31] which contained a theoretical and conceptual approach to legal development applicable not only to Spain but also to other European and non-European countries.[32]

---

26 See, among others, the following articles: BENITO FRAILE, E.J.: "Notas para el estudio de la sentencia en el proceso civil ordinario desde la recepción del Derecho común hasta la Ley de Enjuiciamiento Civil de 1881", *GLOSSAE. Revista de Historia del Derecho Europeo* I (1988), pp. 135–159; COING, H.: "Unidad en el desarrollo del Derecho en los países de Europa", *Glossae. Revista de Historia del Derecho Europeo* 2 (1989–1990); MONTAGUT ESTRAGUÉS, T. de: "La recepción del Derecho feudal común en Cataluña. I. (1211–1330). (La alienación del feudo sin el consentimiento del Señor)", *Glossae. Revista de Historia del Derecho Europeo* 4 (1992), pp. 9–145; BELLOMO, M.: "Tenemos por bien de fazer estudio de escuelas generales. Tra Italia e Castiglia nel secolo XIII", *Glossae. Revista de Historia del Derecho Europeo* 5–6 (1993–1994), pp. 115–129; MONTAGUT ESTRAGUÉS, T. de: "Sobre la recepció del ius commune a Catalunya en matèria de retiment de comptes: els racionals i els oïdors de comptes", *Glossae. Revista de Historia del Derecho Europeo* 5–6 (1993–1994), pp. 365–390; TOMÁS y VALIENTE, F.: "El 'ius commune europaeum' de ayer y hoy", Glossae. Revista de Historia del Derecho Europeo 5–6 (1993–94), pp. 9–16; WOLF, A.: "Los iura propria en Europa en el siglo XIII", *Glossae. Revista de Historia del Derecho Europeo* 5–6 (1993–1994), pp. 35–44; ARVIZU, F. de: "Ilusiones y realidades de la Historia del Derecho europeo", *Glossae. Revista de Historia del Derecho Europeo* 7 (1995), pp. 155–167; GARCÍA y GARCÍA, A.: "El derecho común en Castilla durante el siglo XIII", *Glossae. Revista de Historia del Derecho Europeo* 5–6 (1996), pp. 255–277.

27 LALINDE ABADÍA, J.: "El Derecho común en los territorios ibéricos de la Corona de Aragón", *España y Europa. Un pasado jurídico común*, Murcia, 1986, pp. 145 a 178; "La penetración diferenciada del Derecho romano en la Península Ibérica", Studi Sassaresi (Napoli, Edizioni Scientifiche Italiane, VIII (1987), pp. 416–426.

28 LALINDE ABADÍA, J.: "Perspectiva europea de la Monarquía hispana", *AHDE* 58 (1988), pp. 205–275.

29 LALINDE ABADÍA, J.: "La iushistoriografía española y europea en el umbral del siglo XXI", *AHDE* 56 (1986), pp. 977–993.

30 LALINDE ABADÍA, J.: *Las culturas represivas de la Humanidad.* Zaragoza, 1992.

31 LALINDE ABADÍA, J.: *Iniciación Histórica al Derecho Español. Barcelona, 1970 (whose 4th edition appeared in two vols.*, Barcelona, 1989); LALINDE ABADÍA, J.: Derecho Histórico Español. Barcelona, 1974 (which was reedited several times, the last one in 1989).

32 See, for example, LALINDE ABADÍA, J.: *El Derecho en la Historia de la Humanidad*, Barcelona, 1991.

Aquilino Iglesia Ferreirós, professor of legal history at the University of Barcelona, along with the publication of some articles on the reception of the *ius commune* in the Iberian Peninsula, particularly in Catalonia,[33] organized several conferences called *Dret Comú i Catalunya* with the participation of prestigious Spanish and non-Spanish legal historians.[34]

Along with the reception of *ius commune* in Spain, a topic that other legal historians have explored, studied and published,[35] other topics have been approached comparatively: some contributions on legal historiography,[36] feudalism,[37] the creation of law in the Middle ages,[38] parliaments and royal

---

[33] See, for example, IGLESIA FERREIRÓS, A.: «Derecho municipal, derecho señorial, derecho regio», *H.I.D.* 4 (1977), pp. 155–197; «La creación del Derecho en Cataluña», *AHDE* 47 (1977), pp. 99–423; «¿El primer testimonio de la recepción del Derecho en Cataluña?», *Revista Jurídica de Cataluña* 2 (1978), pp. 277–311; "La Cataluña altomedieval y el Código de Justiniano", *Revista Jurídica de Cataluña* 3 (1983).

[34] See, for example, IGLESIA FERREIRÓS, A.: "La difusión del Derecho común en Cataluña", *El Dret Comú i Catalunya*, Barcelona, 1991, pp. 95–278; «La recepción del Derecho común: estado de la cuestión e hipótesis de trabajo», *El Dret Comú i Catalunya*, Barcelona, 1992, pp. 213–330; «O leiro do dreito común», *El Dret Comú i Catalunya*, Barcelona, 1995, pp. 19–27.

[35] See, on this matter, the bibliography cited in previous footnotes; besides, see SÁNCHEZ-ARCILLA, J.: "La pervivencia de la tradición jurídica romana en España y la recepción del Derecho común", *Estudios jurídicos en homenaje al maestro G. Floris Margadant*, México, 1988, pp. 379–413; see also GUZMÁN, A.: *Ratio Scripta*, Frankfurt, 1981; "Decisión de controversias jurisprudenciales y codificación del derecho en la Epoca Moderna", *AHDE* 50 (1980), pp. 851–890; "Historia de las nociones de 'Derecho común' y 'Derecho propio'", *Homenaje al Profesor Don Alfonso García-Gallo*, Madrid, 1996, vol. I, pp. 207–240.

[36] See ESCUDERO, José Antonio: *Historia del Derecho: historiografía y problemas* (Madrid, 1988), which contained three interesting contributions published between 1965 and 1969; TOMÁS y VALIENTE, F.: "La historiografía jurídica en Europa continental (1900–1975)", *HID* 5 (1978), pp. 431–467; "LXXV años de evolución jurídica en el mundo", *Historia del Derecho y Derecho comparado*, México, 1979, II, pp. 7–42; PÉREZ-BUSTAMANTE, R.: "Tendencias actuales de la historiografía romanística y jurídica europea", *Estudios de Historia del Derecho Europeo. Homenaje al P. G. Martínez Díez*, vol. I, Madrid, 1994, pp. 15–20.

[37] On this matter, see FREY, H., *La feudalidad europea y el régimen señorial español*, México, 1988; MASFERRER, A. / HEIRBAUT, D.: "La contribución de F.L. Ganshof a la historiografía feudal europea. Una revisión crítica a la historiografía española en torno al feudalismo ganshofiano", *Anuario de Historia del Derecho Español* 75 (2005), pp. 595–636; HEIRBAUT, D. / MASFERRER, A.: "François Louis Ganshof, a Belgian view of the Middle Ages", *Rewriting the Middle Ages in the Twentieth Century* (ed. by J. Aurell and F. Crosas). Tornhout (Belgium), Brepols International Academic Publishers, 2005, pp. 223–241.

[38] ÁLVAREZ CORA, Enrique: *La producción normativa medieval según las Compilaciones de Sicilia, Aragón y Castilla*. Milano, 1998.

power,[39] universities,[40] legal doctrine,[41] some private law institutions,[42] Indian law,[43] and the history of the European Union,[44] among others.

During the last twenty years some legal historians have made considerable efforts to approach the development of criminal law from a European or comparative perspective, as the Spanish historiography shows.[45]

Tomás y Valiente was probably the first who made a considerable effort in this

---

[39] DÍEZ DEL CORRAL, L.: *La monarquía hispánica en el pensamiento político europeo. De Maquiavelo a Humboldt*, Madrid 1976; GÓMEZ RIVERO, R.: «Análisis comparado del pase foral en el País Vasco a partir del siglo XVIII», *Boletín de la Real Sociedad Vascongada de Amigos del País* 39, 3–4, (1983); FERNÁNDEZ ALBALADEJO, P.: «Cortes y poder real: una perspectiva comparada», *Las Cortes de Castilla y León en la Edad Moderna. Actas de la Segunda Etapa del Congreso Científico sobre la Historia de las Cortes de Castilla y León*, Valladolid, 1989, pp. 477–499.

[40] PESET REIG, M., "Universidades españolas y universidades europeas", *Ius commune* 12 (1984), pp. 71–89; on this matter, see also the bibliographical references already cited in the footnotes containing some publications of Antonio Pérez Martín.

[41] PETIT, C.: "La categoria giuridica nella cultura europea del Medioevo (with Jesús Vallejo), Storia d'Europa, III: Il Medioevo (secoli V–XV), a cura di Gherardo Ortalli, Torino, Einaudi, 1994, pp. 721–760; "Derecho común y Derecho castellano. Notas de literatura jurídica para su estudio (siglos XV–XVII)", *Revue d'Histoire du Droit* / TvRG 50 (1982), pp. 157–195.

[42] See, for example, ALEJANDRE GARCÍA, J.A.: «El arte de la Notaría y los formularios notariales del Derecho común hasta la Ley del Notariado», *Revista de Historia del Derecho*, II-1, Granada, 1977–1978, pp. 189–220; TATJER PRAT, M.T., «Survivance du ius commune dans le droit des succesions en Catalogne. Une institutution concrète: le fidéicommis», *Revue Internationale des Droits de l'Antiquité*, Brussels, 3rd serie, vol. 40 (1993), pp. 427–443.

[43] BRAVO LIRA, B.: «El Derecho Indiano y sus raíces europeas. Derecho común y propio de Castilla», *AHDE* 68 (1988), pp. 5–80.

[44] PÉREZ-BUSTAMANTE, Rogelio: *Los Estados de la Unión Europea: Historia política y constitucional.* Madrid, 1994; PÉREZ-BUSTAMANTE, Rogelio: *Historia política de la Unión Europea (1945–1995).* Madrid, 1995; PÉREZ-BUSTAMANTE, Rogelio / WRANA, Javier: *La unión económica y monetaria en Europa: una introducción histórica (1969–1998).* Madrid, 1999; PÉREZ-BUSTAMANTE, Rogelio / CONDE, Elena: *La unión política Europea (1968–1999).* Madrid, 1999; PÉREZ-BUSTAMANTE, Rogelio: *Cronología de la Unión Europea, 1914–2004.* Madrid, 2004.

[45] On this matter, see MASFERRER, A.: "El *ius commune* en la historiografía penal española. Una apuesta metodológica de apertura hacia lo supranacional y europeo", O. Condorelli, E. Montanos-Ferrín, K. Pennington, Hgg., *Studi in Onore di Manlio Bellomo*, Roma, 2004, t. III, pp. 563–587; MASFERRER, A.: "La historiografía penal española del siglo XX. Una aproximación a su alcance temático", *Rudimentos Legales* 5 (2003), pp. 29–125; BARÓ PAZOS, Juan: "Historiografía sobre la Codificación del Derecho penal en el siglo XIX", *Doce Estudios de Historiografía Contemporánea.* Santander, 1991, pp. 11–40; ALVAREZ ALONSO, Clara: "Tendencias generales de la historiografía penal en España desde el s. XIX", *Hispania. Entre derechos propios y derechos nacionales. Atti dell'Incontro di Studio (Firenze-Lucca, 25–27 maggio 1989).* Milano, 1990, 2 vols. (vol. 34/35 de la colec. *Per la Storia del Pensiero Giuridico Moderno*), pp. 969–984; interesting outlooks on the history of criminal law can be seen in GACTO FERNÁNDEZ, Enrique: "Aproximación a la Historia del derecho penal español", *Per la storia pensiero giuridico moderno 34/35. Hispania. Entre derechos propios y derechos nacionales. Atti dell'Incontro di Studio (Firenze-Lucca, 25–27 maggio 1989).* Milano, 1990, 2 vols. (vol. 34/35 of the *Per la Storia del Pensiero Giuridico Moderno*), pp. 501–530; OTERO VARELA, Alfonso: "Historia del Derecho criminal en Compostela", *Dereito* 8 (nº 1), 1999, pp. 141–186.

regard.[46] Some years later, several works followed Tomas y Valiente's footsteps by focusing on the *ius-commune* approach to criminal law tradition.[47] In 1999 a young criminal lawyer also published a book on self-defense from a comparative perspective.[48] I have also been doing research on this field – taking the European approach – and published several works in the last ten years. I started with my PhD work, published in 2001, which dealt with the punishment of infamy and its development from the Romanization period until its suppression in 1848.[49] A year later I wrote a paper whose main purpose was describing the legal regime of some humiliating punishments which were common not only in Catalonia but all over Europe, suggesting some methodological ideas for the research of the criminal law development.[50] In 2003 I published a book on the codification

[46] TOMÁS y VALIENTE, Francisco: *El Derecho penal de la Monarquía absoluta (siglos XVI–XVIII).* Ed. Tecnos, Madrid, 1969 (2nd edit., 1992); Tomás y Valiente affirmed to have knowledge of the work written by SCHAFFSTEIN, Friedrich: *Die Europäische Strafrechtswissenschaft im Zeitalter des Humanismus* (Göttingen, 1954), although he used the Spanish version (*La Ciencia europea del Derecho penal en la época del Humanismo.* Madrid, Instituto de Estudios Políticos, 1957), translated by JMª Rodríguez Devesa. Surprisingly enough, he did not seem to know about Schaffstein's main work (*Die allgemeinen Lehren vom Verbrechen in ihrer Entwicklung durch die Wissenschaft des gemeinen Strafrechts. Beiträge zur Strafrechtsentwicklung von der Carolina bis Carpzov.* Berlin, 1930 –reed. by Verlag Aalen, 1986–), although Tomas y Valiente's book presents such a similar methodological approach to that of Schaffstein's *Die allgemeinen Lehren…* that it makes me think that Tomas y Valiente did know that book and used it in writing his *Derecho penal de la Monarquía absoluta* (on this matter, see MASFERRER, "El *ius commune* en la historiografía penal española. Una apuesta metodológica de apertura hacia lo supranacional y europeo", pp. 577–578).

[47] See, for example, MONTANOS FERRÍN, Emma: "An de die vel de nocte", *Rivista Internazionale di Diritto Commune* 9 (1998), pp. 49–80; MONTANOS FERRÍN, Emma: "¿Por qué suena la campana?, *Rivista Internazionale di Diritto Commune* 10 (1999), pp. 37–52; see also ORTEGO GIL, Pedro A.: "La literatura jurídica como fundamento en la aplicación práctica de la ley penal en la edad Moderna", *La Historia de la Filosofía Jurídica Española* (F. Puy Muñoz and S. Rus Rufino, eds.). Santiago, 1998, pp. 77–108; ORTEGO GIL, Pedro A.: "Algunas consideraciones sobre la pena de azotes durante los siglos XVI–XVIII", *Hispania*, LXII/3, n. 212 (2002), pp. 849–906.

[48] IGLESIAS RÍO, Miguel Ángel: *Perspectiva histórico-cultural y comparada de la legítima defensa.* Burgos, 1999.

[49] MASFERRER, A.: *La pena de infamia en el Derecho histórico español. Contribución al estudio de la tradición penal europea en el marco de ius commune.* Dykinson, Madrid, 2001; for its review see, for example, José SARRIÓN GUALDA (*Revista d'Història del Dret català* I, 2001, pp. 296–298 y *Anuario de Historia del Derecho Español* 71, 2001, pp. 836–837); Antonio PÉREZ MARTÍN (*Anuario de Historia del Derecho Español* 71, 2001, pp. 758–759); Jan HALLEBEEK (*Tijdschrift voor rechtsgeschiedenis* 70, 2002, pp. 356–360).

[50] MASFERRER, A.: "La dimensión ejemplarizante del Derecho penal municipal catalán en el marco de la tradición jurídica europea. Algunas reflexiones iushistórico-penales de carácter metodológico", *Anuario de Historia del Derecho Español* 71 (2001), pp. 439–471.

of Spanish criminal law,[51] and an article on the codification of French criminal law, both from a European perspective.[52] In 2005 two other papers were published, one on the influence of the canon law and theology over the modern criminal legal science in Europe,[53] the other on a comparative approach to the humiliating punishments in the Spanish and German constitutionalism.[54] In 2009 a comparative legal history research was published, presenting not just the historical development of an institution from a European or comparative perspective, but describing it and its evolution in different jurisdictions belonging to both the civil law and common law traditions. More specifically, the book analyzed the disqualification from holding public office in the European and Anglo-American criminal law tradition.[55] In 2009 and 2010 I published two papers set in the Anglo-American context,[56] presenting English versions of the outcomes accomplished in previous works dealing with the history of Spanish criminal law from a comparative perspective.[57]

---

[51] MASFERRER, A.: *Tradición y reformismo en la Codificación penal española. Hacia el ocaso de un mito. Materiales, apuntes y reflexiones para un nuevo enfoque metodológico e historiográfico del movimiento codificador penal europeo*. Prólogo de J. Sainz Guerra. Universidad de Jaén, 2003; its review can be seen in Juan Alfredo OBARRIO MORENO (*Anuario de Historia del Derecho Español* 86, 2006, pp. 808–810); Patricia ZAMBRANO MORAL (Revista de Estudios Histórico-Jurídicos, Universidad Católica de Valparaíso, Valparaíso, XXVI, 2004, pp. 658–659).

[52] MASFERRER, A.: "Continuismo, reformismo y ruptura en la Codificación penal francesa. Contribución al estudio de una controversia historiográfica actual de alcance europeo", *AHDE* 73 (2003), pp. 403–420.

[53] MASFERRER, A.: "Contribución de la Teología y ciencia canónica al Derecho penal europeo moderno. Materiales y breves notas para su estudio", *Europa, sé tú misma. Actas del VI Congreso Católicos y Vida Pública (Madrid, 19–21 de noviembre de 2004)*. Madrid, 2005, vol. I, pp. 185–200.

[54] MASFERRER, A.: "El alcance de la prohibición de las *penas inhumanas y degradantes* en el constitucionalismo español y europeo. Una contribución histórico-comparada al contenido penal del constitucionalismo español y alemán", *Presente y futuro de la Constitución española de 1978* (editado por la Facultad de Dret de la Universitat de València y Tirant lo Blanch, ISBN 84-8456-248-4). Valencia 2005, pp. 515–544.

[55] MASFERRER, A.: *La inhabilitación y suspensión del ejercicio de la función pública en la tradición penal europea y anglosajona. Especial consideración a los Derechos francés, alemán, español, inglés y norteamericano* (galardonado con el 1er Accésit del Premio Nacional Victoria Kent 2008). Prólogo de José A. Escudero. Madrid, Servicio de Publicaciones del Ministerio del Interior, 2009, 483 pp. Several reviews of it have been written: Juan Alfredo OBARRIO MORENO (*Iustel. Revista General de Derecho Romano* 12, diciembre 2009); Juan SAINZ GUERRA (Anuario de Historia del Derecho Español 78–79, 2008–2009).

[56] MASFERRER, A.: "Codification of Spanish Criminal Law in the Nineteenth Century. A Comparative Legal History Approach", *Journal of Comparative Law* Vol. 4, no. 1 (2009), pp. 96–139; MASFERRER, A.: "Liberal State and Criminal Law Reform in Spain", Sellers, Mortimer; Tomaszewski, Tadeusz (Eds.), *The Rule of Law in Comparative Perspective*. Series: *Ius Gentium: Comparative Perspectives on Law and Justice*, vol. 3 (2010), pp. 19–40.

[57] MASFERRER, A.: "La ciencia del Derecho penal en la Codificación decimonónica. Una aproximación panorámica a su contenido y rasgos fundamentales", *Estudios de Historia de las ciencias criminales en España*, Madrid, Dykinson, 2007, pp. 273–349; see also my book cited in the footnote number 42.

The constitutionalism or history of Spanish constitutions (1808-1978) has been studied in comparative perspective by some scholars, not all of them legal historians. In this regard, García de Enterría explored the influence of the French revolution to the making of the European public law.[58] It is also worthwhile to note the contribution of authors like Bartolomé Clavero,[59] Varela Suanzes,[60] Garriga and Lorente,[61] Petit,[62] Álvarez Alonso,[63] Portillo Valdés[64] and Blanco Valdés,[65] who have all been publishing interesting works that seek to link the history of Spanish constitutionalism within the European or Anglo-American context. Some of these authors have published frequently in the *Historia Constitucional*, a constitutional history journal, created in 2000, that usually approaches topics on foreign legal texts and literature.[66]

Some general topics like the Liberal political system have been also analyzed comparatively.[67] The same can be said concerning the Spanish monarchy,[68] the separation of powers.[69]

Despite all the efforts made by the aforementioned scholars to approach the Spanish constitutional history from a comparative perspective, there are no handbooks on this subject adopting the comparative approach. This is particularly surprising when there have been authors whose profound knowledge would have enabled them to do it successfully. This would be the case of

---

58 GARCÍA DE ENTERRÍA, Eduardo: *Revolución francesa y Administración contemporánea*. Madrid, Taurus, 1972 (2nd ed., 1981); GARCÍA DE ENTERRÍA, Eduardo: La lengua de los derechos. *La formación del Derecho Público europeo tras la Revolución Francesa*. Madrid, 1994.

59 See, for example, CLAVERO, Bartolomé: *Happy Constitution. Cultura y lengua constitucionales*. Madrid 1997.

60 VARELA SUANZES, Joaquín "La Monarquía en el pensamiento del Benjamín Constant (Inglaterra como modelo)", *Revista del Centro de Estudios Constitucionales* 10 (1991); Varela Suanzes edited the *Textos básicos de la Historia constitucional comparada* (Madrid, CEPC, 1998), where one can find the Spanish version of the main sources of the Contiental and Anglo-American constitutionalism.

61 C. GARRIGA / M. LORENTE: *Cádiz, 1812. La Constitución jurisdiccional*. Madrid, CEPC, 2007.

62 See, for example, PETIT, C.: "Una Constitución europea para Cádiz, 1812", Andrea Romano (ed.), *Alle origini del constituzionalismo europeo*, Messina, Accademia Peloritana, 1991, pp. 57–71.

63 ÁLVAREZ ALONSO, Clara: "Un Rey, una Ley, una Religión (Goticismo y Constitución histórica en el debate constitucional gaditano)", *Historia Constitucional* (revista electrónica), n. 1, 2000.

64 PORTILLO VALDÉS, José María: *Revolución de nación. Orígenes de la cultura constitucional en España, 1780–1812*. Madrid, CEPC, 2000.

65 BLANCO VALDÉS, Roberto: *El valor de la constitución: separación de poderes, supremacía de la ley y control de constitucionalidad en los orígenes del Estado liberal*, Madrid, 1994.

66 See http://www.historiaconstitucional.com/index.php/historiaconstitucional/index. The current Director of this journal is Joaquín Varela Suanzes-Carpegna.

67 See *El primer liberalismo: España y Europa, una perspectiva comparada. Foro de debate, Valencia, 25 a 27 de octubre de 2001* (E. La Parra and G. Ramírez, eds.). Valencia, Biblioteca Valenciana, 2003.

68 PAPELL, Antonio: *La monarquía española y el Derecho constitucional europeo*. Barcelona, Edit. Labor, 1980.

69 ALVARADO PLANAS, Javier: *De la ideología trifuncional a la separación de poderes*. Madrid, 1993.

Bartolomé Clavero;[70] and Joaquín Varela promised to publish a comparative constitutional history some years ago, but we are still waiting for it.[71] Meanwhile, some constitutional lawyers have published interesting historical introductions to constitutional law whose approach is more comparative than those which have been written by legal historians.[72]

The same could be said of handbooks on Spanish legal history. Despite the efforts made. Despite the efforts made by some legal historians to deal with the *ius commune* and its reception, or to approach some aspects of the legal development comparatively, Spanish legal history handbooks have barely paid attention to the *ius commune* and seem to ignore the European perspective.

There are also some exceptions in this regard. Jose A. Escudero's handbook, for instance, inasmuch as it tends to describe the main institutions taking into account Spanish and foreign literature, following their creation and historical development within a broader context than the Spanish one. This is particularly clear in its treatment of some institutions like feudalism, royal power, municipalities, parliaments, Indian laws, etc.[73]

The same can be said – although to a less extent – regarding Tomás y Valiente's handbook,[74] though it does not contain legal institutions as Escudero's handbook does. However, it does treat the *ius commune* and its development much better and more extensively than any other – perhaps, except one –[75] Spanish legal history handbook.

Emma Montanos made an effort to describe a panoramic view of Spanish legal history from a European perspective.[76]

The main source of the European approach to Spanish legal history teaching is the emergence and reception of *ius commune*, and, to a lesser extent, the codification movement that would not be clearly explained without resorting to

---

70 See, for example, his elementary –but thoroughful– *Evolución histórica del Constitucionalismo español.* Madrid, 1984 (reedited several times); see also his *Manual de historia constitucional de España.* Madrid, 1989 (also reedited several times).

71 Joaquín Varela, in his prologue to his *Textos básicos de la Historia constitucional comparada* (Madrid, CEPC, 1998), expressed his intention of writing a comparative constitutional history handbook that has not been published yet.

72 This would be the case, for example, of JIMÉNEZ ASENSIO, Rafael: *Introducción a una historia del constitucionalismo español.* Valencia, tirant lo blanch, 1993; JIMÉNEZ ASENSIO, Rafael: *El Constitucionalismo.* Oñati, IVAP, 2001.

73 ESCUDERO LOPÉZ, José Antonio: *Curso de Historia del Derecho. Fuentes e Instituciones Político-administrativas.* Madrid, 2003.

74 TOMÁS y VALIENTE, Francisco: *Manual de Historia del Derecho Español.* Madrid, 1992.

75 CLAVERO, B.: *Temas de Historia del Derecho: Derecho Común*, Sevilla, 1977, (2ª ed., Salamanca, 1994).

76 MONTANOS FERRÍN, E.: *España en la configuración histórico-jurídica de Europa. I. Entre el mundo antiguo y la primera edad medieval,* Il Cigno Galileo Galilei, Roma, 1997.

the French and German codifications. Leaving aside the *ius commune* and the codification movement, and despite the research projects of few legal historians, it would not be true to state that Spanish legal history has been traditionally taught from a European or comparative perspective. Moreover, only a few universities in Spain have offered optional courses on European legal history. In fact, as far as I know, these courses have only been offered at the universities of Murcia and Illes Balears (in Majorca), in the former taught by Antonio Pérez Martín, in the latter by Román Piña Homs.[77]

Spanish case is quite the opposite to some other European countries, such as Belgium, which have to some extent lacked a national legal history.[78] Political and historical reasons explain the different path followed by Belgium, whose legal historians have tended to write more on European legal history than on their own national legal tradition,[79] and the same could be said about other European countries whose small seize led their legal historians to look beyond their own national borders.[80]

Some may think that Spain belongs to the group of the big European countries like France, Germany and Italy, among others, whose legal traditions are rich enough to "ignore" a bit the European legal context, particularly considering that their legal histories constitute an important part of the European legal tradition. This may be partly true but should not justify, however, a narrow-minded approach to national legal history, since any national legal tradition can be only explained within a geographical context which goes beyond the national boundaries. In my view, it is undeniable that an important part of the European legal tradition, particularly as cultural and scientific realities, cannot be confined to the political circumstances which caused the boundaries to move from one place to another over the centuries.

---

[77] To that purpose the following handbook was written, published and recommended to the students enrolled in that course, PIÑA HOMS, R.: *Fundamentos jurídicos de Europa. Apuntes para una Historia del Derecho europeo*. Palma de Mallorca, 2001; as far as we know, this is the only European legal history handbook which until today has been published in Spain.

[78] HEIRBAUT, Dirk: "The Belgian legal tradition: does it exist?", H. Bocken / W. De Bondt, *Introduction to Belgian law*, Kluwer, 2001 (2000), 1–22.

[79] See, for example, some books written by CAENEGEM R. VAN: *Judges, legislators and professors: chapters in European legal history*, Cambridge, 1987; *An historical introduction to western constitutional law*, Cambridge, 1995; *European law in the past and the future. Unity and diversity over two milennia*, Cambridge, 2002; on this matter, see Dirk Heirbaut's article contained in this volume (with the title "European comparative legal history as a necessity: the Belgian experience"), particularly its first part entitled "The impossibility of a national legal history in Belgium".

[80] On this matter, see Heikki Pihlajamäki's article (in this volume) according to which a distinction between small and big countries should be made: while the latter already have a great history of their own and thus there is less need of looking beyond the borders, in smaller countries the situation is the opposite.

3. What Should Happen

Now that it is clear what has happened in Spain concerning the teaching of Spanish legal history, I want to focus on what it should happen. In other words, let me explain now how – at least, in my opinion – Spanish legal history should be taught.

a) Law and Legal History

Anyone who has even a summary knowledge of Spanish legal tradition knows that current law is in debt, and sometimes quite in debt heavily, to ancient traditions, no matter whether we talk about criminal, private, commercial, or procedural law. Consequently, the study of legal history is not an activity merely for scholarly minds seeking to satisfy their curiosity, but also for jurists pursuing a thorough understanding of contemporary Spanish law. And the same could be said regarding other national legal traditions. Looking back at the legal tradition one may find many concepts that are out of phase with current thinking, yet there are also a number of elements and principles that are maintained in modern European legal systems. There are even occasions when trends and concepts that had seemed to be buried by history centuries ago resurface and gain new relevance.

It would be incorrect to maintain that once legal tradition was codified according to a rationalist conception of law, legal history lost its *raison être*. This idea would be false at least for three reasons. First, it is untrue that codification constituted an absolute break with tradition. Second, only history enables us to approach the present law with perspective enough to understand our current legal institutions and their development over the time. Third, both legal rules and legal institutions contained in the codes need to be interpreted before their application to specific cases, so the legislator laid down, among others, the historical interpretation of the provisions. Hence, Art. 3.1 of the Spanish civil code prescribes that laws should be interpreted, among other criteria, "according to the context, historical and legislative antecedents". The same criterion can be seen in other European civil codes.

There is another reason which explains the importance of historical approach to the current law: the historicity of law. Let us explain it briefly. Law has been, is and will be in continual flux. The law in each historical period is thus the result of centuries of development, at the same time the law of each period contains the seed for future changes. Yet while all this is certainly true, it is also the case that the law needs a certain degree of stability, without which it lacks meaning.[81] In other words, although it is undeniable that law is constantly developing, there would be no legal security or certainty if it had no continuity at all. The people would never know what the law says. For this reason, although legal certainty will not ever be entirely attained, the validity of law constitutes an important notion and tool to grant a minimum degree of stability to the law. Consequently, citizens feel legally secure when they know for sure that, because some legal sources and institutions are "in force", they will be applied by courts if a legal dispute arises.

The law requires a certain degree of stability, without that law becomes meaningless. A key route for this is that once it has been promulgated in the form of legislation and comes into force, that law becomes valid and accepted to regulate future cases and situations. Nonetheless, nobody can deny that, in fact, such a legal norm or regulation belongs to the past, since it was enacted in the past and according to a historical, social, economic and cultural context. This is precisely the meaning of the expression "historicity of law" because legal sources are promulgated or approved at a moment which belongs to history, although they remain in force unless are they explicitly suppressed or implicitly abrogated (e.g., by falling in disuse

b) Legal History and Comparative Law? A Comparative Approach to Legal History

As noted above –and according to the historicity of law– the law belongs to the past, since it was made in the past and according to a historical, social, economic and cultural context. It is precisely such historical, social, economic and cultural context which, going beyond national boundaries, makes the comparative approach absolutely necessary. In the case of Spain or any other European country, the European perspective is unavoidable. The resort to Comparative law is not just a means to contrast a national legal history with others, so that students may broaden their knowledge on legal culture. It is not just a matter of relating two disciplines (legal history and comparative law) which should assist and support

[81] On this matter, see some German historiography: MITTEIS, Heinrich: *Die Rechtsgeschichte und das Problem der historischen Kontinuität*, Berlin, 1947; BETTI, Emilio: *Das Problem der Kontinuität im Lichte der Rechtshistorischen Auslegung*, Roma, 1957; THIEME, Hans: "Ideesgeschichte und Rechtsgeschichte", *Ideesgeschichte und rechtsgeschichte. Gesammelte Schriften von Hans Thieme*, Böhlau Verlag Köln-Wien, 1986, pp. 3–26; THIEME, Hans: "Kontinuität – Diskontinuität in der Sicht der Rechtsgeschichte", *Ideesgeschichte und Rechtsgeschichte. Gesammelte Schriften von Hans Thieme*, Böhlau Verlag Köln-Wien, 1986, pp. 63–79.

one another.[82] It is something more. The problem is that the comparative approach constitutes a necessary –not just an optional– requirement to deal with legal history; otherwise, legal history would not be real legal history because both law and history need such comparative approach. In this regard, to talk about the relationship between legal history and comparative law is somehow redundant and would be a tautology because legal history itself brings with it the comparative approach. This does not imply denying that there are different ways of approaching legal tradition comparatively. Let us briefly describe some reasons which demonstrate to what extent it is true that a comparative approach constitutes a necessary requirement to study any legal tradition.

First, any legal historian should take seriously the comparative approach for no legal history of a particular jurisdiction can be considered a self-contained and self-sufficient legal order, disconnected or isolated from others which were made and developed within the same or similar historical, social, economic and cultural context. Hence, we can talk about the civil law tradition and the common law tradition, belonging both to the Western legal traditions.[83]

Second, the existence of such Western legal traditions implies some common features whose reception and validity in different jurisdictions could not be explained unless legal history goes beyond the national boundaries. Cultural movements and other historical realities like feudalism, seigniorial regime, the emergence of the royal power, municipalities and parliaments, the *ius commune*, the Enlightenment and the legal codification cannot –and should not– be explained just from a national perspective. Otherwise, the historical reality would be considerably distorted. In this regard, it has been claimed that the falsehood of the traditional view of the English common law as an exceptional legal tradition, independent from the European *ius-commune* legal science.[84] A prestigious legal historian rightly stated that lawyers "applied a mixed legal system whose components were on the one hand local statutes and customs

---

[82] On the relationship between legal history and comparative law (or viceversa), which has become a classical topic, see the recent work written by GORDLEY, James: "Comparative Law and Legal History", *The Oxford Handbook of Comparative Law* (ed. by Matthias Reimann and Reinhard Zimmermann). Oxford University Press, 2006, pp. 753–773.

[83] On the convenience to emphasize the common features of the European and Anglo-American legal systems for they belong all to the Western legal traditions, see, for example, LAWSON, C.M.: "The Family Affinities of Common-Law and Civil-Law Legal Systems," 6 *Hastings Int'l and Comparative Law Review* 86 (1982–1983), pp. 85–131.

[84] DONLAN, Seán Patrick: "'All this together make up our Common Law': legal hybridity in England and Ireland, 1704–1804", ÖRÜCÜ, E, *Mixed legal systems at new frontiers* (2010). This article grew out of DONLAN, "'Our laws are as mixed as our language': commentaries on the laws of England and Ireland, 1704–1804", *Journal of Comparative Law* 3 (2008) 178 (also available as *Electronic Journal of Comparative law* 12 (2008) at www.ecjl.org/121/abs121-6.html).

and on the other hand the law books of Justinian and the Canon Law".[85] And the same has been recognized by some common-law legal historians.[86]

Third, if different jurisdictions were born and developed within the same cultural context, as, for example, the Western legal traditions, it is reasonable to think about the existence of exchanges of legal components or particularities between jurisdictions. In this regard, it has been said that "no legal tradition is a purely native growth".[87] I could not agree more with Donlan, who, recognizing that "significant and explicit legal hybridity was, in fact, the norm across Europe before the nineteenth century", states clearly that "the failure to acknowledge legal hybridity and diffusion both distorts the past and obscures our understanding of the present. This neglect is arguably most significant in the Anglo-American legal traditions".[88] In this regard, the notion of legal transplant was conceived in the last century – and has been used and developed until today –[89] as a way to express that "borrowing is the name of the legal game and is the most prominent means of legal change".[90]

Hence, to research and teach legal history without taking into account such a comparative approach would be a considerable mistake, with deplorable consequences for both legal historians (in their research and teaching) and law students. It would certainly deprive the latter of a clear understanding of the current law to which they devote several years in the law school.

---

[85] COING, H.: "The Roman Law as Ius Commune on the Continent", *Law Quarterly Review* 89 (1973), p. 510.

[86] See, for example, DONAHUE, C. Jr.: "Ius commune, canon law, and common law in England' *Tulane Law Review* 66 (1992), p. 1748: "[I]n the realm of basic principles, organizing ideas, techniques of argumentation, and habits of thought, the parallels are sufficiently great that one might want to call the common law simply a variant, admittedly an eccentric variant, of the multitude of legal systems that ultimately derive from the ius commune"; and DONLAN, Seán Patrick: "*The Debt Is Forgotten': A Compendious View of Arthur Browne, c1756–1805*, vol 13.3 (September 2009) *Electronic Journal of Comparative Law* (available at http://www.ejcl.org/133/art133-3.pdf).

[87] ÖRÜCÜ, E.: "A general view of 'legal families' and of 'mixing systems'", ÖRÜCÜ, E. / NELKEN, D.: *Comparative law: a handbook* (2007), p. 177; see also Palmer, "Mixed legal systems ... and the myth of pure laws", *Louisiana Law Review* 67 (2007), p. 1207; see also DONLAN, "'All this together make up our Common Law': legal hybridity in England and Ireland, 1704–1804", cited above.

[88] DONLAN, "'All this together make up our *Common* Law': legal hybridity in England and Ireland, 1704–1804", p. 267; see also McKNIGHT, J.: "Some historical observations on mixed systems of law", *Juridical Review* 22 (1977), p. 178, where he affirmed: "However mixed his system is in fact the English lawyer does not think of it as such". (cited by Donlan); on this matter, see also CASTELLUCCI, Ignazio: "How Mixed Must a Mixed System Be?", vol 12.1 (May 2008) *Electronic Journal of Comparative Law* (available at http://www.ejcl.org/121/art121-4.pdf); and the –almost already, classical– work written by TETLEY, William: "Mixed Jurisdictions: Common Law vs. Civil Law (Codified and Uncodified) (Part I)", *4 Unif. L. Rev.* 591 (1999), pp. 591–619.

[89] On this concept, see WATSON, Alan: *Legal Transplants: An Approach to Comparative Law*. Athens, GA: University of Georgia Press, 2nd ed., 1993; further information on Watson's publications concerning the notion of "legal transplants", see http://www.alanwatson.org/home.htm.

[90] Alan Watson, http://www.alanwatson.org/law_reality_society.pdf.

c) How Spanish Legal History Should Be Taught

Any national legal history should be approached comparatively. Thus, questions as to whether legal history needs to be European to be comparative, or whether it needs to be comparative to be European, are pointless. I maintain that legal history needs to be comparative anyway; whether it is European, Anglo-American, or Spanish. Otherwise, it would not be real legal history.

Consequently, I understand that it should not be necessary to add the expression "comparative" or "European" to the legal history of any European jurisdiction since such "European" or "comparative" approach should be taken for granted, being assumed just by the fact of dealing with legal history. In this regard, I wonder whether there is today in Europe any legal historian who really thinks that it is possible to teach legal history without the European perspective, or that it is possible to teach legal history without the comparative approach. They are probably a rare breed indeed.

The Spanish legal history clearly reveals that it is not possible to reconstruct the history of Spanish law without resorting to both the European and comparative perspectives. A Spanish law student enrolled in a legal history course should acquire a minimum degree of knowledge about the making and development of both legal sources and legal institutions from a comparative perspective, including both the European legal tradition and the Anglo-American legal tradition (devoting logically to the former more time than to the latter though).[91]

In teaching Spanish legal history, several aspects should be approached comparatively:[92]

aa) Historical periods

In describing the historical development of law in Spain –like in other European countries– it is not surprising to realize the parallels between the Spanish and the European, historical periods as well as the existence of common, cultural movements.

Many legal historians –though not all of them– have divided Spanish legal history into the following epochs:

[91] In practice, nonetheless, it is well known that the lack of time makes it difficult to deal with both the history of legal sources and the history of legal institutions.

[92] This part of the article has been heavily drawn from my own experience in teaching Spanish legal history (see MASFERRER, Aniceto: *Spanish Legal Traditions. A Comparative Legal History Outline*. Madrid, Dykinson, 2009, 429 pp.).

aaa) Ancient times

This epoch includes the Primitive Spain (up to 218 B.C.) and the Roman conquest (218 B.C. – 476 AD). What is referred to as Primitive Spain stretches from the beginnings of civilization in the Spanish Peninsula until the arrival of the Romans in the third century BC. The Law of this period is referred to as Archaic or Primitive Law. The Romanization of the Peninsula began in the year 218 BC. The Romanization period comprises the time of the Roman conquest of the Peninsula, beginning with the disembarkation of Roman soldiers in *Ampurias* (Emporia) in the year 218 BC, until the year 476 AD.

bbb) The Middle Ages

This epoch contains various periods: Early [, High] and Late Middle Ages:
– The earliest stage is the Visigothic period, which has two phases:
– The Gallic phase (from the year 476 until the year 568).
– The Hispanic phase (from the year 568 until the year 711).
– The Muslim invasion of the Peninsula began in the year 711.

Muslim Law was completely different from the legal systems that had existed on the Peninsula before the invasion. During this period of occupation the Roman legal traditions persisted, as we will see, although in intimate coexistence with Germanic Law (through the legal texts of the Visigoths).

This period also saw the elaboration of the first collections of Canon law. The Reconquest began before the middle of the eighth century (Covadonga Battle, 722). It is a common opinion among historians that the Middle Ages began at this moment. So, the strict Middle Ages are divided into…
– Early Middle Ages, which designates the period between the 8th century and the 11th century, and the
– Late Middle Ages, which covers the period from the 11th century to the 15th century (1469).

ccc) The Early Modern Age

The start of this period coincides with the reign of the Catholic Monarchs at the end of the fifteenth century (19th October 1469, Isabel and Fernando's marriage) and lasts until 1812.

ddd) The Modern Age (or Constitutional epoch)

The final phase starts in the nineteenth century with the collapse of the *ancien régime*. This is the phase in which a Constitutional regime begins and is later consolidated. The first Spanish Constitution was promulgated on 19th March 1812, (known as the Cádiz Constitution), which set up a new political system:

liberal regime or Constitutional regime, state or nation. (By comparison, from 1808 Constitution was granted by the French King José Bonaparte but not freely assumed by the Spanish nation.)

As is evident, the main features of the law in the majority of these periods are common to all over the European countries: the pre-Roman (or Primitive) laws; the first Romanization of many European countries; the influence of the Germanic laws; the impact of Canon law (also by adopting Roman laws –"*Ecclesia vivit secundum legem romanam*"–, but somehow modifying it); the second Romanization (or *ius commune*) all over Europe from 11th century onwards, being first developed by the school of glossators (11th-13th centuries), and then the post-glossators or commentators (14th-15th centuries), the school of the *usus modernus pandectarum* (16th-17th centuries), the natural law theory of the Enlightenment (18th century); the nationalization of law through its codification (19th century); the process of de-codification, the creation of the European Union and the attempts to codify the European private law by elaborating drafts to harmonize the law from different jurisdictions which somehow share the same legal tradition, based mainly upon the old, European *ius commune* (20th-21st centuries).

bb) Common European tendencies and shifts

Besides the parallel historical periods between the Spanish and the European legal histories, the comparative approach is also highly convenient in analyzing some important tendencies or shifts to which both the law both in Spain and in Europe went through. In this regard, and concerning the History of legal sources, it is important to emphasize:

aaa) The decisive role and influence of Roman law

The law in Spain, like in other European countries, was particularly influenced by Roman law, first the Post-classical and vulgar, from the Roman conquest until the downfall of the West Roman Empire in 476 AD,[93] later the emergence

---

93 On this matter, see, for example, LEVY, E.: "West Roman Vulgar Law. The Law of Property", *Memoirs of the American Philosophical Society* 29 (1951); WIEACKER, F.: "Vulgarismus und Klassizismus im Recht der Spätantike", *Sitzungsberichte der Heildelberger Akademie der Wissenschaften* 3 (1955); BOLIN, S.: *State and Currency in the Roman Empire to 300 AD*. Stockholm, 1958; BROUGHTON, T.R.S.: "The Romanization of Spain: the Problem and the Evidence", *Proceedings of the American Philosophy Society* 103 (Philadelphia, 1959); ARNOLD, W.T.: *The Roman System of Provincial Administration to the Accession of Constantine the Great* (1914, 3rd edit. revis. by E.S Bouchier, Roma, 1968); BOSWORTH, A.B.: "Vespasian and the Provinces. Some Problems of the Early 7C's AD", *Athenaeum* 51 (1973), 49 ff.; WIEACKER, F.: "Vulgarrecht und Vulgarismus: alte und neue Diskussionen", *Studi in honore di Arnaldo Biscardi*. Milan, 1982, vol. I, pp. 33–51; BARNES, T.D.: *Early Christianity and the Roman Empire*. London, 1984; KULIKOWSKI, Michael: Late Roman Spain and Its Cities. JHU Press, 2004.

of the *ius commune* or Classical both Roman law[94] and Canon law,[95] and the reception and development of them –with varieties– in the different European jurisdictions from 11th to 18th centuries). Such tendency is common to all the European jurisdictions.

bbb) Shift from a local, customary law to a law based upon territorial, legal enactments
While the law of some periods (Pre-Roman epoch, Early and High Middle Ages) was based on custom, from the Late Middle Ages onwards the law started to be based upon legal enactments. This shift took place substantially in the Late Middle Ages because of the legal enactments emanating from the monarch and the parliaments (*Cortes*). Legislation did not generally abolish customary law, but customs lost protagonism. Consequently, the late medieval law was characterized by the preservation of the early medieval customs and the emergence of legislation coming from the monarch and parliaments. This shift brought with it two other common tendencies, experiencing the law two important changes concerning its: b.1) validity, going from the local to a territorial (or general) one; and b.2) making, going from a private (or popular) to an official one through legal enactments.

In the Early Middle Ages the law was essentially local in origin and application, being this trait a clear consequence of the customary nature of law. Nonetheless, several institutions emerged in the early Middle Ages (*Curia Regia*, Councils and Assemblies of Peace and Truce of God), would constitute important exceptions

---

94 On this matter, see, for example, CANNATA, Carlo Augusto: *Historia de la ciencia jurídica europea* (trans. by L.Gutiérrez-Masson). Madrid, 1989; PENNINGTON, K.: *The prince and the Law, 1200–1600: Sovereignty and Rights in the Western Legal Tradition*. Berkekey, 1993; BELLOMO, Manlio: *The Common Legal Past of Europe, 1000–1800*. The Catholic University of America Press, 1995; STEIN, Peter: *Roman Law in European History*. Cambridge University Press, 1999; ROBINSON O. F. / GORDON, W. M. / FERGUS, David: *European Legal History* (3rd ed., Abingdon: LexisNexis UK, 2000), pp. 107–124 and 169 ff.; PÉREZ MARTÍN, Antonio: "Ius commune", *Power, Law and Legislation* (Spain and Sweeden: Encounters throughout History). Puertollano, Marcial Pons-B.W Foundation, 2001; CAENEGEM, R. C. van: *European Law in the Past and the Future: Unity and Diversity over Two Millennia*. New York and Cambridge, England: Cambridge University Press, 2002.

95 On this matter, see, for example, LINEHAN, P.: *The Spanish Church and the Papacy in the Thirteenth Century* (1971) (*The Library of Iberian Resources Online* http://libro.uca.edu/title.htm); GRATIAN: *Treatise on Laws* (translated by Augustine Thompson and James Gordley). Washington, DC: Catholic University Press, 1993; HELMHOLZ, R.H.: *The Spirit of Classical Canon Law*. London-New York, 1995; BRUNDAGE, James A.: *Medieval Canon Law*, Longman, 1995; WINROTH, A.: *The Making of Gratian's Decretum*. Cambridge, 2000; LOGAN, F. Donald: *The History of the Church in the Middle Ages*. London-New York: Routledge, 2002; DONDORP, H. / HALLEBEEK, J.: "The Church as Promoter of the Law: The Emergence of Canon Law as a Separate Discipline in the Middle Ages", *Kultur- und rechtshistorische Wurzeln Europas. Arbeitsbuch* (ed. by Jörg Wolff). MG, Forum Verlag Godesberg, 2005, 43–62; PENNINGTON, K. / HARTMANN, W. (eds.): *The History of Canon Law in the Classical Period, 1140–1234: From Gratian to the Decretals of Pope Gregory* IX. Washington, D.C.: The Catholic University of America Press, 2008.

whose development would have important consequences in the Late Middle Ages. Local, customary diversities remained, but were gradually changed by the fact that the provisions from both the king and parliaments were called to have validity over the whole kingdom. That was also due to the development of the afore-mentioned institutions which arose in the early Middle Ages. Nonetheless, it is also true that they also contributed to increase the amount of legislation by enacting different kinds of legal dispositions. The local, customary law was, however, importantly threatened by the emergence of the *ius commune*, a new legal science based mainly upon the Justinian compilation of Roman law which disseminated all over Europe. Consequently, from the late Middle Ages onwards law can be characterized by a gradual process of legal unification due to both, the legislation of general validity emanating from the king and Parliaments, and the emergence and reception of *ius commune*.

ccc) Shift from a non-technical and rudimentary law to a technical and specialized juridical science

All over Europe – and not just in Spain – the law essentially evolved from ancient and popular practices. In the Early Middle Ages, for example, the law did not contemplate complex juridical problems but rather sought to satisfy the fundamental needs of the community that it served. Crude and primitive methods acquired juridical force.[96] In the Late Middle Ages, the law changed completely in this regard because of the revival and reception of *ius commune*. Thus the late medieval law was characterized by *its scientific nature*, being the law (both the civil and canon law: *utrumque ius*) one of the three disciplines (along with Philosophy-Theology and Medicine) studied at the new-founded medieval universities. As already said, from then onwards –and until today–, law would be scientifically approached and developed.[97]

---

[96] One example of these methods was the *ordalías* that allowed God to be called upon as a witness in trials. The most famous of these "*Ordalías*" had the revealing name of the "red hot iron" ("*hierro candente*", in Spanish).

[97] All over Europe from 11th century onwards, law was first developed by the school of glossators (11th–13th centuries), and then the post-glossators or commentators (14th–15th centuries), the school of the *usus modernus pandectarum* (16th–17th centuries), the natural law theory of the Enlightenment (18th century); the national law and legal positivism: the French School of Exegesis and the German Historical School of Law (19th century); etc.

ddd) Shift from a theological concept of natural law to a philosophical conception of the natural law theory and its deviation to legal positivism

The notion and historical development of natural law is complex and belongs more to the European context than to the Spanish one. There are different conceptions of natural law. However, roughly speaking, natural law or the law of nature (*lex naturalis*, in Latin) is a theory that posits the existence of a law whose content is set by nature and that therefore has universal validity. The expression *natural law* is sometimes opposed to the positive law of a given political community, society, or nation-state, thus can function as a standard by which to criticize that law. So man-made law would be only legitimate in so much as it respects the divinely created natural order of things.

In the Middle Ages, the main contribution on the natural law was done by Aquinas. According to him, the natural law is a participation in the eternal law. Eternal law, for Aquinas, is that rational plan whereby all creation is ordered; natural law is the way that the human being "participates" in the eternal law. While non-rational beings partake in eternal law only by being determined by it – their non-free action results from their determinate natures, natures the existence of which results from God's will in accordance with God's eternal plan – rational beings like us are able to grasp our share in the eternal law and freely act on it. It is this feature of the natural law that justifies, on Aquinas's view, our calling the natural law "law." Law, as Aquinas defines it, is a rule of action put into place by one who takes care of the community; and as God takes care of the entire universe, God's choice to bring into existence beings who can act freely and in accordance with principles of reason is enough to justify our thinking of those principles of reason as law.

While the scholastic model of natural justice posited the existence of a natural law that reflected the harmonious essence of the divine, the rationalist (or philosophical) model proposed a system of natural laws based on reason (following the philosophy of Descartes).[98] According to this rationalist model, laws could be written in manner that could be considered the fruit of pure reason. Such laws could be valid for all time and among all nationalities (with periodic revisions over time to account for linguistic variations). The philosophical conception of a rational natural law was intimately connected with the idea of the superiority of written law over all other sources. Written law displaced custom,

[98] Thus Rationalist philosophy, which elevated human reason to the category of the supreme attribute of the individual and humanity, was first formulated in the Renaissance (René Descartes). This philosophy was furthered in different fields throughout the ages. Grotius and Puffendorf working in the 17th century were its most celebrated jurists, Rousseau its most significant theologian, and Kant its most profound philosophical exponent. Rationalism was a truly European intellectual movement.

jurisprudence and the opinion of legal experts in the legal hierarchy. Again, this happened in general terms across Europe, not just in Spain.[99]

eee) Shift from a non-equality juridical model to the recognition of the principle of equality

In the Ancient times and in the Early Middle Ages there were different legal regimes for different classes of person. Each legal order accorded a different juridical status to subjects depending on their religion or ethnic origin, social class, profession, or the region in which they lived. In the Late Middle Ages and Early Modern Age the law did not change much, keeping the same characteristic trait. Furthermore, in emerging a new social class, the merchants, a new law and jurisdiction were born, the commercial law and its own tribunals which settle the legal disputes between merchants according to their own laws.

The desired change was partly a result of the liberal system and its partner idea, modern constitutionalism (18th and 19th centuries, although in England that happened in the 17th century). From then onwards – and by comparison – if the social order of the *ancien régime* can be seen as the division of society into estates (the nobles, the clergy, the universities) and privileged members of corporations, then the new social order was individualistic and egalitarian. This move entailed the abolition of class based privileges. The beneficiaries of this new "equality" were, at first, the bourgeoisie, and then men in general.[100] More importantly, all juridical privileges and distinctions made on grounds of class, race, religious belief, or gender were to be abolished.[101]

cc) The necessary, European Approach to the Late-Medieval, legal context:

Historical periods need a geographical context which goes beyond national boundaries. In other words, it needs, at least, the European context and, if possible, the context of the Western legal cultures. This broad perspective can be applied to all historical periods but it is particularly necessary from the Late Middle Ages onwards. Let us try to present a brief synthesis which could be

---

[99] The political events that convulsed Europe at the end of the eighteenth century and the beginning of the 19th century favoured the adoption and the spread of new and unfamiliar ideas of different kinds among certain sectors of Spanish society, while at the same time provoking rejection amongst other sectors. The differences among these ideas can perhaps be said to originate with the strong influence that humanism exerted over "ius commune", to the point where it enabled the development of a theoretical basis for a juridical system that was separate from that derived from the scholastic theories of natural law.

[100] In Spain, the working class male was given the vote in 1868, while women were finally extended this right in 1931.

[101] In Spain, a decree dated the 6th of December 1868 unified legal jurisdiction and gave all Spanish citizens equal juridical status. The abolition of the "estates" cleared the way for a new social hierarchy based primarily on wealth.

useful to clarify the shift which the law underwent from the Early to the Late Middle Ages, a shift whose context was clearly European.

The majority of the changes of the law in the Late Middle Ages were caused by the emergence of several political institutions without which the law had probably remained as it was in the Early Middle Ages, and from which emerged other relevant institutions. The main political institutions emerged in Europe between the 12th and 13th centuries were:

– The monarchy;[102]
– The city, from which emerged the merchant class;[103]
– The Parliament.[104]

Within this political, social and economic context, two important things concerning the legal development happened all over Europe:

– the creation of universities,[105] where law was one of the three original university degrees;[106] and

[102] Once the figure of the Emperor declined, the main secular authority was the monarch, who succeeded in consolidating his authority before the cities since the reconquest, and started to organize a political burocracy which, formed by royal offices (most of them jurists), gradually developed during the Late Middle Ages, enabling him to create a consistent State in the Early Modern Age. The law which had conferred legal legitimacy to the Emperor and the Pope was now used to support the monarchy (*rex superiorem non cognoscens in regno suo est imperator*), affirming his absolute power (*plenitudo potestatis*).

[103] In some territories the cities developed more than in others. Within the Spanish context, for example, in Castile, where the nobility was particularly strong, there was not a relevant merchant class, which limited the power of the cities. In Catalonia, on the contrary, where the nobility almost disappeared in the 15th century, the cities, populated by an active merchant class, were stronger than in Castile.

[104] As known, parliaments originated when the king started to convoke and summon, along with the nobility and the clergy, the representatives of the cities.

[105] The university (group of students and professors), also called *Studium Generale* (because several disciplines were taught), or the *Third Power* (because its culture enabled students to free from the Empire and the Church or Pontificate), born in the urban context, played since its creation an important role in the development of law, the political power, the monarchy, the parliaments, the cities, etc. The universities, which substituted the Early medieval schools which taught the *Trivium* (Gramatics, Rethoric –including *ars loquenda* and *ars dictandi*–, and Logics or Dialectics) and *Quadrivium* (Aritmetics, Geometry, Music and Astrology), taught only three disciplines: Philosophy-Theology (being Paris the best University for that), Medicine (Salerno) and Law (Bologne). The universities had to be located in a pontifical or imperial (or royal) city, since their titles had universal character (*licentia ubique docendi*). They employed the scholastic method, which was based on: a) the authority of old texts: Articela or collection of writings from Hipocrates (Medicine), *Sentences*, by Pedro Lombardo (Theology), and *Corpus Iuris Civilis / Corpus Iuris Canonici* (Law); and b) the analysis of the texts by using the Aristotelian logic to elaborate *propositiones, genera y differentia specifica*, etc.

[106] Bologne was the first Faculty of Law (1088, founded by Irnerius), followed by many others all over the medieval Europe. In the 13th century there were in Bologne over 1000 students. Later on, other universities were created in Italy and in other European countries; in Italy: Padua (1222), Vercelli, Vicenza, Arezzo, Reggio, Parma, Siena, Pavia (1361), Ferrara (1391), Turin (1405) Catania (1443); in France: Paris, Montpellier (1260), Orleans (1230), Avignon (1256), Orange (1265), Cahors (1332), Poitiers (1431), Caen (1432), Burdeos (1441), Nantes (1460), Bourges (1464); in Spain: Palencia (at the end of 12th century), Salamanca (1218), Valladolid, Lleida (1300), Perpignan (1349); in Germany: Praga (1348), Vienne (1365), Heidelberg (1386), Cologne (1388), Erfurt (1392), Leipzig (1409), Rostock (1419), Fribourg (1457), Tubingen (1477), Uppsala (1477), etc.

– the emergence and reception of *ius commune* in all the European jurisdictions. It would not be wrong to affirm that the discovery of the Justinian Compilation by Irnerius in the 11th century and the subsequent progressive study and reception of the *Corpus Iuris Civilis* and the *Corpus Iuris Canonici* in Europe were not only the most relevant aspect of the High and Late medieval law. They marked a shift that would last until the 19th century and still influences contemporary law. But, most important, they represent the most important event of the European legal tradition. Again, the rediscovery of Roman law (or Justinian Compilation) by the end of the 11th century was a unique event in legal history and would mark the future of European law.[107] Shadowy figures with unusual names like Pepus and Irnerius began to teach the law of the ancient Romans at Bologna.[108]

In short, the *ius commune* was a legal science based on Roman Law, Canon law and Lombardian feudal law, which was valid and in force throughout Europe with the exception of England to some extent. That *ius commune* would not have been possible without its legal sources (*Corpus Iuris Civilis* and the *Corpus Iuris Canonici*), is indeed true. However, it is also true that it would neither have existed without universities, where the jurists received not only the legal education based upon the afore-mentioned legal sources, but also the legal methods which enabled them to apply the Roman and Canon rules and principles in different chronological periods and geographical contexts. This explains why the *ius commune* was, first of all, a legal science and a law of jurists, since nobody else was able to manage it.[109]

---

[107] Justinian Compilation consisted of four parts: the Institutes, an introduction to Roman law originally written for first year law students; the Codex, containing imperial legislation from the second to the sixth century; the Digest, a compilation of excerpts from the writings of the Roman jurists; and finally, the Novellae, a compilation of Justinian's legislation. The Digest was of particularly fundamental importance for understanding the intricacies of Roman law. The excerpts from the Roman jurisconsults defined terms, discussed theoretical difficulties, cited court cases, and made the mass of legislation found in the Codex understandable and, therefore, usable. Without the Digest Roman law would have had little influence for European legal systems of the Middle Ages.

[108] The jurists in Bologna recovered the key text of Roman law, the Digest, in stages during the late eleventh and early twelfth centuries. These Bolognese jurists were the first to recognize the importance of the Digest, and, like their Humanist successors in the 15th century, they must have searched for manuscripts copies of it. The law that they taught was late imperial law that had been compiled by the Emperor Justinian in the 6th century. This codification, the *Corpus iuris civilis*, yielded the material for teaching Roman law in the 11th century. Its doctrines provided medieval jurists with a sophisticated model for contracts, rules of procedure, family law, testaments, and a strong monarchical constitutional system. Six hundred years after his death, Justinian's name became eponymous for legislator and codifier.

[109] As Peter Stein affirmed in his book entitled *Roman Law in the History of Europe*, what explains how a legal compilation of the 6th century can provide the needed legal rule for completely different geographical and chronological contexts, is the fact that the *Corpus Iuris Civilis* was, for the jurists, *like a legal supermarket*, from which they could take what they needed, and applied it after a proper legal interpretation to update or adapt such old legal provision to the present social, economic and political context.

Such *ius commune*, or common law, co-existed with the particular law of every European kingdom or jurisdiction, called *ius proprium*. As a result, from the Late Middle Ages to the Modern Ages, there was a duality between the *ius commune* and *ius proprium*. This duality,[110] which was consolidated during the reception of *ius commune* all over Europe, explains the situation of the law in the different European kingdoms up until the codification period (19th century).

The characteristics of *ius commune* could be summed up as follows:

- It was based upon the *corpora iura* (*Corpus Iuris Civilis* and the *Corpus Iuris Canonici*).
- It was scientifically developed by jurists through a legal doctrine with its ideology, methodology and different legal schools: glossators and commentators (*mos italicus, mos gallicus, usus modernus pandectarum*, etc.).[111]
- It was a legal science common to all Western Europe (*Respublica Christiana*), different from that of other religions (Jews and Muslims), of Eastern Europe (Byzantine law / Ortodox Church), or of England (which had its own *common law*).
- It was a law technically sophisticated (a law of jurists who have studied it at the University).
- It was composed of three different elements (Roman law, the Canon law and the Lombardian feudal law) which were strongly connected and worked together (particularly the Roman law and Canon law). With canon law, Roman law formed the medieval *ius commune* of Western Europe. To separate the two legal systems would be artificial and even misleading. Both laws were taught in law schools throughout Christendom, students studied both laws as a part of their legal education, and the medieval jurisprudence can only be understood with knowledge of each. The vocabulary and structures of Roman and canon law shaped academic and secular law.
- It was dynamic, being able to adopt other legal orders and transform them (it is the case of the feudal law, the commercial law, or the statutory law).
- It was different from the *iura propria* (laws of the kingdoms: customs, priviledges, royal law, municipal law, etc.), but co-existed with, and influenced them.

---

[110] The *ius proprium* and *ius commune* duality came from the First Book of Gaius' Institutions (I.1, later transcribed in Digest 1, 1, 9: "Omnes populi"). The text stated that all the cities ruled by laws and customs, "in part" use their "own" law or "civil law", and "in part" the law common to all men.

[111] The most significant accomplishment of the *ius commune* in the Middle Ages consisted of encouraging literary activity of the jurists all over Europe. From the 12th century onwards they explored every nook and cranny of Justinian's Corpus *iuris civilis* and produced a massive legacy of juristic writings. They interpreted Roman law by writing glosses (comments on individual words or phrases), commentaries and *summas* (an extended analysis of a law book, title, or law), *questions* (disputations on legal points held as academic exercises), *consilia* (briefs written for an actual case).

– Latin was its main language, being also the official university language. The language of medieval legal Latin creates significant problems for the modern reader.
– It strongly influenced the current law and institutions.

If the social, political and cultural context in which law and legal institutions developed was not just Spanish, French, German, Dutch, etc., but European, it would be wrong to approach legal development just from a national perspective.

What should be said about some Early-medieval legal institutions? It would be also wrong to think that there was a break up between the early and the late Middle Ages. We would be mistaken by not keeping in mind the existence and survival of the two different early medieval legal regimes, namely, the seigniorial regime and the municipal regime. In fact, the cities had arisen in the Early Middle Ages, constituting the alternative to the seigniorial regime. And this did not occur just in Spain, but in many other European countries.

What about the feudal system? Did it exist still in the Late Middle Ages? The answer will depend upon which is understood by the expression "feudalism". According to its economic conception, feudalism would remain up to the French revolution; according with its juridical-institutional conception, feudalism would have collapsed with the emergence of the monarchy in the 13th century; according with its social conception, some feudal institutions could be witnessed in the Late Middle Ages and even in the Early Modern Age.[112]

Anyway, it would be erroneous not to bear in mind what has been said regarding the social, economic, legal and political context of the Early Middle Ages, forgetting about the seigniorial regime, the municipal regime and the possible survival of some feudal institutions. In fact, without keeping them in mind it would be rather difficult to understand the emergence of the monarchy, the development and autonomy of the cities, the rise of the merchant class and the origin of the Parliaments, etc., since the emergence and development of all these realities are strongly connected.

If not, try to explain how the monarch could have managed to affirm his authority before the nobility without resorting to the cities and the Roman law; how the Parliament could have originated without the previous existence of the cities; how the cities could have developed their autonomy without the rise of the merchants and the royal support; how the *ius commune* could have been so appealing and successful without the existence of cities which needed an urban law, or without the support of the king, who, in turn, saw his legitimacy and public authority reinforced;

[112] On this matter, see the bibliography cited in the footnote n. 37.

how the *ius commune* could have developed without universities; how universities, created at the beginning by the Church, could have emerged without the social and economic stability provided by the municipal environment, and later survived without the royal support; etc. To understand properly the shift of the law from the Early to the Late Middle Ages is convenient to observe the mutual relationship between all the afore-mentioned institutions within the European context.[113]

dd) The necessary, comparative approach to any legal tradition with a plurality of laws: One of the features of the European legal traditions is the existence of a plurality of laws within each jurisdiction. In other words, the legal tradition of any European jurisdiction consisted of a plurality of laws whose study and analysis require a comparative approach.

Such plurality of laws – or legal pluralism –[114] does not refer just to the aforementioned duality between *ius commune* and *ius proprium* (or *iura propria*).[115]In Spain, for example, the variety of legal sources of the different kingdoms was, like in other European territories, considerable. In exploring and describing such complexity, a comparative approach is highly recommended. Otherwise, it would be difficult to capture a clear picture of the different Spanish legal traditions. In doing so, the legal systems of Castile, Catalonia, Aragon, Valencia, Majorca, Navarre and Basque territories (Guipúzcoa, Alava and Vizcaya) need to be analyzed from different aspects, revolving all of them around the plurality of legal sources:

a) brief presentation of the main legal sources;
b) the *Cortes* and the King as lawmakers;
c) the role of the *ius commune* in the different Spanish legal traditions;
d) The enforcement of the law in a juridical system of divergent legal sources: the hierarchy of legal sources; and
e) the role of the judicial precedent and legal doctrine in developing law and legal science.

---

[113] In this regard, it is particularly useful to analyze the whole development from the royal perspective, since the monarchy eventually needed to deal with the cities (the merchants and the municipal regime), the nobility (seigniorial regime), the clergy (seigniorial regime and the Church), the universities and the *ius commune* (upon which his legislative and political power was grounded).

[114] I used both expressions –plurality of laws or legal pluralism– as synonymous, although some authors tend to distinguish between these concepts; on this matter, see DONLAN, "'All this together make up our *Common* Law': legal hybridity in England and Ireland, 1704–1804", and some of the bibliographical references concerning this matter contained in Donlan's article.

[115] As said, the *ius commune*, or common law, co-existed with the particular law of every European kingdom or jurisdiction, called *ius proprium*. As a result, from the Late Middle Ages to the Modern Ages, there was a duality between the *ius commune* and *ius proprium*.

Applying the comparative approach to the Spanish mixed, complex legal system constitutes a necessary requirement to appreciate a plurality of laws and legal traditions in force as of today. Although these legal traditions underwent a significant process of legal unification, it is important to keep in mind that in Spain legal unification never was entirely achieved.

Leaving aside political and ideological tendencies, the historical approach of Spanish Law shows the existence of diverse cultures – Christian, Muslim, and Jewish, and different ethnic groups that populated the Iberian Peninsula. Spain was – and is – "an aggregation of different regions, diverse populations and languages, with historical struggles to maintain a centralized national "Spanish" State in the face of cultural pluralism".[116] When the Spanish occupied the New World, for example, they also recognized Indian laws and courts. On August 6, 1555, Emperor Don Carlos (Charles V) and Queen Dona Juana issued a decree that "ordered and commanded" that "the laws and good customs" of Indians, along with their "usages and customs," must "be kept and enforced." This principle, firmly accepted in Spanish Indian Law, was lost when new states emerged in Latin America following the period of revolutions.[117]

In short, a Spanish Legal History which, ignoring the cultural history of Spain, would not emphasize an ongoing struggle between local autonomy and central authority, would not be consistent enough. The comparative approach cannot be avoided for juridical pluralism requires necessarily a comparative approach. In this regard, a Spanish legal history handbook should include at least three levels of comparative perspective: the Spanish level, comparing the different legal traditions within the Iberian Peninsula; the European level, comparing and analyzing the duality *ius proprium* and *ius commune*, looking at the diverse kinds of reception of the latter to both the Spanish and European contexts; and the Anglo-American level, considering and contrasting it with the European legal tradition.

The reader may think that, considering the short amount of time available

---

[116] CROW, John A.: *Spain: The Root and the Flower*, 1985; in this sense, it has been said that following the complete reconquest of Spain by Christians in 1492, the national legal system that emerged was based on beliefs "that there was a natural law binding on all people and peoples whoever they might be," and there was "a variety of human observance, all of it permissible so long as it did not conflict with natural law and *ius gentium*," "a common body of law and custom that might be found in the practices of all peoples" (BORAH, Woodrow: *Justice by Insurance: the General Indian Court of Colonial Mexico and the Legal Aides of the Half-Real* 6, 1983). It has also recognized that, when Christians retook control of Spain, "Moslems were allowed to live under their own law and custom and to resort to their own courts for matters concerning themselves" (SEED, Patricia: *Ceremonies of Possession in Europe's Conquest of the New World 1492– 1640*, 1995, pp. 69, 99).

[117] JUNEAU, Donald: "The Light of Dead Stars," 11, 1 *American Indian L. Rev.* 1, 13.

to teach a legal history course, such a comparative perspective is unrealistic. It may be true, but it depends on how deep the comparative approach is employed. Sometimes, it would be enough to state explicitly that some historical process, cultural movement or legal institution are common to all Europe, and it is not just a Spanish, French or Belgian reality. Other times, it would be useful to add something else; for example, in dealing with the creation of the medieval parliaments (*Cortes*) in Spain, it could be added that "the representative assemblies received different names throughout Europe. While in the Anglo-Saxon territories were used the expression "Parliament", in Spain it was known as *Cortes* (General Estates, in France and in the Low Countries; Diet, in Germany) (...). Since the beginning of the 12th century, and due to the development of urban life in Western Europe, the bourgeoisie became a social and economical power aware of their common interests, and united by mutual protection and supporting defence. Thus both the king and this new social class of traders and merchants recognized the convenience of allowing the cities' representatives to take part in the royal assemblies, in which they could give advice and financial support to the king. It was, then, a matter of mutual interest."[118]

Let me give another example. When lecturing law students, I usually explain that the bourgeoisie formed social groups characterised by its particular legal and social status. Throughout Spain, the bourgeoisie was known by the denomination of *ciudadanos* (citizens). In Catalonia and Valencia they were sometimes called *burgueses* (bourgeois), and in Leon and Castile with the special name of *hombres buenos de las ciudades y villas* (good men of the cities and villages). Having said this, I usually add that "in the rest of Europe the names also differed from region to region. In England they received the name of *commons*; and in France, since the 14th century, they were called *common estate* or *Third estate*. During the 13th century, the sessions of the extraordinary assemblies of the royal *Curia* became "estate assemblies" or *Parlamentos* (Parliaments). The participation of the *Third estate* in public life was clearly backed up by the growing economical power of the bourgeoisie. Since the 12th century, the bourgeoisie entered into

[118] It would also be clarifying to add a terminological explanation of the expression "parliament" to avoid possible misunderstandings: "Since the English expression "courts" refers to the tribunals, and not to the Spanish "Parlamento" or "Cortes", it is important not to confuse the Spanish "Cortes" with the English "courts". The expression "Parliament" was first mentioned in Ireland in the 13th century, following closely on their appearance in England. The word parliamentum meant "parley" or "discussion" (in its proper English sense), and seems to have been a newfangled term for the long established colloquies between kings and their leading lay and ecclesiastical subjects. It acquired additional significance during the disputes between Henry III and his barons (1258–65)." (MASFERRER, Spanish Legal Traditions. A Comparative Legal History Outline, p.142).

the extraordinary *Curias* of all Western Europe, being this access admitted in Spain faster than any other European country."[119]

I do not think it is matter of having much time available for lecturing. It is rather a matter of keeping constantly in mind the comparative approach, teaching – in my case – Spanish legal history within the European perspective. My teaching experience shows me that law students get interested in legal history inasmuch as they discover its real interest, if they feel the necessity to know it. In pursuing so, the comparative approach is really helpful. For this reason, every year I start my first lecture asking why a law student has to deal with legal history. My answer is as follows:

> "On November 23, 1880, an outstanding American lawyer and scholar named Oliver Wendell Holmes, giving a Lowell Lecture at Harvard Law School, stated:
>
> 'The life of the law has not been logic; it has been experience. The felt necessities of the time, the prevalent moral and political theories, intuitions of public policy, avowed or unconscious, even the prejudices which judges share with their fellow men, have had a good deal more to do than the syllogism in determining the rules by which men should be governed. The law embodies the story of a nation's development through many centuries, and it cannot be dealt with as if it contained only the axioms and corollaries of a book of mathematics. In order to know what it is, we must know what it has been, and it tends to become. We must alternately consult history and existing theories of legislation. But the most difficult labor will be to understand the combination of the two into new products at every stage. The substance of the law at any given time pretty nearly corresponds, so far as it goes, with what is then understood to be convenient; but its form and machinery, and the degree to which it is able to work out desired results, depend very much upon its past.'
>
> (Oliver Wendell Holmes, *The Common Law and Other Writings*, Birmingham, The Legal Classics Library, 1881).
>
> The statement that *the life of the law has not been logic; it has been experience*, is clear enough to realise to which extend it is important to know what the law has been in order to understand what the law is in the present. It is the knowledge of our legal past what enables us to have a better understanding of our present legal institutions (...).

---

[119] MASFERRER, *Spanish Legal Traditions. A Comparative Legal History Outline*, p.143.

> Our Western Civilization witnesses two main legal traditions whose knowledge is highly convenient for any law student: the civil law and the common law tradition. The former is also called the "Continental" or "European" legal system, while the latter is also called the "Anglo-American" legal system. While the European countries, besides United Kingdom, South and Central America, as well as many Asian territories belong to civil law tradition, England, USA, Canada, Australia and New Zealand belong to common law tradition.
>
> Only history can explain the existence of these two different legal traditions. Only history can show their main characteristics. Only history can give reason of their development and present state. This has always been so, it is now so, and it will always be so, no matter whether legal history will be taught in the future as a compulsory law course or not."[120]

I have seen several times to which extent this answer captures students' attention from the first day, installing in them an open and positive disposition to know about the Spanish legal history from a comparative approach.

4. Concluding Considerations: What will Probably Happen

Although it is hard to predict what will happen in the future with the Spanish legal history, I do have the conviction – and not just the desire – that a comparative approach will help considerably. This is more than wishful thinking, it is a prediction based upon the facts and the current context of the Spanish legal history scholarship.

It is true that traditionally Spanish legal history has been not really come close to a comparative or European perspective, but it is also true that the contributions written by some legal historians in this regard in the last thirty years have possessed a scientific consistency which goes beyond the common standards. One could be surprised that this literature has not have much influence over the Spanish legal history teaching. That is partly true, since some legal historians have been teaching not only the Spanish legal history course from a European perspective, but also a European legal history course.[121] For example, a course on "Legal history of the European Union" ("Historia Jurídica de la Integración Europea", in Spanish) has been offered and taught by a legal historian, Rogelio

[120] MASFERRER, *Spanish Legal Traditions. A Comparative Legal History Outline*, p.16.

[121] See the footnote n. 77 and its main text, which shows the Spanish universities that offer a course on European legal history, as well as the lecturers who teach it: University of Murcia (Antonio Pérez Martín) and University of Illes Balears, Majorca (Román Piña Homs).

Pérez-Bustamante,[122] at the University of Rey Juan Carlos (Madrid) for some years until today.

Furthermore, I have seen the synopsis of some legal history courses taught today in some Spanish law schools. Looking at their content, they could be called European legal history rather than Spanish legal history. In some universities, the title of the course has been even modified, being called just "legal history" instead of "Spanish legal history".[123] I do not have time now to give concrete examples revealing this move towards the comparative approach, but it is true and understandable considering the current tendency of young –and not that young– legal historians to spend time abroad doing research, and who, back to Spain, tend to look at the Spanish legal tradition from a comparative perspective, using a foreign literature which enables them to write, publish and teach consequently in accordance to their comparative legal mind.

Other factor which is – and will be – encouraging Spanish legal historians to teach legal history from a comparative perspective is the introduction of teaching innovation programs. One of these consists in teaching in English courses towards a law degree. Not only Erasmus students from all over Europe are attracted to spend time (a semester or a year) enrolled in Spanish universities. Spanish students are also given the chance to add some special distinction to a law degree otherwise held by many other law students, enabling them to keep open other professional doors in a broader geographical context, that is, beyond the Spanish borders.

The first Spanish law school which implemented a law degree in English was that of the University of Valencia, where I have taught the Spanish legal history course (in English) in the last three years. During these years, I have realized that to teach a legal history course in English constitutes a challenge which encourages the lecturer to go beyond the national boundaries, since both the lecturer and the students are expecting something more than teaching and learning a strict national legal history. Alongside the Spanish legal history course (which is compulsory), I have also been giving an optional course entitled "History of Codes and Constitutions" devoted to the constitutionalism and the codification movement from a comparative perspective, including both the Continental and the Anglo-American legal traditions. It seems to me that students enjoyed these courses mainly because of the comparative perspective, and it is clear to me that the majority of them like comparative legal history. They are fully aware that

[122] Topic upon which he has published extensively (on that, see the bibliographical references contained in the footnote n. 44).

[123] This has occurred, for example, in the University of Navarre.

they are attending a course on comparative legal history, and not just on legal history or just on comparative law. In my view, it is a course on legal history because I take for granted the comparative approach; otherwise – as said –, it would not be a real or consistent legal history course.[124]

This year the law school of the University of Castilla-La Mancha has offered a similar course called "Comparative legal systems" ("Sistemas Jurídicos Comparados", in Spanish). The course is taught in English by Sara Granda (who has spent time doing research in the UK and in the USA). This year also the law school of the University Rey Juan Carlos (Madrid) has offered a course called "Comparative history of legal institutions", which has been taught in English by Gabriela Cobo del Rosal (who has also spent time abroad doing research). Next year the law school of the University of Navarre will offer an optional course called Comparative history of legal institutions ("Historia comparada de las instituciones jurídicas", in Spanish), which will be taught by Rafael García Pérez (who has been abroad several times: France, Italy and USA).

I am sure that, in the near future, optional courses like these will proliferate, and the compulsory course on Spanish legal history will be taught much more comparatively than it has been done in the past. My prediction is optimistic: Spanish legal historians will be more comparative in both doing research and teaching, so our contribution to the law student's education will be greater than ever. But this will require the student's active engagement with interactive methodological systems of legal education whose goodness and positive results I have already tested and appreciated in the last three years.

[124] Most probably my view on this matter is due mainly to the stays abroad I have made in the last ten years: Visiting Professor at Tasmania Law School (January–February 2010), Visiting Scholar at Melbourne Law School (January–February 2010 and July–September 2008), Visiting Scholar at Harvard Law School (2006–07), Herbert Smith Visiting Professor at Cambridge University (UK, February–July 2005), and Fellow Researcher at Max-Planck Institute for European Legal History (Frankfurt/Main, Germany, May–August, 2000–02). I'm very grateful to Matt Dyson (UK) and Orlando Rivero (USA) for revising my English version.

C.H. van Rhee and J.A.J.M. van der Meer

Teaching European Legal History at Maastricht University in the Netherlands

Introduction

In the Netherlands, there are no specific admission requirements as regards the courses law students should have taken during their pre-university education. Although a sufficient knowledge of, for example, foreign languages (including Latin), economics and history is highly beneficial to such students, many of them cannot be expected to have mastered all these topics in detail. Therefore, at the Maastricht University faculty of law a determined effort is made to teach the various courses in such a way that a lack of the necessary background knowledge can be overcome.

The present paper deals with the way European legal history is taught at Maastricht. Of course, when teaching European legal history, a lack of knowledge as regards European history in general, the major modern European languages (French, German and English) and Latin is especially problematic. In order to overcome this problem, we[1] have designed our compulsory first-year course in such a way that students not only acquire the necessary knowledge of European *legal* history, but also study the main events in European History in general. Additionally, we provide original texts with extensive translations, and encourage students to read both the translation and the original. During the tutorials we frequently refer to the original texts in order to demonstrate their importance. This is not only beneficial from the perspective of legal history, but also from the perspective of other law courses which presuppose that students have some knowledge of the concept of Europe and European integration processes, of the major modern European languages, and of the language that for a long period helped to shape the European intellectual environment (Latin).

After the first-year introductory course on European legal history, which will be discussed below, we aim at integrating legal history into the various (modern) law courses on offer in Maastricht. In our opinion, the integration of legal

[1] Apart from the authors of the present contribution, 'we' refers to Prof. dr. Louis Berkvens, Dr. Pim Oosterhuis, Mr. Emanuel van Dongen and Ms. Mariken Lenaerts.

history helps to demonstrate the relevance of this topic in a modern European legal curriculum, and, where necessary, also keeps the instructor aware of the fact that he/she is teaching in the law faculty and not in the history department of his/her university.

1. General introduction to legal history in year 1 of the Bachelor's programme

In the first year of the Bachelor's programme, European legal history is taught during what may be called a 'crash course' of four weeks in January (4 ECTS) in both English and Dutch (students may choose their preferred language). This is unfortunately a short period of time, although the benefit of concentrating the introductory course in this short period is that it is the only course the students have to focus on (in Maastricht, usually two parallel course are taught during eight-week periods). Consequently, students are expected to devote 40 hours per week to the course, something that is stimulated by not having a written exam at the end of the course, but a series of compulsory student papers (one paper per week) that are graded and that make up the final mark.

Taking into consideration what has been said above, it may not come as a surprise that the introductory course not only puts an emphasis on European *legal* history and its chronology, but also provides – as far as relevant from a legal point of view – the necessary information on European history in general.

The subject matter is divided into three periods: (1) Roman Law in Antiquity, (2) the Ius Commune period (Middle Ages and early modern period),[2] and (3) the Codification Period. The course consists of two weekly lectures and two weekly tutorials.

Lectures

In the two lectures, which are scheduled at the start of each week, external European legal history and European history in general are focused on. The students are required to prepare for the lectures well. This is facilitated by the fact that the various Power Point presentations used during the lectures are made available in advance. The presentations assist the students in focusing on the major issues while reading the relevant parts of Peter Stein's book 'Roman Law in European Legal History'.[3]

Students bring print outs of the Power Point presentations to the lectures in order to make notes on them. The lectures are inter-active in the sense that the

[2] We refer to this period as the "Ius Commune period" only for reasons of convenience.

[3] Cambridge University Press, 1999.

lecturer submits questions to the audience (individual students are selected at random) and gives the students frequent opportunities to ask questions. Students who have not been able to prepare for the lecture well need to mention this at the start of the lecture and will as a result not be asked questions. The lectures are recorded on video and made available on the Intranet site.

After the lecture, both the Dutch and the English language students are required to reread the relevant parts of 'Roman Law in European Legal History'. Although this book might be quite condensed for a beginning law student, the lectures provide the relevant framework needed for a proper understanding of the book. A more extensive book cannot be used during a four-week course. We are, however, currently in the process of writing a book specifically designed for teaching European legal history in Maastricht.

CALI-modules

A further aid to the students in studying 'Roman Law in European Legal History', in addition to the lectures, is offered in the electronic learning modules that have been developed at the Maastricht faculty for the specific purpose of this course.[4] Students need to complete the electronic learning modules covering the subject matter of the particular week. The modules consist first of all of an outline of the subject matter. In addition, and most importantly, the modules contain questions which allow the students to check whether they have studied the materials attentively and suggested further reading and Internet links. The modules provide the students with feedback when they submit the wrong answer, by indicating which parts of the materials should be studied again in order to be able to answer the question in a satisfactory manner.

Tutorials

In the second half of the week the students attend two tutorials. Each of these two tutorials is offered with a particular didactic objective in mind and is geared to a specific element in the individual student papers on the subject matter of the particular week (see below). This is very important, since the papers constitute the course exam and together provide the final grade for the course.

The first tutorial is concerned with external legal history, focusing on the legal history of a series of selected time periods and places within the general historical period of the particular week. The aim is to allow students to analyse primary historical sources in their specific historical context.

---

[4] The modules were developed by prof. dr. A.M.J.A.Berkvens and Prof. Dr. C.H. van Rhee, with contributions of Dr. J.A.J.M. van der Meer. Some of these modules are available on www.cali.nl/.

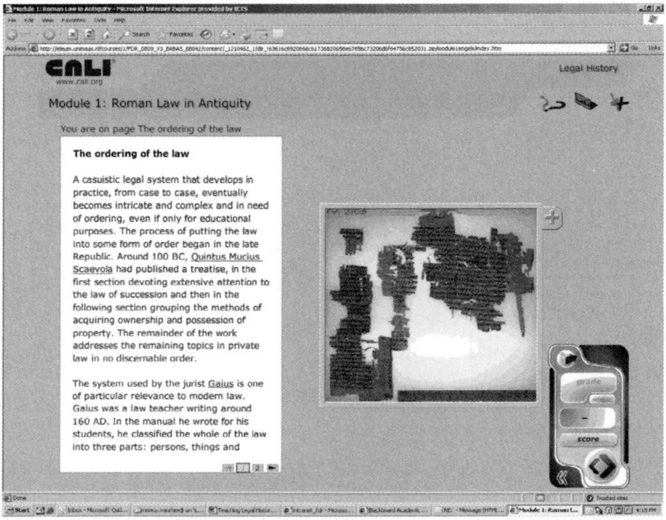

Example of a page from an electronic module with an outline of the subject matter, with hyperlinks and an illustration.

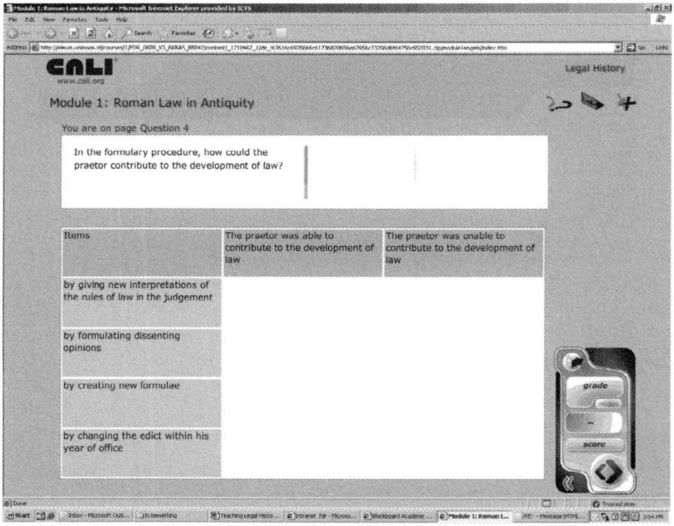

Example of a page from an electronic learning module containing a question. Students have to categorize the four statements on the left ('items') under the correct heading by dragging them into one of the two columns on the right hand-side. It should be noted that each question in the module follows a different format.

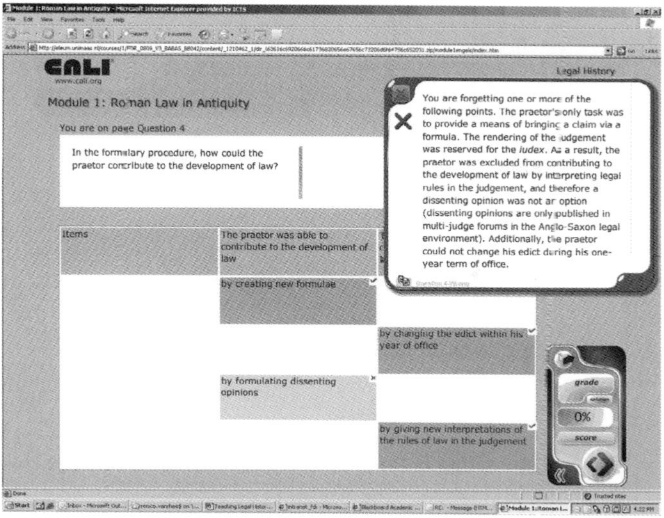

Example of the same page where the student has provided the wrong answer to the question.

Students have to prepare for this first tutorial on the basis of a series of rather broadly formulated assignments. These assignments serve several aims. One of these aims is making the students more familiar with the most important developments in the period under scrutiny. A further aim is familiarizing the students with the components that constitute a legal system, and to help them gain the necessary insights and skills for this element in their student papers. An example of an assignment from the week devoted to Roman law in Antiquity is:

Suppose, you have to write an essay on Marcus Tullius Cicero as lawyer and statesman. To that end, it is important for you to know exactly how things stood in Rome in the years 64–62 BC. Find out what form of government Rome had in those days and who stood at the helm of the Roman state. What territory was encompassed by the Roman state in those days? Discuss the structure of Roman society, the economical state of affairs, the demographic structure of the populace and possible social unrest.

Of course, some of these questions might be hard to answer for a first-year law student, and therefore the tutor devotes a sufficient amount of time to discussing how the relevant information could have been uncovered by using the appropriate research methods

The second tutorial of the week is different in character. During this second tutorial, students who are following the Dutch language programme focus on aspects of the history of the law of delict (*delictum,* i.e. 'tort law'), and the students following the English language programme study aspects of the history of contract law. In each week, developments of the particular period that is focused on in this week are discussed. The books we use for this part of the course are those of Robert Feenstra & Laurens Winkel on Delict (for the Dutch language students)[5] and Robert Feenstra & Margreet Ahsmann on the Law of Contract (translated into English for the English language students).[6] We use these books since they are sufficiently short for our four week period and, most importantly, because they contain a large selection of relevant historical texts, both in the original language and in translation, from the various periods studied by the students.

In Week One of their course, the Dutch students concentrate on the *Lex Aquilia* (ca. 286 BC), one of the sources of the modern continental law of delict, and the English language students focus on the system of contracts and *pacta* in Roman Law. For both groups of students, the aim is to contrast the modern continental situation, with its general law of delict and contract respectively, with a situation where a general law of delict and contract are virtually absent. The difficulties which lawyers encountered as a result of this are highlighted, and accordingly students are offered the necessary tools to appreciate the advantages and disadvantages of the modern approach. Additionally, students study early developments pointing in the direction of a more general approach to delict and contract. As regards delict, this means that they concentrate on the application of the *Lex Aquilia* in its original domain, i.e. specific types of damage inflicted directly and with *iniuria* to a specified series of physical objects. In addition, the development in the types of objects and damage covered by the *Lex Aquilia* is discussed, as well as the development in the interpretations of *iniuria* and the relaxation of the causal link between the act causing damage and the resulting damage. As regards contract, students study the *numerus clausus* of contracts recognized in Roman law, the transformation of *consensus* into a general requirement for contracts, as well as the late post-classical growth of the number of binding agreements due to the introduction of the *actio praescriptis*

[5] R. Feenstra & L.C. Winkel, *Vergelding en vergoeding. Enkele grepen uit de geschiedenis van de onrechtmatige daad*, Deventer: Kluwer.

[6] R. Feenstra & M. Ahsmann, *Contract: 'Contract' and 'Freedom of Contract' in Historical Perspective*, available on the Intranet site. This is a translation with modifications and additions of R. Feenstra & M. Ahsmann, *Contract. Aspecten van de begrippen contract en contractsvrijheid in historisch perspectief*, Deventer: Kluwer, 1988.

verbis (available to parties having performed on the basis of a non-binding agreement (*pactum*), enabling them to obtain restitution or performance of the opposing party; consequently, the non-binding agreement becomes binding, at least to a certain extent).

Developments in these particular fields from the 'rediscovery' of the Roman Law in the High Middle Ages until (and including) the codification period are the subject of the tutorials in the subsequent weeks. This means that the Dutch language students study the contributions of Canon Law, Natural Law and the *ius proprium* to the development of a general, uniform law of delict, and the extent to which this development has influenced the various codifications of private law in Europe (with an emphasis on the Netherlands). The English language students concentrate on the contributions of Canon Law, Natural Law and the Law Merchant to the development of a general law of contract in which both formal and substantive freedom of contract are central issues.

As stated above, students have to use original texts with a translation to answer a set of questions and to solve cases. The relevant texts are to be selected by them from a larger group of texts prescribed in a particular week which can be found in the books of Feenstra & Winkel and Feenstra & Ahsmann mentioned above. In the area of contract law, an obvious text to be studied is printed below.

Decretals of Gregorius IX (Liber Extra) 1,35,1 (c. Antigonus, title De pactis = 'On pacta'; text based on manuscripts and 16th century editions)
Ex concilio Africano
Pacta quantumcumque nuda servanda sunt
Antigonus episcopus dixit et infra. Aut inita pacta suam obtineant firmitatem aut conventus (si se non cohibuerit) ecclesiasticam sentiat disciplinam. Dixerunt universi: pax servetur et pacta custodiantur.

From the text of the African Council [Council at Carthago 348 AD]
Agreements, however naked, must be honoured
Bishop Antigonus etc. etc. [the Liber Extra omits the charge pronounced by bishop Antigonus against his opponent as well as the beginning of an opinion put forward by one of the bishops present at the Council; after 'etc. etc.' follow immediately his conclusion and the verdict of the assembly:] 'either agreements must be in force or the defendant, if he does not contain himself, must undergo ecclesiastical discipline'. All said: 'peace must be maintained and agreements must be honoured'.

Students are first of all required to put the texts in their historical context. To this end and in this particular case, they need to make use of their knowledge about the role of the Church and Canon Law in the medieval context. They need to be precise and, for example, discuss the role and significance of the *Liber Extra*. They also need to discuss the link between Roman Law and Canon Law. Subsequently, after having studied all the relevant texts in their context, they will have to reflect on a series of cases. An example of such cases is provided below. As regards this case, students need to mention that it took place before the *Liber Extra* came into being and must reflect on the possible relevance of the older text cited in the text above.

> Falco is a young man who lives in Padua. He was born in 1125, and is now 23 years old. Five years ago, he started working for Ricardo, who is a master tapestry weaver. They agreed that Ricardo would teach Falco how to design and weave tapestries. If Falco worked hard in Ricardo's atelier for five years and did well, Ricardo would help Falco being admitted to the guild of tapestry weavers. In addition, he would help him to found his own atelier and eventually to attain the master status. Falco worked hard and is now the designer and supervisor of half the tapestries that come out of Ricardo's atelier. Ricardo does not want to lose such a good employee only to create a formidable competitor. Consequently, he changes his mind: he forgets about his promise made to Falco: he will not make him a guild member, let alone help him found his own atelier. Falco decides to take Ricardo to court, but as he asks the advice of a lawyer he hears that his agreement with Ricardo, though valid as such, is not actionable according to Roman law since that law only recognizes a set series of contracts. Falco cannot, therefore, force Ricardo to comply with his earlier promises by going to a secular court that applies Roman law. In confusion, he wanders into his parish church, where the local priest is reading his breviary. The kind old man asks Falco what is the matter, and Falco tells him about his problems. The priest advises him not to go to the secular court, but to the ecclesiastical court. There Falco might win his case …

By having the students study the relevant texts, they simultaneously reflect on the context in which these texts functioned as well as on their possible legal significance in a particular historical period. In this way, students are made aware once more that knowledge of external legal history, i.e. the historical context, is a necessary prerequisite for understanding the law in action.

After having attended the last tutorial in a particular week, the students are well prepared to write their paper for that week. An example of a case about which the students have to write their paper can be found below:

> Mario Benedetto is a carpenter in Perugia. His business is booming, especially after he decided to specialize in making coffins. Unfortunately, many of his customers do not have the money to pay him immediately. Consequently, he lacks the money to buy enough wood for his business and proposes his supplier, Claudio Fregoli, to exchange a series of expensive gems for a large amount of wood to be delivered

in June 1352. Claudio agrees, especially when Mario states that he intends to deliver the gems to Claudio in April 1352, i.e. before the delivery of the wood. Early 1352, the number of customers interested in coffins declines dramatically. Mario despairs, especially because it seems that the amount of wood promised in exchange for his gems is much more than he will need in the coming few years. Additionally, he would rather keep the gems to support his family in the months to come, given the fact that he has realized that many of the unpaid coffins will most likely never be paid for given the fact that in the meantime most of the people who bought these coffins for their family members have also died. Claudio, however, is of the opinion that 'pacta sunt servanda'.

In despair, Mario consults you. He asks you whether he is bound by the agreement reached with Claudio. Since you are *doctor utriusque iure*, you have a tendency to base your answer on the so-called 'learned laws' and to advise your clients to litigate before courts where these laws are taken into consideration. What would your advice be?

Individual student paper

We aim for students to start preparing their paper early in the week during which the lectures and tutorials for the particular period at hand take place. Therefore, we post the case description that is the basis for the paper at the beginning of the week in the Intranet environment rather than at the end.

The paper consists of three parts. The first part is devoted to situating the case in its general historical context. The second part focuses on the legal developments in the period of the case. The questions that have to be answered explicitly in these two parts have been rehearsed during the first tutorial of the week, although for a different place and a different time period. Examples of such questions are:

- Where does the case take place?
- In the period in question, what was the political, administrative and social situation in the area in which the case took place?
- What important legal developments can be identified in this period?
- What sources of law were known in the period in question?
- What was the relationship between these sources of law?
- Name at least two important jurists who practiced in the period in question. Discuss their influence on the development of law.

The third part of the paper is devoted to solving the case. In doing this, students have to make sure that they use all relevant texts that have been provided. Just as in the first two parts of their paper, students should use footnotes referring to their sources. In the third part, this also means that explicit references to the relevant historical legal texts from the books by Feenstra & Winkel and Feenstra & Ahsmann should be included.

The papers need to be submitted electronically in order to allow for a plagiarism test (papers are checked both against the Internet, and against the papers that have been handed in by other course participants, both current ones and those who participated in previous years) and in order to be able to check whether the papers have been submitted at or before the deadline indicated in the course materials (papers submitted after the deadline will not be taken into consideration). After the papers have been submitted, students are provided with an example of what their paper ideally should have looked like and they are allowed to ask questions during the tutorial and lectures. They can apply the additional knowledge obtained in this way in more adequately researching and structuring subsequent papers.

As stated, the final mark for the course is based on the various papers submitted by the students. We have opted for taking into consideration only a specific part of each paper due to constraints as regards the number of staff available for grading the papers. It may, for example, happen that in a certain academic year, we decide to grade the section on the general historical context of the case in the paper submitted for Roman Law, the section on the legal context from the paper submitted for the codification period and the part devoted to solving the case from the paper submitted for the Ius Commune period. Each year a different combination is chosen.

In the introductory course, the emphasis is on the learned laws (Roman and Canon Law). Nevertheless, some attention is given to customary law/the *ius proprium* whenever this is necessary, e.g. as regards delictual liability for bodily harm (Grotius). Additionally, some attention is given to English legal history, although time constraints do not allow us to pay sufficient attention to this important subject, which is unfortunate, especially in the European Law School programme.

2. Legal History in other courses of the Bachelor's programme

As stated, after the introductory first year course, solely devoted to European legal history, legal history is taught within the context of other courses devoted to modern topics. In the course on Comparative Contract Law, for example, the focus is on good faith (*bona fides*), fraud (*fraus*), duress (*metus*) and *causal consideration*. In the course on Property Law, the historical origins of the consensual and traditional systems of transfer of ownership are discussed, as well as the origins of abstract and causal systems of transfer. In the course on International & European Law, the history of public international law, especially in the 18th and 19th centuries, is focused on, while European integration before the establishment of the European Coal and Steel Community also gets some attention.

Additionally, legal history forms part of a course called *Metajuridica* in the

Dutch language programme. This course is taught in the third year of the Bachelor's programme and its main aim is to demonstrate the use of disciplines like history, philosophy, economics and the social sciences in the study of law. A considerable part of the course materials is devoted to legal history, while much of the rest is philosophical in nature. The legal history materials concentrate on the history of constitutional law, criminal law and private law. It is in this course that attention is paid to customary law and the *ius proprium*. The focus is more on the history of ideas than on legal dogmatics.

There is also an elective course solely devoted to legal history at the end of the third year of the Bachelor's programme. Its content varies each year and depends largely on the interests of the participants. Students have to choose topics from a series indicated in the course book and, on the basis of these materials and additional sources, they have to prepare presentations and discussion sessions. The tutorials are supervised by a legal historian, but the emphasis is on student input. This course is graded on the basis of a final paper, class participation and the slides of the various Power Point presentations prepared by the individual students.

3. Legal History in the Master's programmes

In the various Master's programmes, legal history is again taught in an integrated manner. An example is the course Civil Litigation in Europe. This course, which is comparative in nature, discusses the differences between, and the similarities of, the various systems of civil procedure in Europe. A central question is to what extent harmonisation of procedural law is necessary from the perspective of the proper functioning of the internal market, to what extent harmonisation has already been achieved, as well as the chances of further harmonisation. In this course the starting point is always historical. For example, students are familiarized with the distinction between pre-trial and trial in the Anglo-American system of civil procedure by looking at the history of the jury in civil matters. Additionally, they study the continuing existence of these two procedural phases despite of the fact that the civil jury has nearly disappeared in England and many other Common Law countries. The advantages of this division from the perspective of expediency and efficiency are discussed and subsequently parallel developments on the European Continent are taken into consideration. The ideas of the 19th-century Austrian jurist Franz Klein are especially interesting from this perspective.[7]

---

[7] See C.H. van Rhee (ed.), *European Traditions in Civil Procedure*, Antwerp 2005.

As regards the feasibility of a further harmonisation of civil procedural law, we take into consideration various 19th and 20th century authors who have claimed that civil procedure is a topic that is purely national in character and is not fit for harmonisation. We contrast these views with the history of the Romano-canonical procedure, taking into consideration that this procedure served as an international framework while allowing national particularities.

In the Advanced Master in International and European Economic Law, the class in Legal Foundations of Economic and Political Integration is offered in the first course period. The course is one of the few mandatory ones in this advanced master programme, indicative of the importance attached to legal history by the Maastricht law faculty. In this course the students study the historical roots of the legal elements contributing to the economic integration process. An assessment is made of law as an integration fostering instrument, as well as of law as an impediment to such integration. Specific attention is given to the integrative force of organizations such as the WTO, NAFTA, EFTA and the EU in past, present and future. Within this context, the role of regulatory frameworks in the broad sense (e.g. customary, legislative and conventional frameworks) is analysed. Additionally, the role of regional, supra-regional, national and supra-national courts, and, in their absence, alternative types of dispute settlement, is discussed. Finally, the spill-over mechanism in developing international and supranational legal systems and its influence on economic integration is scrutinized.

The emphasis of the course is on student-driven research. Students are divided into teams, each team having two participants. Each team gets assigned a task for particular seminars. The information provided for each task consists of a case story and some basic literature references. Through team research, students have to develop an insight into the historical context of the principle or concept involved in the task. One of the team members will then construct and hold a Power Point presentation on the relevant historical features of the principle or concept, while the other team member writes a paper presenting the team's general findings and analysis to the group. Afterwards an integratory lecture will be offered in which the course coördinator or a guest speaker fills in possible gaps, where necessary providing further structure to the research materials.

The students may choose one of their Power Point presentations and one of their papers for grading. In exceptional cases, the final grade may be augmented or diminished by a bonus or malus point, depending on the overall participation of the particular student during the course. Students invariably find the course a daunting prospect at the start, but are invariably happy with the knowledge and skills gained during the course.

Final remarks

Obviously, the approach to the teaching of legal history in Maastricht described above has many virtues. In our opinion, the most important virtue is that it necessarily establishes a strong link with modern law. There is no possibility of adopting an antiquarian approach, since the professor of legal history continually needs to link his teaching to the contemporary issues taught in the various law courses. This forces him or her to follow developments in contemporary law thoroughly. Without such knowledge, it is obviously hard to explain these developments from an historical perspective. At the same time, the Maastricht approach allows him or her to demonstrate the relevance of legal history for the future studies and legal career of the students and, most importantly, to make the largest number of students enthusiastic about the topic. When this approach is combined with a willingness to teach students with an interest in legal history, one that goes beyond the interest of ordinary law students, in small seminars – or even individually when they have opted for writing a thesis on legal history – we find the Maastricht approach very satisfactory, which may, however, not come as a surprise for the reader.

Ann-Christine Petersson Hjelm

A Comparative Bridge: Challenges in Teaching Comparative Legal History

The Texan boasted to one of his ranch-hands: 'You can drive my car all day long and still be on my land'. 'Yeah', responded the worker, 'I had a car like that myself once'.
Lawrence Rosen, *Beyond Compare*, p. 496.

1 Introduction

The topic for this workshop is *How to teach European Comparative Legal History*. Lawrence Rosen's humoristic quotation, followed by two other selected quotations, initiates my contribution. The following three quotations also open the theory and methodology curriculum at Karlstad University, where comparative legal history is an important element previous to the students' master thesis. In a time when earlier approaches in comparative legal history has been challenged I find it important to grasp this change in teaching. Hopefully the following quotations and this article demonstrate how we have tried to undertake this challenge.

Lawrence Rosen underlines efforts made to reach the "heart" of the matter through comparison. The comparatist's understanding can easily be obscured and Rosen states: "when we fall into the trap of thinking that the ways we have come to view the connections among various aspects of a culture are the ways those connections 'naturally' tend to take shape. Much depends, of course, on the assumptions and position from which one starts the comparison."[1] Rosen's point – explained with the Texan who boasted – is to be aware of different mistakes, and unforeseen connections and consequences in our work.[2] Mitchel de S.-O.-l'E. Lasser explains a similar point distinctly when a colleague of his tried to get a 'short' espresso the Italian way from a busy Chicago waiter who

[1] Rosen, 2003, p. 496. The notion of *culture* depends on the context and the meaning changes depending on the comparatist's position.
[2] Rosen, 2003, p. 496.

had no intention to search for the actual meaning.[3] The waiter just offered to pour half of the coffee out, to the Italian's surprise; when the Italian was requesting a "short pull" on the machine, he wanted only the first strong part of the stream of espresso.

Zweigert and Kötz, on the other hand, with their functionalistic view, maintain that "the legal system of every society faces essentially the same problems and solves these problems by quite different means, though very often with similar results."[4] The way we put the questions in our work is therefore important: "One must never allow one's vision to be clouded by the concepts of one's own national system; always in comparative law one must focus on the concrete problem."[5] Therefore, Zweigert and Kötz find that we must be aware of the consequences if we – sometimes unconsciously – look at the problem with the eyes of our own system. Being a legal foreigner and trying to find the core of other countries' legal functions is sometimes problematic and we tend to wear the famous spectacles where we focus on functions known from our own country. A danger, according to Zweigert and Kötz, could be that we put too much emphasis or do not put enough emphasis on our interpretation of the foreign countries' legal systems. In some cases, the comparatist's ambition to find other systems' solutions/functions fails completely or even ends with the wrong conclusion.

In this seminar the focus is on *the need for a common European discourse regarding teaching methods, theoretical approaches and class material in European Comparative Legal History*. My starting point in the course is more of a broad acceptance of different theoretical and methodological approaches, as my choice of the opening voices of leading comparatists hopefully illustrates. Instead I devote time to clarify significant aspects in the progress from the old schools (David, Zweigert and Kötz) and the new representatives of the postmodern generation (Legrand). Having said that, some essential remarks must initially be made about the course where this subject is taught at Karlstad University.

It is important to know that comparative legal history are studied at the end of the programme when the students also write their master thesis. Comparative legal history are compulsory in the first theoretical part, but students may choose to specialize in these areas as the course continues throughout the semester. These students obtain basic knowledge in comparative legal history but it is not a question of detailed knowledge, instead it is significant that

3 Lasser, 2003, p. 238.
4 Zweigert and Kötz, 1998, p. 34.
5 Zweigert and Kötz, 1998, p. 35.

students acquire a methodological and scientific skill and critical thinking in the subject. Learning different theoretical and methodological approaches is therefore an important part of the education regardless of specialization. One of the challenges of a teacher at Karlstad University is to encourage students to work with comparative legal history; an opportunity they have in their articles and master theses. But this is a demanding task and the question may be raised if the basic skills that students attain are enough. My intention in the following article is also to discuss this methodological demanding walk on a tightrope that is the question: "What is good enough?"

When tutoring, I use a pragmatic model in the shape of a methodological bridge: a construction that, of course, may be rebuilt and reconstructed endlessly depending on the student's legal interest. Increased methodological and theoretical knowledge is a useful introduction to the students regardless of their legal field of interest. One challenge in teaching is to discuss different approaches in comparative legal history and what problems it entails.[6] It is demanding to interpret legal matters when they are dealt with in another legal context and sometimes it is easy to use our Swedish frames of jurisprudence – maybe the famous spectacles mentioned above.

This article starts with a short presentation of the students at Karlstad University and their prior knowledge in law. I approach comparative studies with an open mind in the shape of a bridge, whose construction must be clearly shown to be firm. Then a short discussion follows about knowledge of legal systems as a tool. To make my point, some bridge abutments are presented in the following section, for example interdisciplinary approaches such as the sociology of law. I also reflect upon what might be good enough knowledge in comparative legal history. Finally there are some concluding remarks about what is good enough and the importance that a course keeps pace with developments and new methods and critically evaluates central areas.

2 Teaching goals and objectives at Karlstad University

To achieve a Master in Jurisprudence at Karlstad University, the students take an advanced course in jurisprudence.[7] In this last semester they 1) take an exam in theoretical, methodological, comparative legal history (7,5 hp), 2) write an article based on an individual reading course (7,5 hp) and 3) write

[6] Discussed in Bogdan, 2003, p. 40–41.

[7] This in accordance with the former educational system whereas the curriculum has now been redesigned to adapt to a programme based on the Bologna model.

a final essay, master thesis (15 hp). In part 1 they initially study legal history and comparative law but they also challenge their positivistic approach to law with different interdisciplinary approaches. Several students use their reading course – which concludes with an article and an oral presentation – to immerse themselves in relevant fields. It is popular among students, in part 2, to improve their legal history in the field that they find crucial to their legal training. Some students are also interested in comparative studies in their master thesis in part 3.

The course is presented as a broad methodological and scientific *smorgasbord* where part of it consists of comparative legal history.[8] It is important – as illustrated below – that comparative legal history itself contains a rich toolbox. It is worthwhile to discuss possible funding for a broad overview of the field, for example, by presenting the approaches of different scientists, but also to give students an alternative scientific appropriation. In part 1 Bogdan's work *Komparativ rättskunskap* is used as an introduction to the subject.[9] Thereafter follows a short presentation of problems encountered in comparative law: considerations in comparative law essential in order to make meaningful comparisons. According to Bogdan, it is important to provide "accurate and current knowledge of the laws and legal institutions that we want to compare.".[10] Bogdan also stresses the importance "to liberate themselves from their own legal system, conscious and unconscious mind shackles",[11] without providing students with the illusion that there is an objective truth to be pursued. Recent articles, written by authorities representing the contextual approach to comparative legal history, have been included in a compendium to explain what Whitman describes as "The Neo-Romantic Turn".

Our ambition is that students should be aware of different authorities' views and may perhaps find an approach that is right for the area they wish to study for their article or master thesis. These obstacles – or legal turns – are discussed, hopefully, without deterring students from further work on comparative legal history. Students who are interested are encouraged to develop their knowledge in the field and to search for further information in the light of their purpose in writing the article or master thesis. Then, in discussions with the supervisor, they may justify their choice of comparatist, subject matter etc and show

---

8 The course literature includes, for example, Alvesson, Mats och Sköldberg, Kaj, (2008).

9 Bogdan, Michael, Komparativ rättskunskap, Norstedts juridik AB, 2 uppl., Stockholm 2003.

10 Bogdan, 2003, p. 39. My translation: "korrekta och aktuella kunskaper om de rättsregler och rättsinstitut som man vill jämföra".

11 Bogdan, 2003, s. 40. My translation: "att befria sig från det egna rättssystemets medvetna och omedvetna tankebojor".

that they have enough knowledge to manage a walk on the comparative legal historical bridge.

As regards legal history, there is no ambition in the course to provide a comprehensive review of legal developments; instead the discussion in the lectures focus on the meaning and weight of various sources, how to approach legal history chronologically, thematically, etc. The students then have the option, in parts 2 and 3, to immerse themselves in the areas of law that they intend to work on. A skeptical person might ask if it is possible to accomplish this when their major studies concern Swedish law and they often have a shallow knowledge of legal history per se.[12] Here, the answer must be that the students are learning a skill and they just need more time and knowledge to immerse themselves further in the field.

Most of the students have a legal positivistic point of departure in their work from their previous compulsory course. In my experience, students are often interested in the comparison of institutions and rules on a micro level and research concerning specific legal problems. They often prefer to use a functionalistic methodological approach of studying rules in order to solve actual problems or particular conflicts of interests.[13] Macro comparison, comparing the spirit and style of different legal systems and the methods of thought and procedures in use, is considered difficult. Often students may to some degree reflect on matters such as looking into procedures for resolving and deciding disputes or the roles of those engaged in the law. Finally, most of the students come from a background in public law.[14]

So, do many students write their articles or final essays in comparative legal history? The answer is no, not yet. At the same time, comparative legal history is a key element of the course and is appreciated by the students. Therefore, it is noteworthy that the students' work stops at the reading course in part 2. This probably happens because the requirements are too demanding – not least on the part of the supervisor – for the implementation of such work. Lasser's discussion concerning his students perhaps represents the kind of *good enough* arguments I have raised here. He starts by asking: "[H]ow can a non-New Yorker ever truly grasp the field of referents in a Woody Allen movie?"[15] He continues that it is fairly easy to discover the basic structure but it is hard to gather the background knowledge: Lasser refers to "becoming culturally fluent". The only

---

[12] David, 1985, p. 309. Also Zweigert and Kötz, 1998, p. 181.

[13] Zweigert and Kötz, 1998, p. 5.

[14] Nordic law, 2007, p. 4. Here an anthology like Nordic law is valuable – not just for emphasizing the area – but also for "expanding the scope well beyond the boundaries of private law".

[15] Lasser, 2003, p. 202.

obstacle is that, in some cases, the basic structure of a foreign legal system can be compared with the tip of the iceberg. On the other hand, Lasser emphasizes that students, after a course in comparative legal studies, can identify "the origin of assorted legal arguments".[16] Independent of the researcher's methodological background, I think this is worth considering.

To sum up, it is often a challenge for students to explain their theoretical and methodological steps to prove that they can cross the bridge. In the following chapter I will try to explain the methodological bridge (simplified in this article) I use in teaching.

3 A bridge of comparative legal historical blocks

3.1 The building constructor's outline

It is important to start with an overview – like the building constructor's outline – of the attitudes towards legal families, legal cultures etc. and, in my view, these are academic constructions created as working tools.[17] First, it is important to carefully and systematically explain the construction of the bridge. The validity and reliability of the legal historical comparatist's work depends on its stability or the ability to explain the procedure of constructing a bridge.[18] For example in the initial part we discuss the various problems to be overcome: a legal family is not an exact empirical description, instead it is an analytical structure which provides a first step for comparative studies.[19] In this article I simplify the construction with just a few aspects to make my point. Thus, my strategy for this construction work seems obvious: the bridge can be built in many different shapes, some parts must be emphasized, some can be widened and others can be demolished depending on the individual comparatist's purpose in the work.[20]

Initially, it is crucial to find a comparative model which suits the students and the problems they want to answer in their work. Knowledge of comparative legal history is necessary and a first abutment often consists of work that concerns the grouping of legal families or a comparative authority to lean on in a contextual work. If the student wears poor spectacles, there is a methodological risk of

---

16 Lasser, 2003, pp. 200–201.

17 Munday, 2003, p. 20.

18 Lasser points out that "awareness of one's position does not solve any of the dilemmas of comparative practice". Lasser, 2003, p. 219.

19 Nordic law, 2007, p. 7.

20 Compare Karl Llewellyn (1960) on a trained instinct, *situation-sense*, to find the best method concerning the group of people to whom the study is addressed.

failing to find, explain or interpret the sources. Previously I have mentioned the need to reflect upon and have an open approach to methodological and theoretical innovation. Already in the preceding compulsory course at Karlstad University the students study different perspectives so they have methodological and theoretical pre-understanding. In this course we shortly discuss comparatists with different approache, from Montesquieu, Rabel, Arminjon, Nolde and Wolff, David, Zweigert and Kötz until Legrand and Lasser attack on the functionalistic perspective. I find it important to have the right lens regardless of the comparatist's background. By that I mean adopting a critical approach to avoid short-sightedness. Another abutment is knowledge of the actual issue in current laws, especially if the student has *good enough* knowledge of the foreign system. This subject is often highlighted; Nelken, for example, asks: How far is it possible to understand other peoples' law?[21] My point is that – regardless of the point of departure – it is important to question one's vision of the foreign legal system, to use clearly focused spectacles.

The comparative bridge – illustrated in the form of Palmstedtska bron (now demolished). Lithograph of Ferdinand Tollin 1841, Stockholm City Museum.

[21] Nelken, 2003, p. 437.

The many abutments show the number of possible methodological constructions. The different abutments may consist of knowledge in comparative law, the legal systems concerned etc. The sociology of law as an interdisciplinary challenge can be constructed as an abutment or maybe just a stone in the bridge. It is important for the student to methodologically explain how they have constructed the bridge. Even if it is a weak bridge, it is easier to rebuild it if there is strong methodological concern. The water under the bridge represents pragmatic concerns like language skills, the ability to find sources etc. On the other side of the bridge the receiver of the research is waiting. For a bridge constructor it is important to critically evaluate every stone in the construction.

In this context an interdisciplinary approach may also become an abutment in the comparative bridge. Sociology of law is the most emphasized abutment on the basis of the students' orientation at Karlstad University. The sociology of law sometimes enriches studies in comparative law to clarify issues about how laws in different legal systems really function in societies. Roger Cotterrells point of departure is often used in the education to show the closeness and the use of the sociology of law and he indicates several ways in which legal sociology can be fruitful to comparative law.[22]. Most scholars agree with Cotterrell that law is far wider in scope than the norms created and applied by the state institutions. Few scholars think they have detailed knowledge of the sources in both comparative law and sociology and some are questioning an interdisciplinary approach.[23] For some of my students it is fruitful to use an interdisciplinary approach. This topic has been reduced in the curriculum, for example literature by Cotterrell has been removed, but only for reasons of time.

3.2 An abutment: knowledge of legal systems and the development

> I shall examine all these relations; together they form what is called THE SPIRIT OF THE LAWS.
> Montesquieu, *The Spirit of the Laws*, Book I, Chapter III, On positive laws.

This broad introduction with different comparative strategies, from Zweigert's and Kötz's to Legrand's anthology, may seem confusing but also challenging for the students. Without any ambition here to discuss different approaches to comparative legal history *per se,* we initiate with a short discussion of different views on legal families, even if the classification of legal families is not an aim itself.[24] A classification into legal families is a teaching tool, and grouping in

---

22 Cotterrell, 2003, pp. 142 pp.
23 Alan Watson.
24 Bogdan, 2003, p. 78.

legal systems – based on appropriate criteria – is discussed. Law is not static and the grouping of legal systems is often suitable at the time the researcher devised it. Authorities in comparative legal history, like in all sciences, tend to be superseded. Bogdan provides examples of how comparative work, with spectacles from the former socialist countries, could have implications for the classification of legal families: the socialist and the bourgeois.[25] Although David modified his legal families over time, his classification from 1985 appears somewhat dated today.[26] In his third edition, David focuses on what he calls the three major systems: Romano-Germanic, Common Law and the family of Socialist Law, where the socialist family is often devalued today.[27] Zweigert and Kötz also speak of this movement in comparative law and show how researchers tend to emphasize different criteria in grouping legal families.[28] They think that much depends on the period of time of which one is speaking, vulnerable to alteration by historical development and change.[29] In the course, the Swedish legal background, which is and always has been discussed, is vital.

As mentioned above, a functionalistic perspective has earlier dominated our education, *praesumptio similitudinis*: similar solutions to the same problem.[30] Other perspectives discussed, often with a cultural perspective, challenge this approach.[31] Today we discuss for example how Graziadei writes about the functionalist heritage and challenges this functionalistic perspective with Zweigert and Kötz's methodological approach as the focus of his critique.[32] Legal culture will be given more attention in the education even though we have not satisfactorily reached that point yet. This first part of the course is completed after a traditional examination. After this exam the students are given opportunities to work with comparative legal history in part 2 or/and part 3 according to the curriculum.

3.3 Methodological concern: some initial reflections about the tools in the box

After the first course the students have basic knowledge in comparative legal history. My intention is to open up a rich tool box and with this knowledge

---

25 Bogdan, 2003, p. 77.

26 Bogdan, 2003, p. 81.

27 Nordic law, 2007, p. 3 David's macro-comparative law surpassed by Zweigert and Kötz, 1998, p. 64.

28 Zweigert and Kötz, 1998, pp. 63 pp.

29 Zweigert and Kötz, 1998, p. 67.

30 Also Bogdan, 2003, p. 87.

31 Zweigert and Kötz, 1998, p. 67. Zweigert's and Kötz's comment on, for instance, Legrand's cultural perspective, is just to continue with the functional perspective, even if it is only "second-best", until a better system is on offer.

32 Michele Graziadei, 2003, p. 111.

leave it to the students' ability to form their tool, depending on their approach, their topic and earlier studies to use in their article or/and their master thesis.[33] In order to accomplish that, I initially discuss some important starting points in my approach to the subject. This chapter is by no means complete but these areas are important notions for our students to handle.

Which methodological tool box is most suitable for a study in legal comparative history? The answer must be the method best suited to discussing the problem. Like most comparatists, I talk about the idea of family of laws as a construction in some form, irrespective of their scientific background and about comparative work in an ongoing process, an *organic* entity. Changes in law have been made on a regular basis and it is important to have "knowledge of the structure within which the rules and concepts are organized, the meaning of these categories and concepts, and the relationship of the rules among themselves".[34] The suitability of any classification or outline will depend on the context: is the perspective world-wide or regional, public or private law etc?

Law students in Sweden have a fairly good knowledge of *positivism*. Students at Karlstad University devote much of the previous semester to study in the area and often write a legal dogmatic essay based on their area of interest. It is fair to tell that focus in this seminar is on European legal comparison, it may be noted that criticism of the positivistic approach is perhaps harsher outside this area. In Sweden different methods and perspectives have been taught and discussed during the last decade. Some find a strong connection between *functionalism* and positivism.[35] Functionalism has often proclaimed to be the basic methodological principle of comparative law.[36] Leading advocates like Zweigert and Kötz declare that "the legal system of every society faces essentially the same problems, and solves these problems by quite different means though very often with similar results."[37] In the course at Karlstad University the functionalist perspective has had a dominant position, only today to be challenged.[38] The purpose in this paper is not to accentuate the advantages or disadvantages of functionality but just to point out the flora of comparative methods useful in teaching. A critical

[33] It is impossible to develop methods within legal history that will be regarded as common to all legal historians: topics, historical sources, legal and cultural frameworks, the varieties of institutions, geography and, of course, personal interests, are all too disparate factors to provide even a slight possibility of a common notion of what might be called 'the method of legal history'. Dag Michalsen, Reading past legal texts, Unipax, Oslo, 2006, p. 9.

[34] David, 1985, p. 19.

[35] However, compare Michele Graziadei, 2003, p. 111.

[36] Michele Graziadei, 2003, p. 100.

[37] Zweigert and Kötz, 1998, p. 34.

[38] Bogdan, 2003, s. 58.

discussion, involving articles from Legrands anthology, I also find fruitful for the students to share and reflect upon to find their own perception.

4 How to wear spectacles that are *good enough*

In my paper I would finally like to focus on the possibilities of grasping knowledge in a course like the one at Karlstad University, to cope with comparative legal history, with spectacles that have good enough sharpness. This is not a discussion about an abutment or a block in the comparative bridge, instead it is the firmness of the construction (validity and reliability); a poor bridge will collapse. I think this matter is important regardless of the student's methodological standpoint. Firstly, practical difficulty is, of course, always a barrier to good enough work.[39] Secondly, as is pointed out in Zweigert and Kötz, the fact that the beginner "jumps to the conclusion that a foreign system has 'nothing to report' on a particular problem" is often an issue. Then "one must rethink the original question and purge it of all the dogmatic accretions of one's own system".[40] From another perspective Graziadei finds that a successful comparison depends on the comparatist's ability to "eradicate the preconception of his native legal system" while framing comparative research.[41]

The issue I would like to stress may be compared to a walk on a tightrope with, on the one hand, the requirement of in-depth knowledge regarding the chosen legal historical conception and, on the other, a realistic scrutiny concerning what is possible to accomplish during, for instance, a course at the university. The goal of encouraging further comparative studies in legal history must still remain. At the same time, we must have a realistic view of the method and the possibility of handling the comparative legal method. In my opinion we must encourage our students to wear spectacles that are *good enough* for comparative studies in legal matters. The comparatist must "develop a certain familiarity with the foreign 'culture' and its internal view. But complete understanding is not really possible either for those external to, or even those internal to, the system.[42]

---

[39] Pragmatic questions like poor language skills, poor knowledge of other countries' legal matters and lack of opportunity to find original sources etc can also be an obstacle.

[40] Zweigert and Kötz, 1998, p. 35.

[41] Michele Graziadei, 2003, p. 102. Note to Zweigert and Kötz, 1998, p. 35.

[42] Munday, 2003, introduction, p. 20.

5 Some concluding remarks

At Karlstad University we provide education in comparative legal history in the students' final semester for those who want to take the degree of Master in Jurisprudence. These students have different focuses in their education and to bring them together and provide them all with a meaningful course, we have found a theoretical and methodological approach adequate. The students are then able to develop comparative legal history in their article and even in their final essay. In that way the students can develop a skill in areas that are of concern for their potential employment. I find it important in this course to give the students a rich palette of methodological knowledge. It is possible that this more demanding methodological approach – here illustrated by a comparative legal historical bridge – is too challenging. I hope this is a step towards a curiosity towards comparative legal history which also opens our students' eyes to its benefits in their education.

To summarize then, I have stressed that in teaching comparative legal history, one must be aware of short-sightedness when working with systems of law. Therefore this Pufendorf Seminar on How to teach European Comparative Legal History is crucial. In recent years the functional perspective has been challenged and it is interesting to see how researchers approach comparative legal history. Personally, I can point to the importance that we at Karlstad University place on giving more attention to a new perspective which deals with legal culture; we have not yet reached that point satisfactorily. In this article I have also discussed what is *good enough* in comparative work. On a fundamental level researchers from different methodological standpoints can agree that the student must have the ability to grasp some kind of basic knowledge – like the cup of espresso ordered. Regardless of the choice of methodology and different demands regarding what is *good enough* for comparative studies in legal matters, the conclusion is that it must be explicable and defensible. The student must show the teacher/reader that he can walk dry-shod over the bridge. It is also the teacher's obligation to keep up with the ongoing methodological developments because it is necessary to face new demands in the legal arena. I hope this article – like a Woody Allen movie – will encourage students to adopt a *good enough* approach in their comparative legal historical struggles, with spectacles adapted to their vision in question.

References

Alvesson, Mats, och Sköldberg, Kaj, (2008) *Tolkning och reflektion,* uppl. 2, Stockholm, Studentlitteratur AB.

Bogdan, Michael, (2003) *Komparativ rättskunskap*, Norstedts juridik AB, 2 uppl., Stockholm.

Comparative Legal Studies: Traditions and Transitions, (2003) Pierre Legrand and Rodrick Munday, (eds.) Cambridge University Press, Cambridge.

Cotterrell, Roger, (2003) *Comparatists and Sociology*, In *Comparative Legal Studies: Traditions and Transitions*, Pierre Legrand and Rodrick Munday, (eds.) Cambridge University Press, Cambridge, p. 131–153.

David, René, and John E.C. Brierley, (1985) *Major Legal Systems in the World Today: An Introduction to the Comparative Study of Law*, Third Edition, Stevens and Sons, London.

Graziadei, Michele, (2003) *The Functionalist heritage,* In *Comparative Legal Studies: Traditions and Transitions*, Pierre Legrand and Rodrick Munday, (eds.) Cambridge University Press, Cambridge, p. 100–127.

Lasser, Mitchel de S.-O.-l'E., (2003) *The question of understanding*, In *Comparative Legal Studies: Traditions and Transitions*, Pierre Legrand and Rodrick Munday, (eds.) Cambridge University Press, Cambridge, p. 197–239.

Legrand, Pierre, (2003) *The same and the different*, In *Comparative Legal Studies: Traditions and Transitions*, Pierre Legrand and Rodrick Munday, (eds.) Cambridge University Press, Cambridge, p. 240–311.

Montesquieu, (1989) *The Spirit of the laws*, translated and edited by Anne M. Cohler, Basia Carolyn Miller, Harold Samuel Stone, Cambridge University Press, Cambridge.

Nordic Law – Between Tradition and Dynamism, (2007) Editors: Jaakko Husa, Kimmo Nuotio, Heikki Pihlajamäki, Ius Commune Europaeum, Intersentia Antwerpen, Oxford.

Rosen, Lawrence, (2003) *Beyond compare,* In *Comparative Legal Studies: Traditions and Transitions*, Pierre Legrand and Rodrick Munday, (eds.) Cambridge University Press, Cambridge, p. 493–510.

Whitman, James Q., (2003) The neo-romantic turn, In *Comparative Legal Studies: Traditions and Transitions*, Pierre Legrand and Rodrick Munday, (eds.) Cambridge University Press, Cambridge, p. 312–344.

Zweigert, Konrad, and Hein Kötz, (1998) *An Introduction to Comparative Law*, 3rd edition, Oxford.

Per Nilsén and Christian Häthén

How to Teach European Comparative Legal History A Lund Perspective

In this presentation, we would like to shortly address not only the question "how?" as in "How to Teach European Comparative Legal History" but also touch upon the questions "why?" and (being legal historians) "since when?" In other words, the topic for our presentation could, somewhat lengthy, be described as "How and Why to Teach European Comparative Legal History – and Since When?" The geographical limitations are those of Sweden and, more restricted, those of Lund University and its Faculty of Law.

I.

Per Nilsén

In order to answer the question "since when?" we have to go back to the seventeenth century. Many of to-days structures in the Swedish (and Finnish) public sector – including the field of law and legal learning – have their roots in this period of expansion, reorganisation and reform. Politically, the century was characterised by the rise of Swedish military power and in the 1660ies much of the Baltic Sea area was under Swedish domination. This development called for educated staff in the various branches of public administration. After the Reformation, the late medieval university in Uppsala was reopened and in the 1620ies, a number of grammar schools were founded in cathedral cities all over the realm. Of those grammar schools, two were later reorganised as universities: the University of Tartu (Dorpat) in Livonia and Turku/Åbo in Finland. Both universities were structured after the pattern of Uppsala and when Lund University was opened in 1668, the model of Uppsala was followed here as well.[1]

Uppsala University had been granted new statutes in 1655, a set of regula-

[1] A broad presentation of the development (in Swedish) can be found in Sten Lindroth, *Svensk lärdomshistoria. Stormaktstiden*. Stockholm 1975/1989, 15–56.

tions concerning administration and teaching which were to form a long-lived standard for Swedish higher education. Even if a multitude of royal letters, ordinances (and often, bad finances) altered the original picture of the Swedish universities and their faculties, the core remained intact for many years. The Swedish standard law faculty of the period – modelled after the Uppsala prototype – consisted of two chairs. The duties of the professors were duly described in the statutes:

> "The first of the law professors shall, to begin with, interpret the Swedish private law with necessary explanations for them, who recently started the study. Then, when they have made progress in Swedish law, the general law of nations and Roman law, he shall show them how the Swedish law has its origins in the law of nature and in the positive, divine and human laws, especially those of the educated peoples and he shall compare them with the Roman law and the laws of the ancient Swedes and Goths – both within and outside the Realm –; likewise [shall he compare the Swedish law] with the neighbouring laws of the Germans, Danes and other peoples. [...]
>
> The second law professor shall every year read and conclude *institutiones juris civilis romani,* adapted to the laws of the fatherland; after the students have attained the elementary knowledge in law, he shall show them the simplest way to a thorough knowledge of Roman law as it can be obtained by the other parts of the above mentioned law; in doing so he shall demonstrate the foundations of the rules of Roman law, basing his teaching more on the law of nature, the positive, divine and human, as well as on legal regulations, especially such of the educated peoples, than on unnecessary quotations of a multitude of interpreters. [...]"[2]

[2] "Utaf Juris Professorerna skall den förste läsa öfver Svenska Privat-Rätten, först för dem, som äro nybegynnare uti detta studium, helt enkelt och blott med nödvändig utläggning av texten, men sedan skall han för dem, som uti så väl Svenska Lagen som allmänna Folkrätten och Romerska Lagen äro något för sig komne, visa Svenska Lagens källor uti Natur-Rätten, samt positifva [!] Gudomliga och Menskliga, i synnerhet de bildade folkslagens, lagar, och anställa jemförelse med Romerska Lagen, äfvensom med de gamla så väl inländska som utländska Svea och Göthers, våra grannars, Tyskarnas, Danskarnas och andra folkslags lagar. [...] Den andre skall årligen genomgå Institutioner Civilis Romani, lämpade efter Fäderneslandets lagar, och bemöda sig att de studerande, sedan de inhämtat Lagfarenhetens första grunder, ledas den genaste vägen till den djupare kännedom af Romerska lagfarenheten, som af de öfriga delarna af ofvannämnde Lag kan inhämtas, i det han visar de Romerska Lagarnas grunder, mera med åberopande af Natur-Rätten, samt Positiva, Gudomliga och menskliga, i synnerhet de bildade Folkslagens Lagar, än genom onödiga citationer af olika Lagtolkares meningar. [...]" Translated (PN) from the Swedish language version in *Lunds akademis constitutioner med öfversättning* [...] ed. Fredrik Schrevelius. Lund 1832, 119–121.

The emphasis on an educational comparative perspective is striking: the professor in Swedish law should not only teach the students how the national law had its roots in natural law etc. but also compare the positive law with Roman law, older national legislation and the laws of adjacent regions such as Germany and Denmark. The second professor – the one responsible for Roman law – should lecture on the Institutes by adapting the material to the legal order of Sweden and compare Roman law principles with principles of natural law and those of educated peoples.

As a matter of fact, there is a well-known result of this 17th century way of law teaching. It is a book, written by the professor in Swedish law at the University of Turku/Åbo, Johan Stiernhöök (1596–1675)[3], called *De jure Sveonum et Gothorum vetusto* – "On the Ancient Law of the Swedes and Goths" –, printed in 1672.[4] This book, devoted to Swedish legal history, rendered Stiernhöök a long standing (perhaps, even eternal) reputation of being either the "father of Swedish legal science" or "our first [Swedish] legal historian" – or possibly both.[5] In his preface to the benevolent reader Stiernhöök states that the book is a direct consequence of the regulations in the University statutes: as professor in Swedish law, he had to compare the Swedish law with the Roman. In order to do so, he started to sort out obsolete regulations and finally, he had a surprisingly long list with antiquated Swedish law regulations. This list, he planned to use as a short introduction to his course where he – according to the preface – wanted to compare older Swedish institutions with Roman. But the list grew, and finally – very much thanks to the extraordinary support of the Chancellor of the Realm, Count Magnus Gabriel De la Gardie (1622–86) – it was published as a book.[6]

When studying Stiernhöök's text, his underlying comparative perspective becomes clear. And he does not just compare Swedish law with the Roman. All in all, he makes 176 comparisons between Swedish and foreign law. In 28 cases Norwegian law is the object for comparison, in 23 cases Roman law, in 22 Danish, in 19 Germanic (mainly with reference to Tacitus), in 18 Gothic

---

[3] About Stiernhöök, see *Johan Olofsson Stiernhöök. Biografi och studier 1596–1996*. Rättshistoriska studier 20, 1996.

[4] Facsimile edition of the original latin text as Joh. O. Stiernhöök, *De jure Sveonum et Gothorum vetusto*. Rättshistoriskt bibliotek 1, 1962; Swedish translation as Johan O:son Stiernhöök, *Om svears och götars forna rätt*. Rättshistoriskt bibliotek 2, 1981.

[5] "Fadren för den svenska lagfarenhetens studium" (Erik Gustaf Geijer), "vår förste rättshistoriker" (Jan Eric Almquist) – see Kjell Å. Modéer: "Historia, juridik och politik. En skiss till en vetenskapshistorisk Stiernhöök-biografi" in *Johan Olofsson Stiernhöök. Biografi och studier 1596–1996*. Rättshistoriska studier 20, 1996, 97–104.

[6] Johan O:son Stiernhöök, *Om svears och götars forna rätt*. Rättshistoriskt bibliotek 2, 1981, xxi–xxii.

(mainly of Spanish origin), in 14 Saxon, in eight German (in general) and so on. When it comes to conformity between the Swedish law and the foreign, Norwegian law tops the league, followed by Danish, Germanic, Saxon and Roman law. So, it's perhaps not surprising, that Stiernhöök some 270 years before Zweigert and Kötz could draw attention to the fact, that there was some special connection between the legal orders in this part of Europe. He says, that

> "This part of the North, which the ancient authors called [...] Scandinavia, is populated by original inhabitants [...]. Those peoples, who at home neither have tolerated nor have had any acquaintance with foreign powers [...] were in times past ruled by [...] three kings, but to day by two kings. Since they were united by the same heaven and earth and were mixed together by marriage and commerce, they all lived under almost the same laws."[7]

Of course – it's tempting to compare this statement with the statement of Zweigert and Kötz:

> "Die Verwandschaft der nordischen Rechte erklärt sich daraus, daß zwischen den skandinavischen Ländern seit jeher besonders enge politische und kulturelle Beziehungen bestanden haben." [8]

But perhaps even more interesting is, I think, is the fact that Stiernhöök's book "On the Ancient Law of the Swedes and Goths" was the result of his work as a university teacher guided by the provisions in the university statutes – regulations which, as we have seen, had a strong focus on the comparative perspective.

The reason for this emphasis is of to be found in the rather uncertain state of Swedish law at the time. The seventeenth century Swedish society was still ruled by the norms of medieval legislation[9] but was often confronted with "new" areas of legal problems – problems which often only partly were regulated in royal ordinances or other forms of written statements. Therefore the adjudication in cases not regulated in written law, was influenced by Roman law ideas. The formal position of foreign regulations as a legitimate source of law was never

---

[7] English translation (PN) of Johan O:son Stiernhöök, *Om svears och götars forna rätt*. Rättshistoriskt bibliotek 2, 1981, 1–2.

[8] Konrad Zweigert, Hein Kötz, *Einführung in die Rechtsvergleichung auf dem Gebiet des Privatrechts*. 3., neubearbeitete Aufl. Tübingen 1996, 272.

[9] The most important written legal sources were the 1442 edition of the Land Code (Kristofers or yngre landslagen) and the even older Town Code (stadslagen). A shorter German language survey of the most important developments in Swedish legislation from the middle of the 14th century until 1734 can be found in Dieter Strauch, "Quellen, Aufbau und Inhalt des Gesetzbuches" in *Das schwedische Reichsgesetzbuch von 1734*, ed. Wolfgang Wagner. Ius Commune Sonderhefte 29, 1986, esp. 61–66.

the less a bit unclear but – of course – Roman principles could be understood as *ratio scripta.*[10]

During the last part of the seventeenth century, the position of the King was strengthened. As a consequence, a law commission was formed in 1686 and in 1736, after fifty years of legislative work, the new Law of the Realm of Sweden gained legal force.[11] This codification – usually called the Code of 1734 after the year it was approved by the Diet – is still regarded as the fundament of modern Swedish legislation. By the Code and subsequent legislation, Swedish law gained internal strength and the 17th century openness in matters regarding sources of law was slowly replaced with a more and more stable canon of national regulations, finally forming a sturdy hierarchy of norms from ordinances, over acts of laws to constitutional regulations.

To a certain extent, the Swedish 17th century situation can be compared to the situation of the outgoing 20th century and of today. In 1995 Sweden somewhat reluctant became a member of the European Union and – being a dualistic country – incorporated the European Convention on Human Rights. Since then, and according to the act of incorporation (Swedish Code of Statutes 1994:1219), the Convention shall apply "as law here in the country".[12] The formal status of the Convention is nevertheless a bit unclear, since it is also mentioned in the Constitution. The Instrument of Government stipulates, that no act of law or other provision may be adopted which contravenes Sweden's undertakings under the Convention.[13] So – does the convention have the same status in the national legal system as an act of law, or is it to be understood as something between the traditional, hierarchical levels of acts of law and constitutional regulations? In a much discussed case of the Supreme Court in

---

[10] The reception of Roman law in Sweden during the 17th century has been investigated in several books and articles, such as Stig Jägerskiöld, *Studier rörande receptionen av främmande rätt i Sverige under den yngre landslagens tid.* Lund 1963, Heikki Ylikangas, "Kampen mellan naturrätt och romersk rätt i Sverige. Två förklaringar" in *Den svenska juridikens uppblomstring i 1600-talets [...] stormaktssamhälle.* Rättshistoriska studier 9, 1984, 145–159 (including a short summary in English) and Lars Björne, *Patrioter och institutionalister. Den nordiska rättsvetenskapens historia. Del I. Tiden före år 1815.* Rättshistoriskt bibliotek 52, 1995, 22–38, 42–51.

[11] See Dieter Strauch, "Quellen, Aufbau und Inhalt des Gesetzbuches" in *Das schwedische Reichsgesetzbuch von 1734,* ed. Wolfgang Wagner, Ius Commune Sonderhefte 29, 1986, 66–106. The preparatory works of the Code of 1734 (such as the minutes of the law commission and of the Diet etc.) are published in Wilhelm Sjögren (ed.), *Förarbetena till Sveriges Rikes Lag 1686–1734 I–VIII.* Up(p)sala 1900–1909.

[12] "Som lag här i landet [...]". Lag (1994:1219) om den europeiska konventionen angående skydd för de mänskliga rättigheterna och de grundläggande friheterna.

[13] "Lag eller annan föreskrift får ej meddelas i strid med Sveriges åtaganden på grund av den europiska konventionen angående skydd för de mänskliga rättigheterna och de grundläggande friheterna." Regeringsformen (Instrument of Government), 2:23.

Stockholm in November 2005 concerning a sermon of a Pentecostal pastor criticizing homosexual behaviour, the Supreme Court disregarded (at least) the preparatory works to the national statute which criminalized statements of the kind. Instead, the Court launched an interpretation which was said to be in agreement with the case law of the European Court of Human Rights and the pastor was acquitted.[14]

In other words – this hardly being a secret – today's national legal order is in a state of transformation, not only as a consequence of the EU membership but just as well as of the incorporation of the ECHR. The national hierarchy of norms is crumbling. There is openness in the discussion, not totally unlike the situation of the 17th century. A wider perspective – global or, out of necessity, at least European – is thus essential in legal education, also if you look at it from a local and individual perspective.

To a certain degree, this is also reflected in the Higher Education Ordinance,[15] which can be said to be a late successor of the 17th century university statutes. Here, some importance is attached to the fact that the student should not only demonstrate knowledge of the role of the legal system in a national but also in an international context. More details are not given, which means that the universities and their teaching staffs have good possibilities of influencing the curriculum; such local regulations are given in the syllabi of each LL.M. programme,[16] decided by the local Faculty and Educational Boards. The student representatives in the different University and Faculty bodies are always keen on stressing the importance of internationalization but, when it comes to the practicalities, sometimes the interest is more limited: English language text books are not always popular in law courses and literature in other languages (such as German or French) are impossible to use.

Having dealt with the question "why?", let us now turn our attention to "how?" In Lund, the comparative perspective has a central function within the frames of legal history. The basic, compulsory course in the subject is placed in the sixth (out of totally nine) semesters. This course is thematically structured around a range of central topics (such as legal ideologies, law and religion, codification, modernism, law in totalitarian states etc.) and contains a mix of Internet-based chronological lectures – providing the students, who often are lacking (deeper) historical knowledge, the necessary basics –, traditional hall lectures and semi-

[14] The so-called Åke Green case, NJA 2005, 805. Cf. Martin Sunnqvist's article in this volume.

[15] Högskoleförordning (1993:100).

[16] Such as *Utbildningsplan för juristprogrammet vid Lunds universitet. January 18, 2010* and *Kursplan för allmän rättslära och rättshistoria. September 8, 2009*. Both are downloadable the home page of the Lund Law Faculty: www.jur.lu.se.

naries. Per semester, the normal number of students is somewhere between 90 and 120. The developments in Swedish law are centrally positioned but are explained and commented upon from a European (and North American) perspective with the help of the course literature.[17] At the end of the course (*im wunderschönen Monat Mai* or in the somewhat less *wunderschönen* month of January), there is a four hour open book examination. Whether this is the best form of examination or not, is an open question – at the moment, the teachers are discussing to introduce an oral examination instead of the traditional, written one. According to the compulsory course evaluations, a majority of the students seem to like the course, since it apparently does give the legal material a wider dimension and context.

The Faculty is right now preparing to reform the LL.M.-programme in accordance with the Bologna process and in the future, legal history will be combined with positive comparative law into one course of 7.5 ECTS. The two disciplines will remain in the sixth semester – after the course in international law and just before the planned 15 ECTS bachelor thesis. We are very happy about this position within the curriculum: legal history will also in the future be placed late in the program (which saves the discipline from becoming a sort of introductory course to law) and the cooperation with positive comparative law is bound to be even more intensified, hopefully giving inspiration to interesting bachelor thesises (or even research projects).

Since all students of the basic course have finished the early semesters within the national LL.M.-programme and to a large extent already have been socialized into the Swedish lawyer kind of human being, many of the peculiarities – or difficulties – in teaching students more acquainted to other legal systems do not occur here, but on advanced level, we give an English language course, more specifically devoted to comparative European legal history, led by Christian Häthén.

[17] Christian Häthén, *Stat och straff. Rättshistoriska perspektiv*. Lund 2004, Christian Häthén & Per Nilsén, *Svensk historisk lagbok. Rättshistoriska källtexter*. Lund 2004, Kjell Å. Modéer, *Historiska rättskällor. En introduktion i rättshistoria*. Stockholm 1997, Kjell Å. Modéer, *Juristernas nära förflutna. Rättskulturer i förändring*. Stockholm 2009, Peter Stein, *Roman Law in European History*. Cambridge University Press, 1999.

II.

Christian Häthén

In the second part of the 1990ies, the curriculum of the LL.M.-programme in Lund was gradually changed and each subject represented during the first years of study was asked to develop a range of depth courses. Some of these courses had to be open both for Swedish students and exchange students and, of course, these courses had to be given in English. Legal history as a discipline is well suited for this kind of course, but we realized that the theme had to be rather broad to appeal both to Swedish and to students from other European countries. We started to plan a course with a comparative perspective and I must admit that we were inspired by our colleagues from Uppsala: they had described their English language course (open to both Swedish and foreign students) at a national pedagogical conference. We wanted to do something similar – but at the same time do it our own way. One aspect we tried to copy from Uppsala was the idea of trying to make the students active so that they *learnt* rather than they were *taught*. We also wanted to use the knowledge the foreign students brought from their home universities to ad to the comparative aspect of the course. We wanted to make a course where the students could work together in groups but also have a period of individual work. Finally, we wanted to use a system of examination that could make it possible to balance the results of group activities and the results of individual studies and essay writing in a fair way.

The course was given the first time during the autumn semester of 1998 and it has been given twice yearly since then. The first time we had five students – mostly Swedish as I remember – but since then, the group of international students has grown considerably and now, we usually have about 20 to 25 students from all over the world. The course is an appreciated part of our international program and it attracts students from other faculties in Lund as well.

The basic ideas we had when planning the course remains unchanged but, of course, we have learnt much during the years: we have understood that some topics are better to study than others and that some pedagogical ideas are more realistic that others. The course has developed and we have changed literature and examination forms; we have added more lectures and we give more assistance during the students' essay writing period. We have also revised the course syllabus and added new learning outcomes. According to the syllabus, the student shall "[g]ain insight into themes such as *ius com-*

mune, federalism, judiciaries, human rights, legal science and codification, law and politics from a European dimension". The student shall demonstrate knowledge and understanding of

- the cultures and history of the major legal systems of Europe;
- the development of legal science and legal education;
- constitutional ideas, their manifestations and interactions with human rights;
- the various institutional developments within criminal law, civil law and procedural law.

The course runs for ten weeks, always during the first half of the autumn and spring semesters. In today's system, the course is given 15 ECTS credits. Full time studies are required and even if the students try, it is difficult for them to study something else at the time of the course. We organize the course in three stages. First we give some basic lectures. The numbers of these lectures have varied but I must admit that during the years we have gradually added more of these lectures, since we have found that it is necessary to shape a common platform of basic knowledge of European legal history. We have a number of students from other continents as well and their knowledge of European legal history is often rather limited. I will return to this later in my presentation.

After the period of basic lectures we introduce three projects. These projects are group assignments and the students are supposed to work in small groups of three to five participants. They get an introduction and the topic is presented in a general way. We try to give the basic historical and legal background so that the groups understand the context before they start to work with the assignment. About five days later, they make an oral presentation in front of the whole study group; immediately after this presentation we have a question and answer session. The teacher directs this session but the idea is that the other students have to be active, asking questions that are connected to their own topic. In this way, the teachers listen to all the presentations; if the study group is big, it can take most of a day. The groups are also required to make shorter written presentation that can be added to the course home page.

Since a couple of years we have settled for three topics that have proved to be best suited for the group assignments. The topics are also in line with the research interests of the teachers which creates a win-win situation. The projects are: *Constitutional Law*, *Penal Law* and *Legal Science and Education*. I will give an example of the group assignments in the *Penal Law* project:

Group 1
Describe the development of penal theories in *Europe* during the 19th century and try to analyse the influence of Cesare Beccaria and the influence of social and biological science.

Groups 2 and 3
In what way did the modern penal theories change the focus of punishments and the penal structure in *Germany* and *France* (group 2), and *Great Britain* (group 3) during the 19th and 20th centuries.

Group 4
Compare the general development of penal law in *Europe* and the *US* during the 19th and 20th centuries.

The groups are welcome to use the course literature but are also provided with further reading from articles and books. Each group has to buy a reader with a compilation of material but we also encourage them to do research of their own and, of course, to use the knowledge they bring from their home countries.

When the three projects have been presented, the students have to pass a written examination. The form of this examination has changed during the years but today the students have to write a longer text in an open book examination. We have experimented with home examination but that did not prove to be successfulAfter the projects and written examination the students use about four to five weeks for individual essay writing. With the help of a tutor each student chooses a topic within the framework of the course (i.e. it has to be *European*, *comparative* and related to *legal history*). She gets assistance from the tutor on a drop in basis and sometimes the tutors provide literature from their own libraries. At the end of this period, a seminar is arranged: the student presents her essay and another student prepares an oral opposition. Two teachers are acting as tutors and the final seminars can take a day or two.

As was mentioned earlier, we wanted to base the grading of the students both on the results of their group assignments and on the results of their individual studies and writings. To achieve this balance, we developed a three stage grading system. First, the student get a maximum of five points from her group assignment, then she can get a maximum of 35 points from her written examination and finally, she can get a maximum of 50 points from her essay. All in all, this can give a maximum of 100 points (even if no student has achieved that yet).

By using a 100 point maximum we can also easily adopt the grading results to the ECTS grading system.

Finally some words on the literature we use now. I do not think I exaggerate when I say that the question of literature has been the most problematic question we have faced during these years. We have tried a number of different texts, but none of them has been totally satisfying. Some texts have been too limited and others have been too broad. Of course, the text book has to be in English and that limits the choice somewhat. It must also deal with the legal history of England, Scotland and Continental Europe. It must be written as a text book and not in a too scholarly way; it has to give perspectives and not dig down too much in detail. We all know that the number of books available is limited. Since a couple of years, we have used Robinson/Fergus/Gordon: *European Legal History. Sources and Institution* (3 ed.). In some aspects it is much too detailed and in other aspects it focus a little too much upon the legal history of Scotland. Finally it does not cover the most recent legal history development in Europe – which is an important aspect of the course. Even if we give the students reading instructions, this is not a satisfactory situation. Until some of us here or some other colleague(s) decide to write a new text book on the legal history of Europe, we are lost in this situation.

During these years we have been confronted with a number of interesting problems concerning the very different backgrounds of the students. As I mentioned earlier, the students really comes from all over the world and in the same group there can be students from Sweden, Italy, California, Singapore, Japan, New Zeeland and Scotland. Just to take an example from the spring semester this year. To use the modern, politically correct terminology: this creates challenges and opportunities. But it can also create some big difficulties. The outcome of the mixture can be very interesting, with great possibilities for the students (and teachers) to learn from each other. The students can be a source of knowledge. As teachers, we try to use the different backgrounds as a pedagogical resource and I think we have been successful in many ways. This said we also have to admit that the interesting student mix creates some rather tough pedagogical challenges. I think we can identify four problematic student related situations. When I use the word "different" in these situations I just want to express that something is different from the original expectations of the teachers:

– students with different learning backgrounds;
– students from different pedagogical backgrounds;
– students with different language skills;
– students with different attitudes to essay writing;

I will briefly comment on those four situations.

1. Students with different learning backgrounds

In a student group as large as ours and with so many different continents and countries represented it is obvious that all the students can not have an identical basis of legal and historical knowledge. The course is, first of all, aimed at law students but we have accepted students from other fields of study such as economy, history and political science. Normally this works out quite well. The group assignments are, as you have seen from my examples quite open and it is possible for the students to find views points that are not strictly legal history. To sum up this aspect of difference, I don't think that it is such a big problem as long as the teachers are aware of the student backgrounds.

Among the law students in the course, there is another kind of problem. The Erasmus exchange program is open to students from all over Europe but the time during their studies when students choose to go abroad varies a lot. This means that we sometime will get a student being rather early in her studies and sometimes a student that is almost at end of her studies. This is not necessarily a problem either, but the national law studies curricula differ a lot and the study of legal history is not always in the beginning of the law studies. This means that there can be students attending the course with quite advanced knowledge of legal history and they can work in a project group with a student without any knowledge of the discipline. This is a problem and we have tried to confront this difficulty by providing the first basic lectures. As I pointed out, those lectures are pedagogically rather traditional and we do not expect much activity from the students; our ambition is to create an acceptable common ground of knowledge and the lectures serve our aim rather well in that aspect.

2. Students from different pedagogical backgrounds

Even if the first lectures are pedagogically rather traditional we encourage the students to be active and to ask questions so we can establish a pedagogic dialogue, especially since dialogue and student activity is a basic aspect of the course. To put it a little bluntly: the role of the teachers is, as we see it, to assist the student in her own learning process. This means that the teachers are not teaching all the time but they are often listening to student presentations, adding questions to a discussion or commenting upon the presentation. It is also fairly easy for the students to get into contact with the teachers outside the schedule.

Generally, this way of conducting the course is accepted and often highly appreciated but there are always students that are used to study in very big study groups with extremely limited dialogue and with no possibility for questions. These students normally expect the teacher to present the necessary facts that are to be learnt by heart and they are initially not at ease in this more open climate. Perhaps I have exaggerated this difficulty somewhat. Normally the students adjust to the new pedagogic situation and enjoy the possibilities it presents and we get course evaluations with comments such as: "This is the first time during my studies that I have been active in class". The different pedagogical backgrounds are not a major problem. As a problem it can be overcome by informing the students about the pedagogical techniques during the first weeks of the course. The teachers also have to be a little extra observant of how the individual student acts in the group and sometimes the teachers have to encourage some of the students a little extra.

3. Students with different language skills

I think this is a difficulty that all teachers of courses with international students have experienced. If we mix native English speakers with students from Asia and Europe in a study group it is obvious that there will be a difference in language skills. I always start the course by saying that we all have to speak and understand "global English". Normally, the language difference does not constitute an insurmountable problem but, of course, it is a problem if the students do not understand the lectures or if they are unable to do a presentation in understandable English. In the most problematic cases, the students have difficulties in oral performances but are able to write quite good English. I find those cases most often among the Asian students. Probably this has to do with the way languages are taught in school. The training is concentrated on text studies but talking and training dialogue is neglected. I also guess that American and English films and television programmes are dubbed in most countries so they have not heard spoken English.

We do not want to treat the students differently but if it is completely impossible to understand the presentations we normally accept shorter presentations or in exceptional cases a written presentation as a substitute for the oral. Generally the language skills are quite acceptable and I think it is important to state that the course is not a language course but a course in legal history – we have to live with a variation in the (global) English.

4. Students with different attitudes to essay writing

One course related problem that has been difficult to handle is the problem of lacking originality. With this I mean the tendency to copy sources without clear references and to compose a full essay by copy and paste method. This is obviously cheating, or if you want to put it a little bit more elegantly: academic fraud. Of course, this is not acceptable. The difficulty is that in some academic cultures copy and paste is a method of compiling facts and true originality is not encouraged in undergraduate studies. Naturally, we encourage students to think freely and to base the essay on well formulated questions, on literature and on sources. Occasionally, our instructions can come into conflict with the techniques and methods the students have brought with them from their home university.

As I have stated above, the essay is an important part of the examination and it comes right at the end of the course. The text is handed in and we have little possibility to make any changes in the text or to help the student to correct the result. Each student has a tutor and during the supervision the tutors try to instruct the student and to encourage her to be creative and to use the sources without copying them. Apart from our own knowledge and familiarity with the sources, we can get help from a web-based search programme and we do identify some unacceptable essays. But, with a more than ten year perspective, I must say these are quite few. In my experience, this is mostly a problem for a small group of students. We try to avoid the situation by supervision – if we find a text that is mostly copied we fail the student on a preliminary level and instruct her to rewrite the text or to write another essay.

So – there *are* problems in dealing with a student group that is so divers as ours but generally I think these problems are quite manageable and the individual adjustments are acceptable. With the experience we have got from more than ten years of providing this course I think that we can anticipate some difficulties and that we can handle the others in a fair and acceptable way.

During these two days, we have not only discussed our experiences in teaching European comparative legal history, but also been discussing the possibility to establish a network of legal historians on the European level. We are welcoming the idea, being confident that a closer co-operation would be beneficial for both and teaching and research. Perhaps, such a co-operation could result in a new text book with contributions from all over Europe. Perhaps such a co-operation also would enable us to arrange an exchange programme, so that teachers from different universities in different countries could visit each other and each other's courses. There are definitely possibilities in co-operation – and in comparison.

Epilogue

Miloš Vec

Juristischer Polyzentrismus[1] Wie unterrichtet man vergleichende europäische Rechtsgeschichte?

Auch Fragen, die offen klingen, können Suggestionen enthalten. »How to teach European comparative legal history?« lautete der Titel eines Workshops, der vom 19.–21. August 2009 im südschwedischen Lund stattfand. Eingeladen hatten die örtlichen Rechtshistoriker Kjell Å. Modéer und Per Nilsén. Die Vorannahme, die der Titel transportierte, wurde durch das einleitende Referat Modéers begründet und als Imperativ bekräftigt: Ja, wir sollen vergleichende europäische Rechtsgeschichte lehren! Modéer scheint die europäisch-vergleichende Perspektive in diesen Zeiten hochgradig angemessen, da sie nationale Kurzsichtigkeiten und Engführungen überwinde. Den Wandel skizzierte er mit den Stichworten der Europäisierung des Rechts, der Internationalisierung der Studenten in den universitären Kursen und gesellschaftlich allgemeiner mit den zunehmenden Konflikten der Kulturen sowie der »postkolonialen Situation«. Juristisch habe sich die Perspektive von der Pluralität der Rechtssysteme hin zur Pluralität der Rechtsordnungen gewandelt. Unter diesen Umständen sollten, so Modéers Credo, Rechtsgeschichte und Rechtsvergleichung kooperieren und neue Perspektiven auf das Recht entwickeln. Immerhin gebe es ja Theorien der Rechtsvergleichung, allerdings lehre die Erfahrung, dass sie im Unterricht entweder dominierten oder fehlten. Wie aber soll der Rechtshistoriker dieses Programm in der Lehre umsetzen?

Bevor die kleine Schar europäischer Rechtshistoriker ihre Positionen und Bekenntnisse zum Programm einer vergleichend-europäischen Rechtsgeschichte abgeben konnte, durfte sie sich mit dem Blick von außen auseinandersetzen. Eröffnungsrednerin Maeva Marcus (Washington), Präsidentin der American Society for Legal History (ASLH), berichtete von der Lehre der Rechtsgeschichte in Übersee. Ihr Bericht über die dortigen Zustände klang kritisch und war wohl

[1] First published in Rechtsgeschichte. *Zeitschift des Max-Planck-Instituts für europäische Rechtsgeschichte* 16, 2010, 293–299. The editors wish to thank Dr. Vec for kind permission to reprint his report in this volume.

auch so gegenüber ihren europäischen Adressaten gemeint, mit denen sie erkennbar sympathisierte: Obwohl die amerikanische Rechtsgeschichte zunehmend Aufmerksamkeit empfange, stehe es nicht durchgehend gut um das Fach, zumal in der Lehre: »many publish, few read, few graduate«, klagte Marcus. Um die personellen Lücken in der Lehre zu stopfen, würden immerhin viele Gastdozenten in die USA eingeladen. Sie aber sähen sich mit Studierenden konfrontiert, die oft begrenzte Fremdsprachenkenntnisse aufwiesen. Hinzu kämen Fragmentierungen des Fachs, die dem wissenschaftlichen Austausch innerhalb einer als akademische Einheit verstandenen Rechtsgeschichte abträglich sind. Kurz: Aus Marcus' Sicht stellten sich die Verhältnisse in Europa durchaus positiv dar: Vielsprachigkeit, universitäre Verankerung und Austausch zwischen Forschung und Lehre seien auf dem alten Kontinent in höherem Maße vorhanden als in den USA – gut, dass wir verglichen haben.

Die folgende Debatte unter den europäischen Rechtshistorikern griff die Leitfrage des universitären Unterrichts in vielen Variationen auf. Gemeinsam war den Beiträgern das Bemühen um anschauliche Schilderung ihrer konkreten Rahmenbedingungen, Inhalte und Methoden des Unterrichts in Rechtsgeschichte, was zu einer sehr konkreten Diskussion der Chancen und Probleme führte. Die konzise Tagungsorganisation und Diskussionsleitung tat ein Übriges, um einen offenen Schlagabtausch zu ermöglichen. Um diesen Tagungsbericht von Wiederholungen zu entlasten und stattdessen auf die Kontroversen zu fokussieren, soll von der Wiedergabe der Einzelreferate abgesehen werden und vielmehr topisch auf die Themenkomplexe bzw. Leitmotive eingegangen werden, die schon die Titelworte abbilden: Teaching/European/Comparative/Legal History.

I. Teaching

Prämisse des Workshops war, dass die Rechtshistoriker ihr Fach auch lehren. Das traf in Lund durchgängig auf die Teilnehmer zu, ist aber nicht immer gegeben, wie schon Marcus' Blicke auf die USA zeigten. Auch in Europa gibt es Konstellationen, in denen Forschung und Lehre nicht dem Humboldtschen Ideal folgen, sondern auseinanderfallen. Das kann etwa persönlich der Fall sein bei Mitgliedern von Forschungsinstituten, aber auch sachlich bei inhaltlichen Schwerpunkten, die nicht im Curriculum verankert sind, sei es mangels Bedeutung, sei es aus akademischen Traditionen heraus, obwohl die Themen in der Forschung durchaus Konjunktur haben. Am anderen Ende der Skala werden – jedenfalls in Deutschland – zunehmend Lehrprofessuren eingeführt, bei denen die Nähe von Forschung und Lehre wissenschaftspolitisch mit Absicht zerstört wird. Aus Sicht des Rechtsgeschichtsforschers sind solche Anläufe für die Lehre schädlich, denn sie befördern eine Verschulung der Universität bei gleichzeitiger Verflachung der Inhalte. Umgekehrt sollten die Wissenschaftler versuchen, ihre derzeitigen Forschungsschwerpunkte in die Lehre hineinzutragen. Wo es zu Abkoppelungen kommt, ist vermutlich keiner Seite gedient; die Studierenden werden dann mit einem Unterricht abgespeist, der steril anmutet.

Die in Lund diskutierte Unterrichtsform war in der Regel die Vorlesung; Seminare folgten mit deutlichem Abstand, Tutorien wurden nur ausnahmsweise erwähnt. Aber auch innerhalb des Genres der Vorlesung wurden verschiedene Herausforderungen identifiziert. Remco van Rhee, der die Rechtsgeschichte in Maastricht aufgebaut hat, muss einerseits große Massen Studierende im Hörsaal unterrichten. Andererseits wird gerade dort zusätzlich im Internet eine Plattform zum E-learning ausgebaut – den im niederländischen Vergleich üppig sprießenden Geldern sei's gedankt. Van Rhee zeigte bei einem schnellen Durchgang die Versuche, das in der Vorlesung vermittelte Wissen in Kurzfassung auch online abzubilden und den Studierenden Gedächtnisstützen anzubieten. Die Kurve des Vergessens ist steil – Maastricht hat sie sogar wissenschaftlich erforscht – und jede didaktische Ergänzung willkommen, die sie abflachen kann.

Als Adressaten des Unterrichts in Rechtsgeschichte wurden die Juristen wahrgenommen, andere Fakultäten spielten kaum eine Rolle. Das war schade, denn die Erfahrung lehrt, dass gerade in der fachlich gemischten Zusammensetzung der Kurse größeres Potential liegt, als wenn die Juristen unter sich bleiben. Stattdessen wurden die Binnenunterschiede in diesem Kreis ventiliert. Während manche Referenten im Unterrichten von Erstsemestern eher Probleme sahen, etwa im Hinblick auf die Vermittlung dogmatischer Probleme der Jurisprudenz, betonten andere gerade den Zauber, der dem Anfang innewohne: Man könne in einem frühen Stadium den Geist von Juristen formen (Aniceto Masferrer Domingo, Valencia), auch sei das Interesse an Allgemeinbildung höher und den Anfängern manche Arbeitsmethode noch aus der Schule vertraut, die im eigentlichen Jura-Studium an Relevanz und Wertschätzung verliere. Was man den Juristen aber beibringen soll, steht nicht *a priori* fest. Pia Letto-Vanamo (Helsinki) argumentierte, dass ihre Absolventen etwa in Brüssel tätig würden, also gegebenenfalls für Herausforderungen im europäischen Wettbewerbsrecht gerüstet sein müssten: Die Rechtsgeschichte trage dazu bei, sie juristisches Denken zu lehren. Das klang sympathisch, aber ist es genau das, was speziell die Rechtsgeschichte leistet? Mancher würde eher dafür halten, die Studierenden würden methodisch in der historischen Denkweise geschult, die ihnen die Kontingenz rechtlicher Formen und Konfliktlösungsinstrumente vor Augen führt. Ältere Programme der Legitimation hatten auch noch rechtsethische Absichten, und auch die rechtspolitische Untermauerung mancher Rechtsgeschichtsforschung sollte man nicht außer Acht lassen.

Die sich internationalisierende Zusammensetzung der Klassen wurde vielfach angesprochen, zumal von schwedischer Seite (Mats Kumlien, Uppsala; Nina-Louisa Arold, Christian Häthén, Per Nilsén, alle Lund), wo etwa Austauschstudenten zur regelmäßigen Klientel der Vorlesungen gehören. Sie wurden einerseits als wissbegierig und engagiert bezeichnet, manche täten sich aber schwer mit einer Diskussionskultur und der von ihnen erwarteten kritischen Haltung gegenüber dem Gegenstand Recht. Als Abhilfe wurden immer wieder Kleingruppen, direkte Ansprache und Aufbereitungen des Gelernten empfohlen, was selbstverständlich aber arbeitsintensiv für Lehrende und Lernende ist. Sehr kategorisch schloss dabei Jørn Øyrehagen Sunde (Bergen) bestimmte Unterrichtsstile aus, als er *en passant* proklamierte, man solle universitären Unterricht und Unterhaltung nicht verwechseln. Das erstaunte vor allem deswegen, weil gerade sein lebendig vorgetragenes Referat regelrechten Unterhaltungswert für die Zuhörer hatte. Auf Rückfrage erläuterte Sunde dann aber, was er meinte: Als 19-jähriger Museumsführer habe er die Beobachtung gemacht, dass seine norwegischen Kollegen versuchten, die Zuhörer mit Mythen und Fiktionen bei der Stange zu halten – wo doch in Wahrheit die Geschichte Erzählungen bereithalte, die unsere Phantasie überstiegen. Man müsse sie nur zu erzählen wissen.

Hier setzten die Fragen von Remco van Rhee an, der im Kollegenkreis erfahren wollte, wie man die Rechtsgeschichte am besten aufbereiten und präsentieren solle, um die Studierenden für das Fach zu gewinnen. Dafür gab es natürlich kein Patentrezept, aber doch den nachdrücklichen Rat Dirk Heirbauts (Ghent), das mit Leidenschaft zu lehren, was einen selbst interessiere. Der Funke werde dann schon von selbst überspringen, und die überragend positiven Evaluationen belegten auch, dass er gegenüber den Studierenden jedenfalls authentisch und begeistert wirke. Verweise auf eine genuine Didaktik der Rechtsgeschichte, die Lernziele und Lehrziele professionell erarbeitet, gab es hingegen nicht. Anders als bei den Geschichtswissenschaften ist das didaktische Geschäft gewissermaßen in der Hand von Amateuren, was auch daran liegen mag, dass im juristischen Universitätsfach keine Ausbildung von Lehrern mitbedacht werden muss.

Auch bei den Standards der Prüfungen scheint eine vergleichsweise große Freiheit und Vielfalt zu herrschen. »What is good enough?« fragte Ann-Christine Petersson Hjelm (Uppsala) und berichtete von ihren Selbstzweifeln, welche Leistung sie als Lehrende und Korrektorin von den Studierenden erwarten dürfe: Wie hoch sind die Anforderungen und welche Vorleistungen muss die

Universität dabei erbringen, um sie später mit gutem Gewissen abfragen zu dürfen? Anschaulich schilderte sie ihren Umgang mit studentischen Arbeiten, in denen Rechtsgeschichte, Rechtsvergleichung und positives Recht geprüft werden.

Ein weites Feld eröffnete sich beim Problem der Unterrichtsmaterialien, und vor allem der verwendeten Texte; Bilder und der Medieneinsatz spielten hingegen kaum eine Rolle. Dabei wurden sehr verschiedene Bedürfnisse sichtbar: Sanita Osipova, die seit 18 Jahren in Riga Rechtsgeschichte lehrt, wäre schon zufrieden, endlich mal ein Lehrbuch in der eigenen Landessprache zu haben. Die sich zunehmend internationalisierenden Fakultäten andernorts bewegen sich gewissermaßen in die andere Richtung, also weg von den Nationalsprachen: Anglisierung ist angesagt, in den Fächern des geltenden Rechts ebenso wie in den juristischen Grundlagendisziplinen. Was man den Studierenden an fremden Sprachen zumuten könne, wurde dann kontrovers diskutiert, wobei das Englische zunehmend für selbstverständlich genommen werde und die Nationalsprachen nachgerade verdränge. Tatsächlich sind schon jetzt zwei Drittel des Angebots in den Lunder Universitätsbuchhandlungen englischsprachig, neue Unterrichtseinheiten in Englisch werden diesen Trend verstärken (Mats Kumlien, Uppsala; Per Nilsén und Christian Häthén, Lund, berichteten) und entsprechend suchten die Tagungsteilnehmer händeringend ein wissenschaftlich gutes englischsprachiges Werk in Rechtsgeschichte zu identifizieren, das man dem Unterricht zugrunde legen könne. Sie fanden es aber nicht, da es noch an jedem Klassiker etwas auszusetzen gab, wenn man ihn unter der Prämisse studentischer Bedürfnisse las.

So praktizieren denn auch viele Lehrende das Modell des Readers: Sie stellen individuell Texte zusammen, die ihnen für das Thema der konkreten Lehrveranstaltung mit Blick auf die konkreten Adressaten hilfreich erscheinen. Diese Texte können Auszüge aus Büchern oder andere gedruckte Beiträge sein, manchmal sind es aber auch eigens dafür geschriebene Einführungen. Allerdings sehen sich die Lehrenden einem neuen Problem ausgesetzt: Die Universitätsverwaltungen argwöhnen bei diesen Kompilationen neuerdings Verletzungen des Urheberrechts und untersagen die Verbreitung des Materials (vor allem in digitalisierter Form und über ihr Intranet), sofern nicht die ausdrückliche Zustimmung der Rechteinhaber vorliegt. Das den Universitäten hinlänglich vertraute Plagiats-Thema erscheint damit in einer neuen Variante, nämlich nicht als Tatverdacht gegen Studierende oder Forschende als die üblichen Verdächtigen, sondern gegen die Lehrenden.

Etwas kurz kamen jene Fragen, die wissenschaftlich besonders heikel sind: nämlich die nach den strukturellen Grenzen der Übersetzbarkeit von Fach-sprachen und insbesondere das Problem des Umgangs mit Quellen. Überhaupt stand bei der Diskussion des Unterrichts erstaunlicherweise die Sekundärliteratur dominant im Zentrum, die Beschäftigung mit Quellen eher abseits, die aber gerade aus Sicht einer forschenden Rechtsgeschichte auch in der Lehre unverzichtbar ist. Und auch die wohl kaum aufzuhaltende Anglisierung des Fachs wäre die zentrale Frage wert gewesen, inwieweit es sich auch um eine Verlustgeschichte handeln wird. Anders gesagt: Auch Standardisierungen haben ihre Kehrseiten, und ein polyzentrisches, in seinen Quellen und Forschungen multilinguales Fach wie die Rechtsgeschichte muss sich dieser Risiken in besonderem Maße bewusst sein.

II. European

Modéer hatte sein ideales Programm als »europäisch« ausgewiesen, und das war als eine Perspektivenöffnung etikettiert. Auch die skandinavischen Nachbarn sympathisierten offen mit solchen Erweiterungen: Letto-Vanamo verwies auf die Horizonterweiterung, die sie namentlich in Forschungsaufenthalten im Frankfurter Max-Planck-Institut für europäische Rechtsgeschichte während der 1990er Jahre erfahren habe, und das europäische Element habe in erster Linie dazugehört. Heikki Pihlajamäki (gleichfalls Helsinki) bekannte, dass er gegenüber den Studenten die Erweiterung sachlich begründe: Die Finnen hätten ja, so behaupte er es seinen Studierenden gegenüber gleich am Anfang seiner Vorlesungen, ohnehin niemals irgendetwas im Recht erfunden, also müsse man den Rahmen in der Rechtsgeschichte geografisch weiter spannen. Übrigens heiße das aber nicht, dass sie weniger innovativ als die Dänen, Schweden und Norweger seien, denn für die skandinavischen Nachbarn gelte »der gleiche niederschmetternde Befund«. Das wäre seine didaktisch kalkulierte Provokation am Anfang, nach welchem sich die Hörer mit Wortmeldungen und Mails an ihn wenden würden, um Widerspruch und Vorschläge anzumelden.

Doch es gab auch Einwände gegenüber der Europäisierung des Curriculums und dem Titel des Workshops. Er bilde, so Ditlev Tamm (Kopenhagen), längst nicht mehr die aktuellen historiografischen Perspektiven ab, die sich hin zu einer Globalgeschichte gewandelt hätten. Tatsächlich ist die Zusammensetzung der Studierenden eben gerade nicht mehr »europäisch«, sondern umfasst vielerorts zahlreiche Teilnehmer aus außereuropäischen Regionen. Diese wünschen nun etwas über islamisches und chinesisches Recht oder transnationale Ordnungen zu erfahren. Doch wie man eine Rechtsgeschichte in globaler Perspektive unterrichten soll, das scheint eine noch größere Herausforderung zu sein. Am weitesten dürfte noch die Verfassungsgeschichte sein, die sich in den vergangenen Jahren und Jahrzehnten zunehmend auf globalvergleichende Perspektiven eingelassen hat.

III. Comparative

Kjell Å. Modéers entschiedener methodischer Wunsch richtete sich auf die Allianz der europäischen Rechtsgeschichte mit der Rechtsvergleichung. Sein leidenschaftliches Plädoyer wurde von Masferrer in diesem Punkt mit Gelassenheit gekontert, der das als Selbstverständlichkeit empfand: Wie anders als vergleichend solle man denn Rechtsgeschichte unterrichten, fragte Masferrer und schilderte den Zuhörern die Grundrisse seines Kurses. Das fand dann Dirk Heirbaut doch zu harmonisierend und verwies auf seine Eindrücke, die er in Frankreich gewonnen hat. Dort finde tatsächlich eine problematische Fokussierung auf die nationale Geschichte statt. Themen von europäisch-vergleichendem Zuschnitt (insbesondere aus dem 19. und 20. Jahrhundert) hätten vor den Gutachtern in den *concours* keine Chance, und damit würde eine Wissenschaftspolitik getrieben, die weit reichende inhaltliche Implikationen habe. Für ihn selbst hingegen sei eine erweiterte Perspektive auch unverzichtbar, denn eine »belgische« Rechtsgeschichte könne es angesichts der kurzen politischen Geschichte des Landes nicht sinnvoll geben, die Einbeziehung der Niederlande und Frankreichs sei eine Selbstverständlichkeit.

In der Folge wurden verschiedene Zugänge zur Rechtsvergleichung diskutiert, bei denen aber die zivilrechtliche Prägung unausgesprochen vorausgesetzt und akzeptiert wurde. Die Fragen drehten sich um die Tauglichkeit bestimmter Lehrbücher, etwa des klassischen von Zweigert/Kötz und nun Reimann/Zimmermanns Oxford Handbook of Comparative Law (2007). Welche perspektivischen Grenzen der Vergleichung als solcher immanent sind, kam wenig zur Sprache. Zu denken wäre an die Prämisse voneinander getrennter Entitäten, zumeist also der Nationalstaaten, deren Rechtsordnungen verglichen werden. Demgegenüber geraten Transfer- und Rezeptionsvorgänge leicht außer Sicht, ebenso wie transnationale Entwicklungen.

Den vehementesten Einspruch gegen die Allianz mit der Rechtsvergleichung formulierte Ditlev Tamm (Kopenhagen). Er bekannte sich dazu, nur Rechtshistoriker und eben kein Rechtsvergleicher zu sein; vielmehr sei die Rechtsvergleichung ein eigenes Fach »with own methodology, rules and subjects«. Sunde, der in Bergen genau diesen Brückenschlag vollzogen hat, nahm solche Einwände für wenig durchschlagend: Wir seien doch oft Amateure, meinte Sunde und plädierte dafür, solche Allianzen auch unter strategischen Gesichtspunkten einzugehen. Das war ein interessanter Punkt, denn er initiierte eine Diskussion, in deren Verlauf klare Differenzen zwischen den verschiedenen Hochschulstandorten deutlich wurden. Genau diese Unterschiede zeigten, warum mancherorts die Nähe zur Rechtsvergleichung gesucht wurde, während sie anderswo keine Rolle spielte. Erstaunlich blieb trotz alledem, dass der Blick der Lunder Tagung nur auf dieses Grundlagenfach gerichtet blieb, andere aber nicht ernsthaft in vergleichbarer Nähe gesehen wurden; denn weder Rechtstheorie, Rechtssoziologie noch Rechtsphilosophie wurden als Kandidaten ventiliert oder in ihrem gegenwärtigen Verhältnis zur Rechtsgeschichte diskutiert.

IV. Legal History

Rechtsgeschichte war der gemeinsame thematische Nenner bei der Frage nach dem angemessenen Unterricht, aber selbstverständlich werden in den diversen Universitäten inhaltlich und methodisch verschiedene Rechtsgeschichten erzählt. Als Osipova in Riga zu lehren begann, dominierten noch die marxistischen Theorien, in denen die Verbindung zur Ökonomie ebenso stark war wie der Fokus auf das öffentliche Recht; auch spielte das sowjetische Rechtssystem eine große Rolle. Heute sei man dort davon abgekommen und orientiere sich nach Westen und zum Privatrecht hin, berichtete Osipova; dennoch würde man im Curriculum gerne die russische Rechtsgeschichte stärker berücksichtigen, es fehlten aber die passenden Ansprechpartner. Damit war die lokale Prägung der diversen nationalen Rechtsgeschichten angesprochen.

Gegen die Neigung, ein gemeinsames europäisches Curriculum festzuzurren, bekannten sich zahlreiche Redner an diesem Punkt gerade zur Standortgebundenheit ihrer Unterrichtsinhalte. Dies wurde schon bei den Epochengliederungen und Epochenschwerpunkten deutlich, die ganz verschieden gehandhabt werden. In manchen spanischen Lehrbüchern werde das Mittelalter wissenschaftlich überproportional stark abgehandelt, so Masferrer, worunter dann die neueren Epochen litten; andere Redner warteten mit Epochengliederungen auf, die verblüffend voneinander abwichen (Osipova; Heirbaut). Hinzu kommen aber auch spezielle, vor allem geografisch zu erklärende Unterrichtsinhalte, die sich aus lokalen, regionalen oder nationalen Besonderheiten historischer Rechtssysteme ableiten lassen.

Eine internationale Standardisierung des Curriculums, wie man sie naiverweise vielleicht erwarten könnte, wäre schon damit ausgeschlossen. Hinzu kommen aber auch andere bedenkliche Aspekte. Denn die Inhalte eines als wissenschaftlich verstandenen Unterrichts wechseln auch mit der Person des lehrenden Wissenschaftlers, so sehr die Idee der Individualität und Subjektivität der Forschung manchen Universitätsbürokratien ein Dorn im Auge ist. Diese

Vielfalt und Divergenz aber sollte in der Lehre der Rechtsgeschichte ein bewahrungswürdiges Ziel bleiben. Sie würde auch künftig ihren Wert behaupten, ja mehren können, wenn die thematische und methodische Offenheit des Fachs erhaltenbliebe. Festschreibungen aber beinhalten immer auch Abschließungen und sind schon von daher ein bedenkliches Instrument.

Umso erfreulicher war es daher, dass der Workshop in Lund keinen normativen Zugang zu seinem Gegenstand erzeugte, sondern in familiärer Atmosphäre einen reflektierten Austausch über die praktizierten Unterrichtsmodelle erlaubte. Mehr wäre in diesem Fall tatsächlich weniger gewesen. Und mancher mag auch noch den einen oder anderen praktischen Tipp mit nach Hause genommen haben. So gab es nebenbei für ein praktisches Professoren-Problem auch eine konkrete Abhilfeempfehlung: Wie überbrückt man die Zeit, wenn man nichts zu sagen hat? Sein alter Lehrer empfahl, so Pihlajamäki, ein Stück Kreide tollpatschig fallen zu lassen und dann umständlich und lange auf dem Boden des Hörsaals danach zu suchen. Da biete uns der Medienwandel doch ganz andere Möglichkeiten, meinte Pihlajamäki, während er ungeduldig darauf wartete, dass Beamer und Notebook endlich funktionierten.